To:

____

From:

____

Date:

____

DAILY LIGHT
FOR
MEN

CHRISTIAN ART
PUBLISHERS

Selections from *Daily Light on the Daily Path*

Published by Christian Art Publishers, PO Box 1599,
Vereeniging, 1930, RSA

First edition 2020

Cover designed by Christian Art Publishers

Designed by Christian Art Publishers

Images used under license from Shutterstock.com

Set in 11 on 13 pt Avenir LT Std
by Christian Art Publishers

Printed in China

ISBN 978-1-4321-3166-1 (Faux Leather)
ISBN 978-1-4321-3257-6 (Hardcover)

21 22 23 24 25 26 27 28 29 30 – 13 12 11 10 9 8 7 6 5 4

Introduction

The devotional classic ***Daily Light for Your Daily Path*** continues to offer help, meditation and guidance to countless numbers of people.

Composed entirely of selected Scripture verses, with passages revolving around a single theme, ***Daily Light for Your Daily Path*** was credited by the Bagster family more than a century ago for use in their own family devotions. Subsequently published by Samuel Bagster, it achieved instant popularity and has proved to be unmatched in its ability to meet the needs of Christians in every kind of circumstance.

In this edition the beautiful and clear language of the English Standard Version elegantly complements this timeless classic.

January

JAN.
1

But one thing I do: forgetting what lies behind, …
I press on toward the goal for the prize of
the upward call of God in Christ Jesus.

"Father, I desire that they … whom you have given me, may be with me where I am, to see my glory that you have given me." ❖ I know whom I have believed, and I am convinced that he is able to guard until that Day what has been entrusted to me. ❖ He who began a good work in you will bring it to completion at the day of Jesus Christ.

Do you not know that in a race all the runners compete, but only one receives the prize? So run that you may obtain it. Every athlete exercises self-control in all things. They do it to receive a perishable wreath, but we an imperishable. ❖ Let us also lay aside every weight, and sin which clings so closely, and let us run with endurance the race that is set before us, looking to Jesus.

Phil. 3:13, 14. | John 17:24. | 2 Tim. 1:12.
Phil. 1:6. | 1 Cor. 9:24, 25. | Heb. 12:1, 2.

JAN.
2

Sing to the LORD a new song.

Sing aloud to God our strength; shout for joy to the God of Jacob! Raise a song; sound the tambourine, the sweet lyre with the harp. ❖ He put a new song in my mouth, a song of praise to our God. Many will see and fear, and put their trust in the LORD.

"Be strong and courageous. Do not be frightened, and do not be dismayed, for the LORD your God is with you wherever you go." ❖ "The joy of the LORD is your strength." ❖ Paul thanked God and took courage.

Besides this you know the time, that the hour has come for you to wake from sleep. For salvation is nearer to us now than when we first believed. The night is far gone; the day is at hand. So then let us cast off the works of darkness and put on the armor of light. Let us walk properly as in the daytime, not in orgies and drunkenness, not in sexual immorality and sensuality, not in quarreling and jealousy. But put on the Lord Jesus Christ, and make no provision for the flesh, to gratify its desires.

Isa. 42:10. | Ps. 81:1, 2. | Ps. 40:3. | Josh. 1:9.
Neh. 8:10. | Acts 28:15. | Rom. 13:11-14.

JAN. 3

He led them by a straight way.

"He found [Jacob] in a desert land, and in the howling waste of the wilderness; he encircled him, he cared for him, he kept him as the apple of his eye. Like an eagle that stirs up its nest, that flutters over its young, spreading out its wings, catching them, bearing them on its pinions, the LORD alone guided him." ❖ "Even to your old age I am he, and to gray hairs I will carry you. I have made, and I will bear; I will carry and will save."

He restores my soul. He leads me in paths of righteousness for his name's sake. Even though I walk through the valley of the shadow of death, I will fear no evil, for you are with me; your rod and your staff, they comfort me.

"And the LORD will guide you continually and satisfy your desire in scorched places and make your bones strong; and you shall be like a watered garden, like a spring of water, whose waters do not fail." ❖ This is God, our God forever and ever. He will guide us forever. ❖ "Who is a teacher like him?"

Ps. 107:7. | Deut. 32:10-12. | Isa. 46:4. | Ps. 23:3, 4.
Isa. 58:11. | Ps. 48:14. | Job 36:22.

JAN.
4

"For you have not as yet come to the rest and to the inheritance that the LORD your God is giving you."

For this is no place to rest. ❖ So then, there remains a Sabbath rest for the people of God. ❖ Behind the curtain, where Jesus has gone as a forerunner on our behalf.

"In my Father's house are many rooms. If it were not so, would I have told you that I go to prepare a place for you? And if I go and prepare a place for you, I will come again and will take you to myself, that where I am you may be also." ❖ With Christ, for that is far better.

"He will wipe away every tear from their eyes, and death shall be no more, neither shall there be mourning nor crying nor pain anymore, for the former things have passed away." ❖ "There the wicked cease from troubling, and there the weary are at rest."

"But lay up for yourselves treasures in heaven, where neither moth nor rust destroys and where thieves do not break in and steal. For where your treasure is, there your heart will be also." ❖ Set your minds on things that are above, not on things that are on earth.

Deut. 12:9. | Mic. 2:10. | Heb. 4:9. | Heb. 6:19, 20.
John 14:2, 3. | Phil. 1:23. | Rev. 21:4.
Job 3:17. | Matt. 6:20, 21. | Col. 3:2.

JAN. 5

For we who have believed enter that rest.

They weary themselves committing iniquity. ❖ But I see in my members another law waging war against the law of my mind and making me captive to the law of sin that dwells in my members. Wretched man that I am! Who will deliver me from this body of death?

"Come to me, all who labor and are heavy laden, and I will give you rest." ❖ Therefore, since we have been justified by faith, we have peace with God through our Lord Jesus Christ. Through him we have also obtained access by faith into this grace in which we stand, and we rejoice in hope of the glory of God.

For whoever has entered God's rest has also rested from his works. ❖ Not having a righteousness of my own that comes from the law, but that which comes through faith in Christ, the righteousness from God that depends on faith. ❖ "This is rest; give rest to the weary; and this is repose."

Heb. 4:3. | Jer. 9:5. | Rom. 7:23-24. | Matt. 11:28.
Rom. 5:1, 2. | Heb. 4:10. | Phil. 3:9. | Isa. 28:12.

JAN.
6

Let the favor of the Lord our God be upon us,
and establish the work of our hands upon us.

"And your renown went forth among the nations because of your beauty, for it was perfect through the splendor that I had bestowed on you, declares the Lord GOD." ❖ And we all, with unveiled face, beholding the glory of the Lord, are being transformed into the same image from one degree of glory to another. For this comes from the Lord who is the Spirit. ❖ The Spirit of glory and of God rests upon you.

Blessed is everyone who fears the LORD, who walks in his ways! You shall eat the fruit of the labor of your hands; you shall be blessed, and it shall be well with you. ❖ Commit your work to the LORD, and your plans will be established.

Work out your own salvation with fear and trembling, for it is God who works in you, both to will and to work for his good pleasure. ❖ Now may our Lord Jesus Christ himself, and God our Father, who loved us and gave us eternal comfort and good hope through grace, comfort your hearts and establish them in every good work and word.

Ps. 90:17. | Ezek. 16:14. | 2 Cor. 3:18. | 1 Pet. 4:14.
Ps. 128:1, 2. | Prov. 16:3. | Phil. 2:12, 13. | 2 Thess. 2:16, 17.

JAN. 7

Remember [me] for my good, O my God.

Thus says the Lord, "I remember the devotion of your youth, your love as a bride, how you followed me in the wilderness." ❖ "Yet I will remember my covenant with you in the days of your youth, and I will establish for you an everlasting covenant." ❖ "I will visit you, and I will fulfill to you my promise. … For I know the plans I have for you, declares the Lord, plans for wholeness and not for evil, to give you a future and a hope."

"For as the heavens are higher than the earth, so are my ways higher than your ways and my thoughts than your thoughts." ❖ "I would seek God, and to God would I commit my cause, who does great things and unsearchable, marvelous things without number." ❖ You have multiplied, O Lord my God, your wondrous deeds and your thoughts toward us; none can compare with you! I will proclaim and tell of them, yet they are more than can be told.

Neh. 5:19. | Jer. 2:2. | Ezek. 16:60. | Jer. 29:10, 11.
Isa. 55:9. | Job 5:8, 9. | Ps. 40:5.

JAN. 8

And those who know your name put their trust in you, for you, O Lord, have not forsaken those who seek you.

The name of the Lord is a strong tower; the righteous man runs into it and is safe. ❖ "I will trust, and will not be afraid; for the Lord God is my strength and my song, and he has become my salvation."

I have been young, and now am old, yet I have not seen the righteous forsaken or his children begging for bread. ❖ For the Lord loves justice; he will not forsake his saints. They are preserved forever, but the children of the wicked shall be cut off. ❖ "For the Lord will not forsake his people, for his great name's sake, because it has pleased the Lord to make you a people for himself." ❖ He delivered us from such a deadly peril, and he will deliver us. On him we have set our hope that he will deliver us again.

And be content with what you have, for he has said, "I will never leave you nor forsake you." So we can confidently say, "The Lord is my helper; I will not fear; what can man do to me?"

Ps. 9:10. | Prov. 18:10. | Isa. 12:2. | Ps. 37:25.
Ps. 37:28. | 1 Sam.12:22. | 2 Cor. 1:10. | Heb. 13:5, 6.

JAN. 9

You have set up a banner for those who fear you,
that they may flee to it from the bow.

The LORD is my banner. ❖ For he [the enemy] will come like a rushing stream, which the wind of the LORD drives.

May we shout for joy over your salvation, and in the name of our God set up our banners! ❖ "The LORD has brought about our vindication; come, let us declare in Zion the work of the LORD our God." ❖ We are more than conquerors through him who loved us. ❖ But thanks be to God, who gives us the victory through our Lord Jesus Christ. ❖ The founder of their salvation.

Finally, be strong in the Lord and in the strength of his might. ❖ Falsehood and not truth has grown strong in the land. ❖ "Fight the LORD's battles." ❖ "Be strong, all you people of the land, declares the LORD. Work. … Fear not." ❖ "Lift up your eyes, and see that the fields are white for harvest." ❖ "Yet a little while, and the coming one will come and will not delay."

Ps. 60:4. | Exod. 17:15. | Isa. 59:19.
Ps. 20:5. | Jer. 51:10. | Rom. 8:37. | 1 Cor. 15:57.
Heb. 2:10. | Eph. 6:10. | Jer. 9:3. | 1 Sam. 18:17.
Hag. 2:4, 5. | John 4:35. | Heb. 10:37.

JAN. 10

And may your whole spirit and soul and body be kept blameless at the coming of our Lord Jesus Christ.

Christ loved the church and gave himself up for her ... so that he might present the church to himself in splendor, without spot or wrinkle or any such thing, that she might be holy and without blemish. ❖ Him we proclaim, warning everyone and teaching everyone with all wisdom, that we may present everyone mature in Christ.

And the peace of God ... surpasses all understanding. ❖ And let the peace of Christ rule in your hearts, to which indeed you were called in one body.

Now may our Lord Jesus Christ himself, and God our Father, who loved us and gave us eternal comfort and good hope through grace, comfort your hearts and establish them in every good work and word. ❖ Who will sustain you to the end, guiltless in the day of our Lord Jesus Christ.

1 Thess. 5:23. | Eph. 5:25, 27. | Col. 1:28. | Phil. 4:7. Col. 3:15. | 2 Thess. 2:16, 17. | 1 Cor. 1:8.

JAN. 11

Praise is due to you, O God, in Zion.

Yet for us there is one God, the Father, from whom are all things and for whom we exist, and one Lord, Jesus Christ, through whom are all things and through whom we exist. ❖ "That all may honor the Son, just as they honor the Father. Whoever does not honor the Son does not honor the Father who sent him." ❖ Through him then let us continually offer up a sacrifice of praise to God, that is, the fruit of lips that acknowledge his name. ❖ The one who offers thanksgiving as his sacrifice glorifies me; to one who orders his way rightly I will show the salvation of God!

After this I looked, and behold, a great multitude that no one could number, from every nation, from all tribes and peoples and languages, standing before the throne and before the Lamb, clothed in white robes, with palm branches in their hands, and crying out with a loud voice, "Salvation belongs to our God who sits on the throne, and to the Lamb! … Amen! Blessing and glory and wisdom and thanksgiving and honor and power and might be to our God forever and ever! Amen."

Ps. 65:1. | 1 Cor. 8:6. | John 5:23. | Heb. 13:15.
Ps. 50:23. | Rev. 7:9, 10, 12.

JAN.
12

The only [KJV: wise] God, our Savior.

Christ Jesus, whom God made our wisdom and our righteousness and sanctification and redemption. ❖ "Can you find out the deep things of God? Can you find out the limit of the Almighty? It is higher than heaven – what can you do? Deeper than Sheol – what can you know?"

But we impart a secret and hidden wisdom of God, which God decreed before the ages for our glory. ❖ The plan of the mystery hidden for ages in God who created all things, so that through the church the manifold wisdom of God might now be made known to the rulers and authorities in the heavenly places.

If any of you lacks wisdom, let him ask God, who gives generously to all without reproach, and it will be given him. ❖ But the wisdom from above is first pure, then peaceable, gentle, open to reason, full of mercy and good fruits, impartial and sincere.

Jude 25. | 1 Cor. 1:30. | Job 11:7, 8. | 1 Cor. 2:7.
Eph. 3:9, 10. | James 1:5. | James 3:17.

JAN.
13

"You keep him in perfect peace
whose mind is stayed on you."

Cast your burden on the LORD, and he will sustain you; he will never permit the righteous to be moved. ❖ "I will trust, and will not be afraid; for the LORD GOD is my strength and my song, and he has become my salvation."

"Why are you afraid, O you of little faith?" ❖ Do not be anxious about anything, but in everything by prayer and supplication with thanksgiving let your requests be made known to God. And the peace of God, which surpasses all understanding, will guard your hearts and your minds in Christ Jesus. ❖ "In quietness and in trust shall be your strength."

And the result of righteousness [shall be] quietness and trust forever. ❖ "Peace I leave with you; my peace I give to you. Not as the world gives do I give to you. Let not your hearts be troubled, neither let them be afraid." ❖ Peace from him who is and who was and who is to come.

Isa. 26:3. | Ps. 55:22. | Isa. 12:2. | Matt. 8:26.
Phil. 4:6, 7. | Isa. 30:15. | Isa. 32:17. | John 14:27. | Rev. 1:4.

"For the Father is greater than I."

"When you pray, say: Father, hallowed be your name." ❖ "To my Father and your Father, to my God and your God."

"But I do as the Father has commanded me." ❖ "The words that I say to you I do not speak on my own authority, but the Father who dwells in me does his works."

The Father loves the Son and has given all things into his hand. ❖ "You have given him authority over all flesh, to give eternal life to all whom you have given him."

Philip said to him, "Lord, show us the Father, and it is enough for us." Jesus said to him, "Have I been with you so long, and you still do not know me, Philip? Whoever has seen me has seen the Father. How can you say, 'Show us the Father'? Do you not believe that I am in the Father and the Father is in me?" ❖ "I and the Father are one." ❖ "As the Father has loved me, so have I loved you. Abide in my love. If you keep my commandments, you will abide in my love, just as I have kept my Father's commandments and abide in his love."

John 14:28. | Luke 11:2. | John 20:17. | John 14:31.
John 14:10. | John 3:35. | John 17:2. | John 14:8-10.
John 10:30. | John 15:9, 10.

JAN.
15

My soul clings to the dust;
give me life according to your word!

If then you have been raised with Christ, seek the things that are above, where Christ is, seated at the right hand of God. Set your minds on things that are above, not on things that are on earth. For … your life is hidden with Christ in God. ❖ But our citizenship is in heaven, and from it we await a Savior, the Lord Jesus Christ, who will transform our lowly body to be like his glorious body, by the power that enables him even to subject all things to himself.

For the desires of the flesh are against the Spirit, and the desires of the Spirit are against the flesh, for these are opposed to each other, to keep you from doing the things you want to do. ❖ So then, brothers, we are debtors, not to the flesh, to live according to the flesh. For if you live according to the flesh you will die, but if by the Spirit you put to death the deeds of the body, you will live. ❖ Beloved, I urge you as sojourners and exiles to abstain from the passions of the flesh, which wage war against your soul.

Ps. 119:25. | Col. 3:1-3. | Phil. 3:20, 21.
Gal. 5:17. | Rom. 8:12, 13. | 1 Pet. 2:11.

JAN.
16

For in him all the fullness of
God was pleased to dwell.

The Father loves the Son and has given all things into his hand. ❖ Therefore God has highly exalted him and bestowed on him the name that is above every name, so that at the name of Jesus every knee should bow, in heaven and on earth and under the earth, and every tongue confess that Jesus Christ is Lord, to the glory of God the Father. ❖ Far above all rule and authority and power and dominion, and above every name that is named, not only in this age but also in the one to come. ❖ For by him all things were created, in heaven and on earth, visible and invisible, whether thrones or dominions or rulers or authorities – all things were created through him and for him.

For to this end Christ died and lived again, that he might be Lord both of the dead and of the living. ❖ And you have been filled in him, who is the head of all rule and authority. ❖ And from his fullness we have all received.

Col. 1:19. | John 3:35. | Phil. 2:9-11. | Eph. 1:21.
Col. 1:16. | Rom. 14:9. | Col. 2:10. | John 1:16.

JAN.
17

But in love you have delivered
my life from the pit of destruction.

God sent his only Son into the world, so that we might live through him. In this is love, not that we have loved God but that he loved us and sent his Son to be the propitiation for our sins.

Who is a God like you, pardoning iniquity and passing over transgression for the remnant of his inheritance? He does not retain his anger forever, because he delights in steadfast love. He will again have compassion on us; he will tread our iniquities under foot. You will cast all our sins into the depths of the sea. ❖ O LORD my God, I cried to you for help, and you have healed me. O LORD, you have brought up my soul from Sheol; you restored me to life from among those who go down to the pit. ❖ "When my life was fainting away, I remembered the LORD, and my prayer came to you, into your holy temple." ❖ I waited patiently for the LORD; he inclined to me and heard my cry. He drew me up from the pit of destruction, out of the miry bog, and set my feet upon a rock.

Isa. 38:17. | 1 John 4:9, 10. | Mic. 7:18, 19.
Ps. 30:2, 3. | Jonah 2:7. | Ps. 40:1, 2.

JAN. 18

The one who was to come.

But we see him who for a little while was made lower than the angels, namely Jesus, crowned with glory and honor because of the suffering of death, so that by the grace of God he might taste death for everyone. ❖ One has died for all. ❖ For as by the one man's disobedience the many were made sinners, so by the one man's obedience the many will be made righteous. ❖ Thus it is written, "The first man Adam became a living being"; the last Adam became a life-giving spirit. ❖ Then God said, "Let us make man in our image, after our likeness." So God created man in his own image, in the image of God he created him; male and female he created them. ❖ But in these last days [God] has spoken to us by his Son. ... He is the radiance of the glory of God and the exact imprint of his nature. ❖ "You have given him authority over all flesh."

The first man was from the earth, a man of dust; the second man is from heaven. As was the man of dust, so also are those who are of the dust, and as is the man of heaven, so also are those who are of heaven.

Rom. 5:14. | Heb. 2:9. | 2 Cor. 5:14. | Rom. 5:19.
1 Cor. 15:45, 46. | Gen. 1:26-27. | Heb. 1:1-3.
John 17:2. | 1 Cor. 15:47, 48.

JAN.
19

"Serving the Lord with all humility."

"But whoever would be great among you must be your servant, and whoever would be first among you must be your slave, even as the Son of Man came not to be served but to serve, and to give his life as a ransom for many."

For if anyone thinks he is something, when he is nothing, he deceives himself. ❖ For by the grace given to me I say to everyone among you not to think of himself more highly than he ought to think, but to think with sober judgment, each according to the measure of faith that God has assigned. ❖ "So you also, when you have done all that you were commanded, say, 'We are unworthy servants; we have only done what was our duty.'"

For our boast is this: ... that we behaved in the world with simplicity and godly sincerity, not by earthly wisdom but by the grace of God. ❖ But we have this treasure in jars of clay, to show that the surpassing power belongs to God and not to us.

Acts 20:19. | Matt. 20:26-28. | Gal. 6:3. | Rom. 12:3.
Luke 17:10. | 2 Cor. 1:12. | 2 Cor. 4:7.

JAN. 20

And his name shall be called Wonderful Counselor.

And the Word became flesh and dwelt among us, and we have seen his glory, glory as of the only Son from the Father, full of grace and truth. ❖ For you have exalted above all things your name and your word.

"And they shall call his name Immanuel" (which means, God with us). ❖ "And you shall call his name Jesus, for he will save his people from their sins."

"That all may honor the Son, just as they honor the Father." ❖ Therefore God has highly exalted him and bestowed on him the name that is above every name. ❖ Far above all rule and authority and power and dominion, and above every name that is named, not only in this age but also in the one to come. And he put all things under his feet. ❖ He has a name written that no one knows but himself ... King of kings and Lord of lords.

The Almighty – we cannot find him. ❖ What is his name, and what is his son's name? Surely you know!

Isa. 9:6. | John 1:14. | Ps. 138:2. | Matt. 1:23.
Matt. 1:21. | John 5:23. | Phil. 2:9. | Eph. 1:21, 22.
Rev. 19:12, 16. | Job 37:23. | Prov. 30:4.

JAN.
21

"Every branch of mine that does not bear fruit he takes away."

"For he is like a refiner's fire and like fullers' soap. He will sit as a refiner and purifier of silver, and he will purify the sons of Levi and refine them like gold and silver, and they will bring offerings in righteousness to the Lord."

More than that, we rejoice in our sufferings, knowing that suffering produces endurance, and endurance produces character, and character produces hope, and hope does not put us to shame, because God's love has been poured into our hearts through the Holy Spirit who has been given to us. ❖ It is for discipline that you have to endure. God is treating you as sons. For what son is there whom his father does not discipline? If you are left without discipline, in which all have participated, then you are illegitimate children and not sons. ... For the moment all discipline seems painful rather than pleasant, but later it yields the peaceful fruit of righteousness to those who have been trained by it. Therefore lift your drooping hands and strengthen your weak knees.

John 15:2. | Mal. 3:2, 3. | Rom. 5:3-5. | Heb. 12:7, 8, 11, 12.

JAN.
22

This is God, our God forever and ever.
He will guide us forever.

O LORD, you are my God; I will exalt you; I will praise your name, for you have done wonderful things, plans formed of old, faithful and sure. ❖ The LORD is my chosen portion and my cup.

He leads me in paths of righteousness for his name's sake. Even though I walk through the valley of the shadow of death, I will fear no evil, for you are with me; your rod and your staff, they comfort me. ❖ You hold my right hand. You guide me with your counsel, and afterward you will receive me to glory. Whom have I in heaven but you? And there is nothing on earth that I desire besides you. My flesh and my heart may fail, but God is the strength of my heart and my portion forever. ❖ For our heart is glad in him, because we trust in his holy name. ❖ The LORD will fulfill his purpose for me; your steadfast love, O LORD, endures forever. Do not forsake the work of your hands.

Ps. 48:14. | Isa. 25:1. | Ps. 16:5. | Ps. 23:3, 4.
Ps. 73:23-26. | Ps. 33:21. | Ps. 138:8.

JAN.
23

And hope does not put us to shame.

"I am the LORD; those who wait for me shall not be put to shame." ❖ "Blessed is the man who trusts in the LORD, whose trust is the LORD." ❖ "You keep him in perfect peace whose mind is stayed on you, because he trusts in you. Trust in the LORD forever, for the LORD GOD is an everlasting rock." ❖ For God alone, O my soul, wait in silence, for my hope is from him. He only is my rock and my salvation. ❖ But I am not ashamed, for I know whom I have believed.

So when God desired to show more convincingly to the heirs of the promise the unchangeable character of his purpose, he guaranteed it with an oath, so that by two unchangeable things, in which it is impossible for God to lie, we who have fled for refuge might have strong encouragement to hold fast to the hope set before us. We have this as a sure and steadfast anchor of the soul, a hope that enters into the inner place behind the curtain, where Jesus has gone as a forerunner on our behalf.

Rom. 5:5. | Isa. 49:23. | Jer. 17:7. | Isa. 26:3, 4.
Ps. 62:5, 6. | 2 Tim. 1:12. | Heb. 6:17-20.

JAN.
24

The Lord is at hand.

For the Lord himself will descend from heaven with a cry of command, with the voice of an archangel, and with the sound of the trumpet of God. And the dead in Christ will rise first. Then we who are alive, who are left, will be caught up together with them in the clouds to meet the Lord in the air, and so we will always be with the Lord. Therefore encourage one another with these words. ❖ He who testifies to these things says, "Surely I am coming soon." Amen. Come, Lord Jesus!

Therefore, beloved, since you are waiting for these, be diligent to be found by him without spot or blemish, and at peace. ❖ Abstain from every form of evil. Now may the God of peace himself sanctify you completely, and may your whole spirit and soul and body be kept blameless at the coming of our Lord Jesus Christ. He who calls you is faithful; he will surely do it.

You also, be patient. Establish your hearts, for the coming of the Lord is at hand.

Phil. 4:5. | 1 Thess. 4:16-18. | Rev. 22:20.
2 Pet. 3:14. | 1 Thess. 5:22-24. | James 5:8.

JAN.
25

The righteousness of God through faith in Jesus Christ for all who believe.

For our sake he made him to be sin who knew no sin, so that in him we might become the righteousness of God. ❖ Christ redeemed us from the curse of the law by becoming a curse for us. ❖ Whom God made our wisdom and our righteousness and sanctification and redemption. ❖ Not because of works done by us in righteousness, but according to his own mercy, by the washing of regeneration and renewal of the Holy Spirit, whom he poured out on us richly through Jesus Christ our Savior.

Indeed, I count everything as loss because of the surpassing worth of knowing Christ Jesus my Lord. For his sake I have suffered the loss of all things and count them as rubbish, in order that I may gain Christ and be found in him, not having a righteousness of my own that comes from the law, but that which comes through faith in Christ, the righteousness from God that depends on faith.

Rom. 3:22. | 2 Cor. 5:21. | Gal. 3:13.
1 Cor. 1:30. | Titus 3:5, 6. | Phil. 3:8, 9.

JAN.
26

Therefore let us go to him outside the camp and bear the reproach he endured. For here we have no lasting city, but we seek the city that is to come.

Beloved, do not be surprised at the fiery trial when it comes upon you to test you, as though something strange were happening to you. But rejoice insofar as you share Christ's sufferings, that you may also rejoice and be glad when his glory is revealed. ❖ For we know that as you share in our sufferings, you will also share in our comfort. ❖ If you are insulted for the name of Christ, you are blessed, because the Spirit of glory and of God rests upon you. ❖ Then they left the presence of the council, rejoicing that they were counted worthy to suffer dishonor for the name. ❖ Choosing rather to be mistreated with the people of God than to enjoy the fleeting pleasures of sin. He considered the reproach of Christ greater wealth than the treasures of Egypt, for he was looking to the reward.

Heb. 13:13, 14. | 1 Pet. 4:12, 13. | 2 Cor. 1:7.
1 Pet. 4:14. | Acts 5:41. | Heb. 11:25, 26.

JAN. 27

You know that he appeared to take away sins, and in him there is no sin.

But in these last days [God] has spoken to us by his Son. ... He is the radiance of the glory of God and the exact imprint of his nature, and he upholds the universe by the word of his power. After making purification for sins, he sat down at the right hand of the Majesty on high. ❖ For our sake he made him to be sin who knew no sin, so that in him we might become the righteousness of God. ❖ Conduct yourselves with fear throughout the time of your exile, knowing that you were ransomed from the futile ways inherited from your forefathers, not with perishable things such as silver or gold, but with the precious blood of Christ, like that of a lamb without blemish or spot. He was foreknown before the foundation of the world but was made manifest in the last times for your sake. ❖ For the love of Christ controls us, because we have concluded this: that one has died for all, therefore all have died; and he died for all, that those who live might no longer live for themselves but for him who for their sake died and was raised.

1 John 3:5. | Heb. 1:1-3. | 2 Cor. 5:21.
1 Pet. 1:17-20. | 2 Cor. 5:14, 15.

JAN.
28

"As your days, so shall your strength be."

"And when they bring you to trial and deliver you over, do not be anxious beforehand what you are to say, but say whatever is given you in that hour, for it is not you who speak, but the Holy Spirit." ❖ "Therefore do not be anxious about tomorrow, for tomorrow will be anxious for itself. Sufficient for the day is its own trouble."

The God of Israel – he is the one who gives power and strength to his people. Blessed be God! ❖ He gives power to the faint, and to him who has no might he increases strength.

But he said to me, "My grace is sufficient for you, for my power is made perfect in weakness." Therefore I will boast all the more gladly of my weaknesses, so that the power of Christ may rest upon me. For the sake of Christ, then, I am content with weaknesses, insults, hardships, persecutions, and calamities. For when I am weak, then I am strong. ❖ I can do all things through him who strengthens me. ❖ "March on, my soul, with might!"

Deut. 33:25. | Mark 13:11. | Matt. 6:34. | Ps. 68:35.
Isa. 40:29. | 2 Cor. 12:9, 10. | Phil. 4:13. | Judg. 5:21.

JAN. 29

"You are a God of seeing."

O Lord, you have searched me and known me! You know when I sit down and when I rise up; you discern my thoughts from afar. You search out my path and my lying down and are acquainted with all my ways. Even before a word is on my tongue, behold, O Lord, you know it altogether. … Such knowledge is too wonderful for me; it is high; I cannot attain it.

The eyes of the Lord are in every place, keeping watch on the evil and the good. ❖ For a man's ways are before the eyes of the Lord, and he ponders all his paths. ❖ "But God knows your hearts. For what is exalted among men is an abomination in the sight of God." ❖ "For the eyes of the Lord run to and fro throughout the whole earth, to give strong support to those whose heart is blameless toward him."

But Jesus … knew all people and needed no one to bear witness about man, for he himself knew what was in man. ❖ "Lord, you know everything; you know that I love you."

Gen. 16:13. | Ps. 139:1-4, 6. | Prov. 15:3.
Prov. 5:21. | Luke 16:15. | 2 Chron. 16:9.
John 2:24, 25. | John 21:17.

JAN. 30

Let us run with endurance the race that is set before us, looking to Jesus, the founder and perfecter of our faith.

"If anyone would come after me, let him deny himself and take up his cross daily and follow me." ❖ "So therefore, any one of you who does not renounce all that he has cannot be my disciple." ❖ So then let us cast off the works of darkness and put on the armor of light.

Every athlete exercises self-control in all things. They do it to receive a perishable wreath, but we an imperishable. But I discipline my body and keep it under control, lest after preaching to others I myself should be disqualified. ❖ Brothers, I do not consider that I have made it my own. But one thing I do: forgetting what lies behind and straining forward to what lies ahead, I press on toward the goal for the prize of the upward call of God in Christ Jesus. ❖ "Let us know; let us press on to know the Lord."

Heb. 12:1, 2. | Luke 9:23. | Luke 14:33. | Rom. 13:12.
1 Cor. 9:25, 27. | Phil. 3:13, 14. | Hosea 6:3.

JAN.
31

"But if you do not drive out the inhabitants of the land from before you, then those of them whom you let remain shall be as barbs in your eyes and thorns in your sides, and they shall trouble you in the land where you dwell."

Fight the good fight of the faith. ❖ For the weapons of our warfare are not of the flesh but have divine power to destroy strongholds. We destroy arguments … and take every thought captive to obey Christ.

So then, brothers, we are debtors, not to the flesh, to live according to the flesh. For if you live according to the flesh you will die, but if by the Spirit you put to death the deeds of the body, you will live.

For the desires of the flesh are against the Spirit, and the desires of the Spirit are against the flesh, for these are opposed to each other, to keep you from doing the things you want to do. ❖ But I see in my members another law waging war against the law of my mind and making me captive to the law of sin that dwells in my members. ❖ We are more than conquerors through him who loved us.

Num. 33:55. | 1 Tim. 6:12. | 2 Cor. 10:4, 5.
Rom. 8:12, 13. | Gal. 5:17. | Rom. 7:23. | Rom. 8:37.

February

FEB.
1

Though you have not seen him, you love him.

For we walk by faith, not by sight. ❖ We love because he first loved us. ❖ So we have come to know and to believe the love that God has for us. God is love, and whoever abides in love abides in God, and God abides in him. ❖ In him you also, when you heard the word of truth, the gospel of your salvation, and believed in him, were sealed with the promised Holy Spirit. ❖ To them God chose to make known how great among the Gentiles are the riches of the glory of this mystery, which is Christ in you, the hope of glory.

If anyone says, "I love God," and hates his brother, he is a liar; for he who does not love his brother whom he has seen cannot love God whom he has not seen.

Jesus said to him, "Have you believed because you have seen me? Blessed are those who have not seen and yet have believed." ❖ Blessed are all who take refuge in him.

1 Pet. 1:8. | 2 Cor. 5:7. | 1 John 4:19. | 1 John 4:16.
Eph. 1:13. | Col. 1:27. | 1 John 4:20. | John 20:29. | Ps. 2:12.

"Oh … that you would keep me from harm."

"Why are you sleeping? Rise and pray that you may not enter into temptation." ❖ "The spirit indeed is willing, but the flesh is weak."

Two things I ask of you; deny them not to me before I die: Remove far from me falsehood and lying; give me neither poverty nor riches; feed me with the food that is needful for me, lest I be full and deny you and say, "Who is the LORD?" or lest I be poor and steal and profane the name of my God.

The LORD will keep you from all evil; he will keep your life. ❖ "I will deliver you out of the hand of the wicked, and redeem you from the grasp of the ruthless." ❖ We know that everyone who has been born of God does not keep on sinning, but he who was born of God protects him, and the evil one does not touch him. ❖ "Because you have kept my word about patient endurance, I will keep you from the hour of trial that is coming on the whole world, to try those who dwell on the earth." ❖ The Lord knows how to rescue the godly from trials.

1 Chron. 4:10. | Luke 22:46. | Matt. 26:41. | Prov. 30:7-9.
Ps. 121:7. | Jer. 15:21. | 1 John 5:18. | Rev. 3:10. | 2 Pet. 2:9.

FEB.
3

"Be strong ... work, for I am with you, declares the Lord of hosts."

"I am the vine; you are the branches. Whoever abides in me and I in him, he it is that bears much fruit, for apart from me you can do nothing." ❖ I can do all things through him who strengthens me. ❖ Finally, be strong in the Lord and in the strength of his might. ❖ "The joy of the Lord is your strength."

Thus says the Lord of hosts: "Let your hands be strong, you who in these days have been hearing these words from the mouth of the prophets." ❖ Strengthen the weak hands, and make firm the feeble knees. Say to those who have an anxious heart, "Be strong; fear not!" ❖ And the Lord turned to him and said, "Go in this might of yours."

If God is for us, who can be against us? ❖ Therefore, having this ministry by the mercy of God, we do not lose heart.

And let us not grow weary of doing good, for in due season we will reap, if we do not give up. ❖ But thanks be to God, who gives us the victory through our Lord Jesus Christ.

Hag. 2:4. | John 15:5. | Phil. 4:13. | Eph. 6:10.
Neh. 8:10. | Zech. 8:9. | Isa. 35:3, 4. | Judg. 6:14.
Rom. 8:31. | 2 Cor. 4:1. | Gal. 6:9. | 1 Cor. 15:57.

FEB.
4

"The LORD *has said to you,*
'You shall never return that way again.'"

If they had been thinking of that land from which they had gone out, they would have had opportunity to return. But as it is, they desire a better country, that is, a heavenly one ... choosing rather to be mistreated with the people of God than to enjoy the fleeting pleasures of sin. He considered the reproach of Christ greater wealth than the treasures of Egypt. ❖ "But my righteous one shall live by faith, and if he shrinks back, my soul has no pleasure in him." But we are not of those who shrink back and are destroyed, but of those who have faith and preserve their souls. ❖ "No one who puts his hand to the plow and looks back is fit for the kingdom of God."

But far be it from me to boast except in the cross of our Lord Jesus Christ, by which the world has been crucified to me, and I to the world. ❖ "Therefore go out from their midst, and be separate from them, says the Lord, and touch no unclean thing; then I will welcome you."

He who began a good work in you will bring it to completion at the day of Jesus Christ.

Deut. 17:16. | Heb. 11:15, 16, 25, 26. | Heb. 10:38, 39.
Luke 9:62. | Gal. 6:14. | 2 Cor. 6:17. | Phil. 1:6.

FEB.
5

"I came that they may have life and have it abundantly."

"In the day that you eat of it you shall surely die." ❖ She took of its fruit and ate, and she also gave some to her husband who was with her, and he ate.

For the wages of sin is death, but the free gift of God is eternal life in Christ Jesus our Lord. ❖ If, because of one man's trespass, death reigned through that one man, much more will those who receive the abundance of grace and the free gift of righteousness reign in life through the one man Jesus Christ. ❖ For as by a man came death, by a man has come also the resurrection of the dead. For as in Adam all die, so also in Christ shall all be made alive ❖ Our Savior Christ Jesus … abolished death and brought life and immortality to light through the gospel.

God gave us eternal life, and this life is in his Son. Whoever has the Son has life; whoever does not have the Son of God does not have life. ❖ "For God did not send his Son into the world to condemn the world, but in order that the world might be saved through him."

John 10:10. | Gen. 2:17. | Gen. 3:6.
Rom. 6:23. | Rom. 5:17. | 1 Cor. 15:21, 22.
2 Tim. 1:10. | 1 John 5:11, 12. | John 3:17.

FEB. 6

The grace of our Lord overflowed for me with the faith and love that are in Christ Jesus.

For you know the grace of our Lord Jesus Christ, that though he was rich, yet for your sake he became poor, so that you by his poverty might become rich. ❖ But where sin increased, grace abounded all the more.

So that in the coming ages he might show the immeasurable riches of his grace in kindness toward us in Christ Jesus. For by grace you have been saved through faith. And this is not your own doing; it is the gift of God, not a result of works, so that no one may boast. ❖ Yet we know that a person is not justified by works of the law but through faith in Jesus Christ, so we also have believed in Christ Jesus, in order to be justified by faith in Christ and not by works of the law, because by works of the law no one will be justified. ❖ He saved us, not because of works done by us in righteousness, but according to his own mercy, by the washing of regeneration and renewal of the Holy Spirit, whom he poured out on us richly through Jesus Christ our Savior.

1 Tim. 1:14. | 2 Cor. 8:9. | Rom. 5:20.
Eph. 2:7-9. | Gal. 2:16. | Titus 3:5, 6.

FEB.
7

"And you shall eat and be full,
and you shall bless the LORD *your*
God for the good land he has given you."

"Take care lest you forget the LORD your God." ❖ Then one of them, when he saw that he was healed, turned back, praising God with a loud voice; and he fell on his face at Jesus' feet, giving him thanks. Now he was a Samaritan. Then Jesus answered, "Were not ten cleansed? Where are the nine? Was no one found to return and give praise to God except this foreigner?"

For everything created by God is good, and nothing is to be rejected if it is received with thanksgiving, for it is made holy by the word of God and prayer. ❖ The one who eats, eats in honor of the Lord, since he gives thanks to God. ❖ The blessing of the LORD makes rich, and he adds no sorrow with it. ❖ Bless the LORD, O my soul, and all that is within me, bless his holy name! Bless the LORD, O my soul … who forgives all your iniquity … who crowns you with steadfast love and mercy.

Deut. 8:10. | Deut. 8:11. | Luke 17:15-18.
1 Tim. 4:4, 5. | Rom. 14:6. | Prov. 10:22. | Ps. 103:1-4.

FEB.
8

"No longer do I call you servants, for the servant does not know what his master is doing; but I have called you friends."

The LORD said, "Shall I hide from Abraham what I am about to do?" ❖ "To you it has been given to know the secrets of the kingdom of heaven." ❖ These things God has revealed to us through the Spirit. For the Spirit searches everything, even the depths of God. ❖ Hidden wisdom of God, which God decreed before the ages for our glory.

Blessed is the one you choose and bring near, to dwell in your courts! We shall be satisfied with the goodness of your house, the holiness of your temple! ❖ The friendship of the LORD is for those who fear him, and he makes known to them his covenant. ❖ "For I have given them the words that you gave me, and they have received them and have come to know in truth that I came from you; and they have believed that you sent me."

"You are my friends if you do what I command you."

John 15:15. | Gen. 18:17. | Matt. 13:11.
1 Cor. 2:10. | 1 Cor. 2:7. | Ps. 65:4.
Ps. 25:14. | John 17:8. | John 15:14.

FEB.
9

"But now he is comforted here."

Your sun shall no more go down, nor your moon withdraw itself; for the LORD will be your everlasting light, and your days of mourning shall be ended. ❖ He will swallow up death forever; and the Lord GOD will wipe away tears from all faces, and the reproach of his people he will take away from all the earth. ❖ "These are the ones coming out of the great tribulation. They have washed their robes and made them white in the blood of the Lamb. Therefore they are before the throne of God, and serve him day and night in his temple; and he who sits on the throne will shelter them with his presence. They shall hunger no more, neither thirst anymore; the sun shall not strike them, nor any scorching heat. For the Lamb in the midst of the throne will be their shepherd, and he will guide them to springs of living water." ❖ "He will wipe away every tear from their eyes, and death shall be no more, neither shall there be mourning nor crying nor pain anymore, for the former things have passed away."

Luke 16:25. | Isa. 60:20. | Isa. 25:8.
Rev. 7:14-17. | Rev. 21:4.

FEB.
10

*"Your eye is the lamp of your body.
When your eye is healthy, your
whole body is full of light."*

The natural person does not accept the things of the Spirit of God, for they are folly to him, and he is not able to understand them because they are spiritually discerned. ❖ Open my eyes, that I may behold wondrous things out of your law.

"I am the light of the world. Whoever follows me will not walk in darkness, but will have the light of life." ❖ And we all, with unveiled face, beholding the glory of the Lord, are being transformed into the same image. ... For this comes from the Lord who is the Spirit. ❖ For God, who said, "Let light shine out of darkness," has shone in our hearts to give the light of the knowledge of the glory of God in the face of Jesus Christ.

The God of our Lord Jesus Christ, the Father of glory ... give you a spirit of wisdom and of revelation in the knowledge of him ... that you may know what is the hope to which he has called you, what are the riches of his glorious inheritance in the saints.

Luke 11:34. | 1 Cor. 2:14. | Ps. 119:18. | John 8:12.
2 Cor. 3:18. | 2 Cor. 4:6. | Eph. 1:17, 18.

FEB.
11

Then those who feared the LORD spoke with one another. The LORD paid attention and heard them, and a book of remembrance was written before him of those who feared the LORD and esteemed his name.

While they were talking and discussing together, Jesus himself drew near and went with them. ❖ "For where two or three are gathered in my name, there am I among them." ❖ My fellow workers, whose names are in the book of life.

Let the word of Christ dwell in you richly, teaching and admonishing one another in all wisdom, singing psalms and hymns and spiritual songs, with thankfulness in your hearts to God. ❖ But exhort one another every day, as long as it is called "today," that none of you may be hardened by the deceitfulness of sin.

"I tell you, on the day of judgment people will give account for every careless word they speak, for by your words you will be justified, and by your words you will be condemned." ❖ Behold, it is written before me.

Mal. 3:16. | Luke 24:15. | Matt. 18:20. | Phil. 4:3. Col. 3:16. | Heb. 3:13. | Matt. 12:36, 37. | Isa. 65:6.

FEB.
12

"They shall be mine, says the LORD of hosts, in the day when I make up my treasured possession."

"I have manifested your name to the people whom you gave me out of the world. Yours they were, and you gave them to me, and they have kept your word. … I am praying for them. I am not praying for the world but for those whom you have given me, for they are yours. All mine are yours, and yours are mine, and I am glorified in them. … Father, I desire that they also, whom you have given me, may be with me where I am, to see my glory that you have given me because you loved me before the foundation of the world."

"I will come again and will take you to myself." ❖ When he comes on that day to be glorified in his saints, and to be marveled at among all who have believed. ❖ Then we who are alive, who are left, will be caught up together with them in the clouds to meet the Lord in the air, and so we will always be with the Lord. ❖ You shall be a crown of beauty in the hand of the LORD, and a royal diadem in the hand of your God.

Mal. 3:17. | John 17:6, 9, 10, 24. | John 14:3.
2 Thess. 1:10. | 1 Thess. 4:17. | Isa. 62:3.

FEB.
13

Seated above the likeness of a throne
was a likeness with a human appearance.

The man Christ Jesus. ❖ Being born in the likeness of men. And being found in human form. ❖ Since therefore the children share in flesh and blood, he himself likewise partook of the same things, that through death he might destroy the one who has the power of death.

"[I am] the living one. I died, and behold I am alive forevermore." ❖ We know that Christ being raised from the dead will never die again; death no longer has dominion over him. For the death he died he died to sin, once for all, but the life he lives he lives to God. ❖ "Then what if you were to see the Son of Man ascending to where he was before?" ❖ He raised him from the dead and seated him at his right hand in the heavenly places. ❖ For in him the whole fullness of deity dwells bodily. For he was crucified in weakness, but lives by the power of God. For we also are weak in him, but in dealing with you we will live with him by the power of God.

Ezek. 1:26. | 1 Tim. 2:5. | Phil. 2:7, 8. | Heb. 2:14.
Rev. 1:18. | Rom. 6:9, 10. | John 6:62.
Eph. 1:20. | Col. 2:9. | 2 Cor. 13:4.

FEB. 14

"Let it be so now, for thus it is fitting for us to fulfill all righteousness."

"I desire to do your will, O my God; your law is within my heart."

"Do not think that I have come to abolish the Law or the Prophets; I have not come to abolish them but to fulfill them. For truly, I say to you, until heaven and earth pass away, not an iota, not a dot, will pass from the Law until all is accomplished." ❖ The LORD was pleased, for his righteousness' sake, to magnify his law and make it glorious. ❖ "For I tell you, unless your righteousness exceeds that of the scribes and Pharisees, you will never enter the kingdom of heaven."

For God has done what the law, weakened by the flesh, could not do. By sending his own Son in the likeness of sinful flesh and for sin, he condemned sin in the flesh, in order that the righteous requirement of the law might be fulfilled in us, who walk not according to the flesh but according to the Spirit. ❖ For Christ is the end of the law for righteousness to everyone who believes.

Matt. 3:15. | Ps. 40:8. | Matt. 5:17, 18. | Isa. 42:21.
Matt. 5:20. | Rom. 8:3, 4. | Rom. 10:4.

FEB.
15

Who can say, "I have made my heart pure"?

The LORD looks down from heaven on the children of man, to see if there are any who understand, who seek after God. They have all turned aside; together they have become corrupt; there is none who does good, not even one. ❖ Those who are in the flesh cannot please God.

For I have the desire to do what is right, but not the ability to carry it out. For I do not do the good I want, but the evil I do not want is what I keep on doing. ❖ We have all become like one who is unclean, and all our righteous deeds are like a polluted garment. We all fade like a leaf, and our iniquities, like the wind, take us away.

But the Scripture imprisoned everything under sin, so that the promise by faith in Jesus Christ might be given to those who believe. ❖ In Christ God was reconciling the world to himself, not counting their trespasses against them. ❖ If we say we have no sin, we deceive ourselves, and the truth is not in us. If we confess our sins, he is faithful and just to forgive us our sins and to cleanse us from all unrighteousness.

Prov. 20:9. | Ps. 14:2, 3. | Rom. 8:8. | Rom. 7:18, 19.
Isa. 64:6. | Gal. 3:22. | 2 Cor. 5:19. | 1 John 1:8, 9.

FEB.
16

Your name is oil poured out.

Christ loved us and gave himself up for us, a fragrant offering and sacrifice to God. ❖ So the honor is for you who believe. ❖ Therefore God has highly exalted him and bestowed on him the name that is above every name, so that at the name of Jesus every knee should bow. ❖ For in him the whole fullness of deity dwells bodily.

"If you love me, you will keep my commandments." ❖ God's love has been poured into our hearts through the Holy Spirit who has been given to us. ❖ The house was filled with the fragrance of the perfume. ❖ And they recognized that they had been with Jesus.

O LORD, our Lord, how majestic is your name in all the earth! You have set your glory above the heavens. ❖ "Immanuel" (which means, God with us). ❖ His name shall be called Wonderful Counselor, Mighty God, Everlasting Father, Prince of Peace. ❖ The name of the LORD is a strong tower; the righteous man runs into it and is safe.

Song of Songs 1:3. | Eph. 5:2. | 1 Pet. 2:7.
Phil. 2:9, 10. | Col. 2:9. | John 14:15.
Rom. 5:5. | John 12:3. | Acts 4:13.
Ps. 8:1. | Matt. 1:23. | Isa. 9:6. | Prov. 18:10.

FEB.
17

"All the rest of the bull – he shall carry outside the camp to a clean place, to the ash heap, and shall burn it up on a fire of wood."

So they took Jesus, and he went out, bearing his own cross, to the place called the place of a skull, which in Aramaic is called Golgotha. There they crucified him. ❖ For the bodies of those animals whose blood is brought into the holy places by the high priest as a sacrifice for sin are burned outside the camp. So Jesus also suffered outside the gate in order to sanctify the people through his own blood. Therefore let us go to him outside the camp and bear the reproach he endured. ❖ Share his sufferings.

But rejoice insofar as you share Christ's sufferings, that you may also rejoice and be glad when his glory is revealed. ❖ For this slight momentary affliction is preparing for us an eternal weight of glory beyond all comparison.

Lev. 4:12. | John 19:16-18. | Heb. 13:11-13.
Phil. 3:10. | 1 Pet. 4:13. | 2 Cor. 4:17.

FEB.
18

You are my refuge in the day of disaster.

There are many who say, "Who will show us some good? Lift up the light of your face upon us, O LORD!" ❖ But I will sing of your strength; I will sing aloud of your steadfast love in the morning. For you have been to me a fortress and a refuge in the day of my distress.

As for me, I said in my prosperity, "I shall never be moved." You hid your face; I was dismayed. To you, O LORD, I cry, and to the Lord I plead for mercy: "What profit is there in my death, if I go down to the pit? Will the dust praise you? Will it tell of your faithfulness? Hear, O LORD, and be merciful to me! O LORD, be my helper!"

"For a brief moment I deserted you, but with great compassion I will gather you. In overflowing anger for a moment I hid my face from you, but with everlasting love I will have compassion on you," says the LORD, your Redeemer. ❖ "Your sorrow will turn into joy." ❖ Weeping may tarry for the night, but joy comes with the morning.

Jer. 17:17. | Ps. 4:6. | Ps. 59:16. | Ps. 30:6-10.
Isa. 54:7, 8. | John 16:20. | Ps. 30:5.

FEB. 19

For the LORD gives wisdom; from his mouth come knowledge and understanding.

Trust in the LORD with all your heart, and do not lean on your own understanding. ❖ If any of you lacks wisdom, let him ask God, who gives generously to all without reproach, and it will be given him. ❖ For the foolishness of God is wiser than men, and the weakness of God is stronger than men. ❖ But God chose what is foolish in the world to shame the wise … so that no human being might boast in the presence of God.

The unfolding of your words gives light; it imparts understanding to the simple. ❖ I have stored up your word in my heart, that I might not sin against you.

And all spoke well of him and marveled at the gracious words that were coming from his mouth. ❖ "No one ever spoke like this man!" ❖ He is the source of your life in Christ Jesus, whom God made our wisdom and our righteousness and sanctification and redemption.

Prov. 2:6. | Prov. 3:5. | James 1:5. | 1 Cor. 1:25.
1 Cor. 1:27, 29. | Ps. 119:130. | Ps. 119:11.
Luke 4:22. | John 7:46. | 1 Cor. 1:30.

Out of the anguish of his soul
he shall see and be satisfied.

Jesus … said, "It is finished," and he bowed his head and gave up his spirit. ❖ For our sake he made him to be sin who knew no sin, so that in him we might become the righteousness of God.

"The people whom I formed for myself that they might declare my praise." ❖ So that through the church the manifold wisdom of God might now be made known to the rulers and authorities in the heavenly places. This was according to the eternal purpose that he has realized in Christ Jesus our Lord. ❖ So that in the coming ages he might show the immeasurable riches of his grace in kindness toward us in Christ Jesus.

In him you also, when you heard the word of truth, the gospel of your salvation, and believed in him, were sealed with the promised Holy Spirit, who is the guarantee of our inheritance until we acquire possession of it, to the praise of his glory. ❖ But you are a chosen race, a royal priesthood, a holy nation, a people for his own possession, that you may proclaim the excellencies of him who called you out of darkness into his marvelous light.

Isa. 53:11. | John 19:30. | 2 Cor. 5:21. | Isa. 43:21.
Eph. 3:10, 11. | Eph. 2:7. | Eph. 1:13, 14. | 1 Pet. 2:9.

FEB.
21

"I am the LORD who sanctifies you."

"I am the LORD your God, who have separated you from the peoples. … You shall be holy to me, for I the LORD am holy and have separated you from the peoples, that you should be mine."

Beloved in God the Father. ❖ "Sanctify them in the truth; your word is truth." ❖ Now may the God of peace himself sanctify you completely, and may your whole spirit and soul and body be kept blameless at the coming of our Lord Jesus Christ.

So Jesus also suffered outside the gate in order to sanctify the people through his own blood. ❖ Our … Savior Jesus Christ … gave himself for us to redeem us from all lawlessness and to purify for himself a people for his own possession who are zealous for good works. ❖ For he who sanctifies and those who are sanctified all have one origin. That is why he is not ashamed to call them brothers. ❖ "And for their sake I consecrate myself, that they also may be sanctified in truth." ❖ In the sanctification of the Spirit, for obedience to Jesus Christ and for sprinkling with his blood.

Lev. 20:8. | Lev. 20:24, 26. | Jude 1. | John 17:17.
1 Thess. 5:23. | Heb. 13:12. | Titus 2:13, 14.
Heb. 2:11. | John 17:19. | 1 Pet. 1:2.

FEB. 22

Who is the man who fears the LORD? Him will he instruct in the way that he should choose.

"The eye is the lamp of the body. So, if your eye is healthy, your whole body will be full of light."

Your word is a lamp to my feet and a light to my path. ❖ And your ears shall hear a word behind you, saying, "This is the way, walk in it," when you turn to the right or when you turn to the left. ❖ I will instruct you and teach you in the way you should go; I will counsel you with my eye upon you. Be not like a horse or a mule, without understanding, which must be curbed with bit and bridle, or it will not stay near you. Many are the sorrows of the wicked, but steadfast love surrounds the one who trusts in the LORD. Be glad in the LORD, and rejoice, O righteous, and shout for joy, all you upright in heart!

I know, O LORD, that the way of man is not in himself, that it is not in man who walks to direct his steps.

Ps. 25:12. | Matt. 6:22. | Ps. 119:105.
Isa. 30:21. | Ps. 32:8-11. | Jer. 10:23.

FEB. 23

The sprinkled blood that speaks a better word than the blood of Abel.

"Behold, the Lamb of God, who takes away the sin of the world!" ❖ The Lamb that was slain. ❖ For it is impossible for the blood of bulls and goats to take away sins. Consequently, when Christ came into the world, he said, "Sacrifices and offerings you have not desired, but a body have you prepared for me. … And by that will we have been sanctified through the offering of the body of Jesus Christ once for all.

And Abel … brought of the firstborn of his flock and of their fat portions. And the LORD had regard for Abel and his offering. ❖ Christ loved us and gave himself up for us, a fragrant offering and sacrifice to God.

Let us draw near with a true heart in full assurance of faith, with our hearts sprinkled clean from an evil conscience and our bodies washed with pure water. ❖ Therefore, brothers … we have confidence to enter the holy places by the blood of Jesus.

Heb. 12:24. | John 1:29. | Rev. 13:8. | Heb. 10:4, 5, 10.
Gen. 4:4. | Eph. 5:2. | Heb. 10:22. | Heb. 10:19.

FEB.
24

"Thus says the Lord God: This also I will let the house of Israel ask me to do for them."

You do not have, because you do not ask. ❖ "Ask, and it will be given to you; seek, and you will find; knock, and it will be opened to you. For everyone who asks receives, and the one who seeks finds, and to the one who knocks it will be opened." ❖ And this is the confidence that we have toward him, that if we ask anything according to his will he hears us. And if we know that he hears us in whatever we ask, we know that we have the requests that we have asked of him. ❖ If any of you lacks wisdom, let him ask God, who gives generously to all without reproach, and it will be given him. ❖ Open your mouth wide, and I will fill it. ❖ And he told them a parable to the effect that they ought always to pray and not lose heart. ❖ The eyes of the Lord are toward the righteous and his ears toward their cry. The Lord hears and delivers them out of all their troubles. ❖ "In that day you will ask in my name, and I do not say to you that I will ask the Father on your behalf; for the Father himself loves you, because you have loved me. ... Ask, and you will receive, that your joy may be full."

Ezek. 36:37. | James 4:2. | Matt. 7:7, 8.
1 John 5:14, 15. | James 1:5. | Ps. 81:10.
Luke 18:1. | Ps. 34:15, 17. | John 16:26, 27, 24.

FEB.
25

Resist the devil, and he will flee from you.

For he will come like a rushing stream, which the wind of the LORD drives. ❖ "Be gone, Satan! For it is written, 'You shall worship the Lord your God and him only shall you serve.'" Then the devil left him, and behold, angels came and were ministering to him.

Finally, be strong in the Lord and in the strength of his might. Put on the whole armor of God, that you may be able to stand against the schemes of the devil. ❖ Take no part in the unfruitful works of darkness, but instead expose them. ❖ So that we would not be outwitted by Satan; for we are not ignorant of his designs. ❖ Be sober-minded; be watchful. Your adversary the devil prowls around like a roaring lion, seeking someone to devour. Resist him, firm in your faith, knowing that the same kinds of suffering are being experienced by your brotherhood throughout the world. ❖ And this is the victory that has overcome the world – our faith.

Who shall bring any charge against God's elect? It is God who justifies.

James 4:7. | Isa. 59:19. | Matt. 4:10, 11.
Eph. 6:10, 11. | Eph. 5:11. | 2 Cor. 2:11.
1 Pet. 5:8, 9. | 1 John 5:4. | Rom. 8:33.

FEB.
26

Let us test and examine our ways,
and return to the Lord!

Prove me, O Lord, and try me; test my heart and my mind. ❖ Behold, you delight in truth in the inward being, and you teach me wisdom in the secret heart. ❖ When I think on my ways, I turn my feet to your testimonies; I hasten and do not delay to keep your commandments. ❖ Let a person examine himself, then, and so eat of the bread and drink of the cup.

If we confess our sins, he is faithful and just to forgive us our sins and to cleanse us from all unrighteousness. ❖ We have an advocate with the Father, Jesus Christ the righteous. He is the propitiation for our sins. ❖ Therefore, brothers, since we have confidence to enter the holy places by the blood of Jesus, by the new and living way that he opened for us through the curtain, that is, through his flesh, and since we have a great priest over the house of God, let us draw near with a true heart in full assurance of faith, with our hearts sprinkled clean from an evil conscience and our bodies washed with pure water.

Lam. 3:40. | Ps. 26:2. | Ps. 51:6. | Ps. 119:59, 60.
1 Cor. 11:28. | 1 John 1:9. | 1 John 2:1, 2. | Heb. 10:19-22.

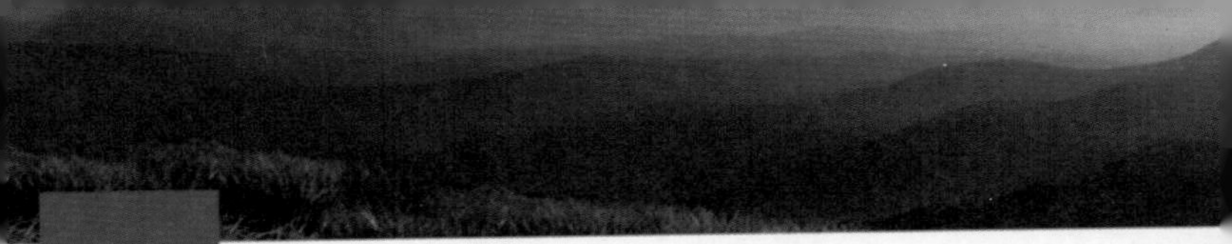

FEB.
27

So you also must consider yourselves
dead to sin and alive to God in Christ Jesus.

"Truly, truly, I say to you, whoever hears my word and believes him who sent me has eternal life. He does not come into judgment, but has passed from death to life." ❖ For through the law I died to the law, so that I might live to God. I have been crucified with Christ. It is no longer I who live, but Christ who lives in me. And the life I now live in the flesh I live by faith in the Son of God, who loved me and gave himself for me.

"Because I live, you also will live." ❖ "I give them eternal life, and they will never perish, and no one will snatch them out of my hand. My Father, who has given them to me, is greater than all, and no one is able to snatch them out of the Father's hand. I and the Father are one."

If then you have been raised with Christ, seek the things that are above, where Christ is, seated at the right hand of God. … For you have died, and your life is hidden with Christ in God.

Rom. 6:11. | John 5:24. | Gal. 2:19, 20.
John 14:19. | John 10:28-30. | Col. 3:1, 3.

FEB.
28

"For God so loved the world, that he gave his only Son, that whoever believes in him should not perish but have eternal life."

All this is from God, who through Christ reconciled us to himself and gave us the ministry of reconciliation; that is, in Christ God was reconciling the world to himself, not counting their trespasses against them, and entrusting to us the message of reconciliation. Therefore, we are ambassadors for Christ, God making his appeal through us. We implore you on behalf of Christ, be reconciled to God. For our sake he made him to be sin who knew no sin, so that in him we might become the righteousness of God. ❖ God is love. In this the love of God was made manifest among us, that God sent his only Son into the world, so that we might live through him. In this is love, not that we have loved God but that he loved us and sent his Son to be the propitiation for our sins. Beloved, if God so loved us, we also ought to love one another.

John 3:16. | 2 Cor. 5:18-21. | 1 John 4:8-11.

FEB.
29

Do not boast about tomorrow, for you do not know what a day may bring.

Behold, now is the favorable time; behold, now is the day of salvation. ❖ "The light is among you for a little while longer. Walk while you have the light, lest darkness overtake you. The one who walks in the darkness does not know where he is going. While you have the light, believe in the light, that you may become sons of light." ❖ Whatever your hand finds to do, do it with your might, for there is no work or thought or knowledge or wisdom in Sheol, to which you are going.

"'Soul, you have ample goods laid up for many years; relax, eat, drink, be merry.' 'Fool! This night your soul is required of you, and the things you have prepared, whose will they be?' So is the one who lays up treasure for himself and is not rich toward God."

What is your life? For you are a mist that appears for a little time and then vanishes. ❖ And the world is passing away along with its desires, but whoever does the will of God abides forever.

Prov. 27:1. | 2 Cor. 6:2. | John 12:35, 36. | Eccles. 9:10.
Luke 12:19-21. | James 4:14. | 1 John 2:17.

March

MAR. 1

But the fruit of the Spirit is love.

God is love, and whoever abides in love abides in God, and God abides in him. ❖ God's love has been poured into our hearts through the Holy Spirit who has been given to us. ❖ So the honor is for you who believe. ❖ We love because he first loved us. ❖ For the love of Christ controls us, because we have concluded this: that one has died for all, therefore all have died; and he died for all, that those who live might no longer live for themselves but for him who for their sake died and was raised.

You yourselves have been taught by God to love one another. ❖ "This is my commandment, that you love one another as I have loved you." ❖ Above all, keep loving one another earnestly, since love covers a multitude of sins. ❖ And walk in love, as Christ loved us and gave himself up for us, a fragrant offering and sacrifice to God.

Gal. 5:22. | 1 John 4:16. | Rom. 5:5. | 1 Pet. 2:7.
1 John 4:19. | 2 Cor. 5:14, 15. | 1 Thess. 4:9.
John 15:12. | 1 Pet. 4:8. | Eph. 5:2.

*"For God has made me fruitful
in the land of my affliction."*

Blessed be the God and Father of our Lord Jesus Christ, the Father of mercies and God of all comfort, who comforts us in all our affliction, so that we may be able to comfort those who are in any affliction, with the comfort with which we ourselves are comforted by God. For as we share abundantly in Christ's sufferings, so through Christ we share abundantly in comfort too.

Now for a little while, if necessary, you have been grieved by various trials, so that the tested genuineness of your faith – more precious than gold that perishes though it is tested by fire – may be found to result in praise and glory and honor at the revelation of Jesus Christ. ❖ But the Lord stood by me and strengthened me.

Therefore let those who suffer according to God's will entrust their souls to a faithful Creator while doing good.

Gen. 41:52. | 2 Cor. 1:3-5. | 1 Pet. 1:6, 7.
2 Tim. 4:17. | 1 Pet. 4:19.

MAR. 3

Trust in the LORD with all your heart, and do not lean on your own understanding. In all your ways acknowledge him, and he will make straight your paths.

Trust in him at all times, O people; pour out your heart before him; God is a refuge for us.

I will instruct you and teach you in the way you should go; I will counsel you with my eye upon you. Be not like a horse or a mule, without understanding, which must be curbed with bit and bridle, or it will not stay near you. Many are the sorrows of the wicked, but steadfast love surrounds the one who trusts in the LORD. ❖ And your ears shall hear a word behind you, saying, "This is the way, walk in it," when you turn to the right or when you turn to the left.

"If your presence will not go with me, do not bring us up from here. For how shall it be known that I have found favor in your sight, I and your people? Is it not in your going with us, so that we are distinct, I and your people, from every other people on the face of the earth?"

Prov. 3:5, 6. | Ps. 62:8. | Ps. 32:8-10.
Isa. 30:21. | Exod. 33:15-16.

MAR. 4

Set your minds on things that are above,
not on things that are on earth.

Do not love the world or the things in the world. If anyone loves the world, the love of the Father is not in him. ❖ "Do not lay up for yourselves treasures on earth, where moth and rust destroy and where thieves break in and steal, but lay up for yourselves treasures in heaven, where neither moth nor rust destroys and where thieves do not break in and steal. For where your treasure is, there your heart will be also."

For we walk by faith, not by sight. ❖ So we do not lose heart. Though our outer nature is wasting away, our inner nature is being renewed day by day. For this slight momentary affliction is preparing for us an eternal weight of glory beyond all comparison, as we look not to the things that are seen but to the things that are unseen. For the things that are seen are transient, but the things that are unseen are eternal. ❖ An inheritance that is imperishable, undefiled, and unfading, kept in heaven for you.

Col. 3:2. | 1 John 2:15. | Matt. 6:19-21.
2 Cor. 5:7. | 2 Cor. 4:16-18. | 1 Pet. 1:4.

MAR. 5

O Lord, I am oppressed; be my pledge of safety!

To you I lift up my eyes, O you who are enthroned in the heavens! Behold, as the eyes of servants look to the hand of their master, as the eyes of a maidservant to the hand of her mistress, so our eyes look to the LORD our God. ❖ Hear my cry, O God, listen to my prayer; from the end of the earth I call to you when my heart is faint. Lead me to the rock that is higher than I, for you have been my refuge, a strong tower against the enemy. Let me dwell in your tent forever! Let me take refuge under the shelter of your wings! ❖ For you have been a stronghold to the poor, a stronghold to the needy in his distress, a shelter from the storm.

Christ also suffered for you, leaving you an example, so that you might follow in his steps. He committed no sin, neither was deceit found in his mouth. When he was reviled, he did not revile in return; when he suffered, he did not threaten, but continued entrusting himself to him who judges justly.

Isa. 38:14. | Ps. 123:1, 2. | Ps. 61:1-4.
Isa. 25:4. | 1 Pet. 2:21-23.

MAR.
6

Watching over the way of his saints.

The LORD your God ... went before you in the way to seek you out a place to pitch your tents, in fire by night and in the cloud by day, to show you by what way you should go. ❖ Like an eagle that stirs up its nest, that flutters over its young, spreading out its wings, catching them, bearing them on its pinions, the LORD alone guided him. ❖ The steps of a man are established by the LORD, when he delights in his way; though he fall, he shall not be cast headlong, for the LORD upholds his hand. ❖ Many are the afflictions of the righteous, but the LORD delivers him out of them all. ❖ For the LORD knows the way of the righteous, but the way of the wicked will perish. ❖ And we know that for those who love God all things work together for good, for those who are called according to his purpose. ❖ "With us is the LORD our God, to help us and to fight our battles."

The LORD your God is in your midst, a mighty one who will save; he will rejoice over you with gladness.

Prov. 2:8. | Deut. 1:32, 33. | Deut. 32:11, 12.
Ps. 37:23, 24. | Ps. 34:19. | Ps. 1:6.
Rom. 8:28. | 2 Chron. 32:8. | Zeph. 3:17.

MAR.
7

"For your Maker is your husband,
the LORD *of hosts is his name."*

This mystery is profound, and I am saying that it refers to Christ and the church. ❖ You shall no more be termed Forsaken … but you shall be called My Delight Is in Her … for the LORD delights in you … and as the bridegroom rejoices over the bride, so shall your God rejoice over you. ❖ He has sent me … to comfort all who mourn; to grant to those who mourn in Zion – to give them a beautiful headdress instead of ashes, the oil of gladness instead of mourning, the garment of praise instead of a faint spirit.

I will greatly rejoice in the LORD; my soul shall exult in my God, for he has clothed me with the garments of salvation; … as a bridegroom decks himself like a priest with a beautiful headdress, and as a bride adorns herself with her jewels.

"And I will betroth you to me forever. I will betroth you to me in righteousness and in justice, in steadfast love and in mercy."

Who shall separate us from the love of Christ?

Isa. 54:5. | Eph. 5:32. | Isa. 62:4, 5. | Isa. 61:1-3.
Isa. 61:10. | Hosea 2:19. | Rom. 8:35.

MAR.
8

You have cast all my sins behind your back.

Who is a God like you, pardoning iniquity and passing over transgression for the remnant of his inheritance? He does not retain his anger forever, because he delights in steadfast love. He will again have compassion on us; he will tread our iniquities under foot. You will cast all our sins into the depths of the sea.

"For a brief moment I deserted you, but with great compassion I will gather you. In overflowing anger for a moment I hid my face from you, but with everlasting love I will have compassion on you," says the LORD, your Redeemer. ❖ "I will forgive their iniquity, and I will remember their sin no more."

Blessed is the one whose transgression is forgiven, whose sin is covered. Blessed is the man against whom the LORD counts no iniquity, and in whose spirit there is no deceit. ❖ The blood of Jesus his Son cleanses us from all sin.

Isa. 38:17. | Mic. 7:18, 19. | Isa. 54:7, 8.
Jer. 31:34. | Ps. 32:1, 2. | 1 John 1:7.

MAR.
9

God … richly provides us with everything to enjoy.

"Take care lest you forget the Lord your God by not keeping his commandments and his rules and his statutes, which I command you today, lest, when you have eaten and are full and have built good houses and live in them … then your heart be lifted up, and you forget the Lord your God … for it is he who gives you power to get wealth."

Unless the Lord builds the house, those who build it labor in vain. Unless the Lord watches over the city, the watchman stays awake in vain. It is in vain that you rise up early and go late to rest, eating the bread of anxious toil; for he gives to his beloved sleep. ❖ For not by their own sword did they win the land, nor did their own arm save them, but your right hand and your arm, and the light of your face, for you delighted in them. ❖ There are many who say, "Who will show us some good? Lift up the light of your face upon us, O Lord!"

1 Tim. 6:17. | Deut. 8:11, 12, 14, 18.
Ps. 127:1, 2. | Ps. 44:3. | Ps. 4:6.

"The LORD will provide."

"God will provide for himself the lamb for a burnt offering, my son."

Behold, the LORD's hand is not shortened, that it cannot save, or his ear dull, that it cannot hear. ❖ "The Deliverer will come from Zion, he will banish ungodliness from Jacob."

Blessed is he whose help is the God of Jacob, whose hope is in the LORD his God. ❖ Behold, the eye of the LORD is on those who fear him, on those who hope in his steadfast love, that he may deliver their soul from death.

And my God will supply every need of yours according to his riches in glory in Christ Jesus. ❖ He has said, "I will never leave you nor forsake you." So we can confidently say, "The Lord is my helper; I will not fear; what can man do to me?" ❖ The LORD is my strength and my shield; in him my heart trusts, and I am helped; my heart exults, and with my song I give thanks to him.

Gen. 22:14. | Gen. 22:8. | Isa. 59:1.
Rom. 11:26. | Ps. 146:5. | Ps. 33:18, 19.
Phil. 4:19. | Heb. 13:5, 6. | Ps. 28:7.

MAR.
11

"The Lord bless you and keep you."

The blessing of the Lord makes rich, and he adds no sorrow with it. ❖ For you bless the righteous, O Lord; you cover him with favor as with a shield.

❖ He will not let your foot be moved; he who keeps you will not slumber. Behold, he who keeps Israel will neither slumber nor sleep. The Lord is your keeper; the Lord is your shade on your right hand. ... The Lord will keep you from all evil; he will keep your life. The Lord will keep your going out and your coming in from this time forth and forevermore. ❖ I, the Lord, am its [the vineyard's] keeper; every moment I water it. Lest anyone punish it, I keep it night and day.

"Holy Father, keep them in your name, which you have given me. While I was with them, I kept them in your name, which you have given me."

The Lord will rescue me from every evil deed and bring me safely into his heavenly kingdom. To him be the glory forever and ever. Amen.

Num. 6:24. | Prov. 10:22. | Ps. 5:12. | Ps.121:3-5, 7, 8. Isa. 27:3. | John 17:11, 12. | 2 Tim. 4:18.

MAR.
12

"The LORD make his face to shine upon you and be gracious to you; the LORD lift up his countenance upon you and give you peace."

No one has ever seen God; the only God, who is at the Father's side, he has made him known. ❖ He is the radiance of the glory of God and the exact imprint of his nature. ❖ The god of this world has blinded the minds of the unbelievers, to keep them from seeing the light of the gospel of the glory of Christ, who is the image of God.

Make your face shine on your servant; save me in your steadfast love! O LORD, let me not be put to shame, for I call upon you. ❖ By your favor, O LORD, you made my mountain stand strong; you hid your face; I was dismayed. ❖ Blessed are the people who know the festal shout, who walk, O LORD, in the light of your face.

May the LORD give strength to his people! May the LORD bless his people with peace!

"Take heart; it is I. Do not be afraid."

Num. 6:25, 26. | John 1:18. | Heb. 1:3.
2 Cor. 4:4. | Ps. 31:16, 17. | Ps. 30:7.
Ps. 89:15. | Ps. 29:11. | Matt. 14:27.

MAR. 13

For there is one God, and there is one mediator between God and men, the man Christ Jesus.

Since therefore the children share in flesh and blood, he himself likewise partook of the same things.

"Turn to me and be saved, all the ends of the earth! For I am God, and there is no other."

We have an advocate with the Father, Jesus Christ the righteous. ❖ But now in Christ Jesus you who once were far off have been brought near by the blood of Christ. For he himself is our peace. ❖ He entered once for all into the holy places, not by means of the blood of goats and calves but by means of his own blood, thus securing an eternal redemption. ... Therefore he is the mediator of a new covenant, so that those who are called may receive the promised eternal inheritance, since a death has occurred that redeems them from the transgressions committed under the first covenant. ❖ Consequently, he is able to save to the uttermost those who draw near to God through him, since he always lives to make intercession for them.

1 Tim. 2:5. | Heb. 2:14. | Isa. 45:22. | 1 John 2:1.
Eph. 2:13, 14. | Heb. 9:12, 15. | Heb. 7:25.

MAR.
14

In everything … may adorn
the doctrine of God our Savior.

Only let your manner of life be worthy of the gospel of Christ. ❖ Abstain from every form of evil. ❖ If you are insulted for the name of Christ, you are blessed, because the Spirit of glory and of God rests upon you. But let none of you suffer as a murderer or a thief or an evildoer or as a meddler. ❖ Be blameless and innocent, children of God without blemish in the midst of a crooked and twisted generation, among whom you shine as lights in the world. ❖ "In the same way, let your light shine before others, so that they may see your good works and give glory to your Father who is in heaven."

Let not steadfast love and faithfulness forsake you; bind them around your neck; write them on the tablet of your heart. So you will find favor and good success in the sight of God and man. ❖ Finally, brothers, whatever is true, whatever is honorable, whatever is just, whatever is pure, whatever is lovely, whatever is commendable, if there is any excellence, if there is anything worthy of praise, think about these things.

Titus 2:10. | Phil. 1:27. | 1 Thess. 5:22. | 1 Pet. 4:14, 15.
Phil. 2:15. | Matt. 5:16. | Prov. 3:3, 4. | Phil. 4:8.

MAR.
15

Perfect through suffering.

"My soul is very sorrowful, even to death; remain here, and watch with me." And going a little farther he fell on his face and prayed, saying, "My Father, if it be possible, let this cup pass from me; nevertheless, not as I will, but as you will." ❖ And being in an agony he prayed more earnestly; and his sweat became like great drops of blood falling down to the ground.

The snares of death encompassed me; the pangs of Sheol laid hold on me; I suffered distress and anguish. ❖ Reproaches have broken my heart, so that I am in despair. I looked for pity, but there was none, and for comforters, but I found none. ❖ Look to the right and see: there is none who takes notice of me; no refuge remains to me; no one cares for my soul.

He was despised and rejected by men; a man of sorrows, and acquainted with grief; and as one from whom men hide their faces he was despised, and we esteemed him not.

Heb. 2:10. | Matt. 26:38, 39. | Luke 22:44.
Ps. 116:3. | Ps. 69:20. | Ps. 142:4. | Isa. 53:3.

MAR.
16

What is your life? For you are a mist that appears for a little time and then vanishes.

"My days are swifter than a runner; they flee away; they see no good. They go by like skiffs of reed, like an eagle swooping on the prey." ❖ You sweep them away as with a flood; they are like a dream, like grass that is renewed in the morning: in the morning it flourishes and is renewed; in the evening it fades and withers. ❖ "Man who is born of a woman is few of days and full of trouble. He comes out like a flower and withers."

And the world is passing away along with its desires, but whoever does the will of God abides forever. ❖ They will perish, but you will remain; they will all wear out like a garment. You will change them like a robe, and they will pass away, but you are the same, and your years have no end. ❖ Jesus Christ is the same yesterday and today and forever.

James 4:14. | Job 9:25, 26. | Ps. 90:5, 6. | Job 14:1, 2.
1 John 2:17. | Ps. 102:26, 27. | Heb. 13:8.

MAR.
17

He shall lay his hand on the head of the burnt offering, and it shall be accepted for him to make atonement for him.

Knowing that you were ransomed from the futile ways inherited from your forefathers, not with perishable things such as silver or gold, but with the precious blood of Christ, like that of a lamb without blemish or spot. ❖ He himself bore our sins in his body on the tree.

He has blessed us in the Beloved.

You yourselves like living stones are being built up as a spiritual house, to be a holy priesthood, to offer spiritual sacrifices acceptable to God through Jesus Christ. ❖ I appeal to you therefore, brothers, by the mercies of God, to present your bodies as a living sacrifice, holy and acceptable to God, which is your spiritual worship.

Now to him who is able to keep you from stumbling and to present you blameless before the presence of his glory with great joy, to the only God, our Savior, through Jesus Christ our Lord, be glory, majesty, dominion, and authority, before all time and now and forever. Amen.

Lev. 1:4. | 1 Pet. 1:18, 19. | 1 Pet. 2:24. | Eph. 1:6.
1 Pet. 2:5. | Rom. 12:1. | Jude 24, 25.

MAR. 18

My eyes are weary with looking upward.

Be gracious to me, O LORD, for I am languishing; heal me, O LORD, for my bones are troubled. My soul also is greatly troubled. But you, O LORD – how long? Turn, O LORD, deliver my life; save me for the sake of your steadfast love. ❖ My heart is in anguish within me; the terrors of death have fallen upon me. Fear and trembling come upon me, and horror overwhelms me. And I say, "Oh, that I had wings like a dove! I would fly away and be at rest." ❖ For you have need of endurance.

And while they were gazing into heaven as he went, behold, two men stood by them in white robes, and said, "Men of Galilee, why do you stand looking into heaven? This Jesus, who was taken up from you into heaven, will come in the same way as you saw him go into heaven." ❖ But our citizenship is in heaven, and from it we await a Savior, the Lord Jesus Christ. ❖ Our blessed hope, the appearing of the glory of our great God and Savior Jesus Christ.

Isa. 38:14. | Ps. 6:2-4. | Ps. 55:4-6. | Heb. 10:36.
Acts 1:10, 11. | Phil. 3:20. | Titus 2:13.

MAR.
19

"God having raised up his servant, sent him to you first, to bless you by turning every one of you from your wickedness."

Blessed be the God and Father of our Lord Jesus Christ! According to his great mercy, he has caused us to be born again to a living hope through the resurrection of Jesus Christ from the dead. ❖ Saved by his life.

Our … Savior Jesus Christ, who gave himself for us to redeem us from all lawlessness and to purify for himself a people for his own possession who are zealous for good works. ❖ But as he who called you is holy, you also be holy in all your conduct, since it is written, "You shall be holy, for I am holy."

The God and Father of our Lord Jesus Christ … has blessed us in Christ with every spiritual blessing in the heavenly places. ❖ For in him the whole fullness of deity dwells bodily, and you have been filled in him. ❖ And from his fullness we have all received, grace upon grace.

He who did not spare his own Son but gave him up for us all, how will he not also with him graciously give us all things?

Acts 3:26. | 1 Pet. 1:3. | Rom. 5:10.
Titus 2:13, 14. | 1 Pet. 1:15, 16. | Eph. 1:3.
Col. 2:9, 10. | John 1:16. | Rom. 8:32.

The unfolding of your words gives light.

This is the message we have heard from him and proclaim to you, that God is light, and in him is no darkness at all. ❖ For God, who said, "Let light shine out of darkness," has shone in our hearts to give the light of the knowledge of the glory of God in the face of Jesus Christ. ❖ The Word was God. … In him was life, and the life was the light of men. ❖ But if we walk in the light, as he is in the light, we have fellowship with one another, and the blood of Jesus his Son cleanses us from all sin. ❖ I have stored up your word in my heart, that I might not sin against you. ❖ "Already you are clean because of the word that I have spoken to you."

For at one time you were darkness, but now you are light in the Lord. Walk as children of light. ❖ But you are a chosen race, a royal priesthood, a holy nation, a people for his own possession, that you may proclaim the excellencies of him who called you out of darkness into his marvelous light.

Ps. 119:130. | 1 John 1:5. | 2 Cor. 4:6.
John 1:1, 4. | 1 John 1:7. | Ps. 119:11.
John 15:3. | Eph. 5:8. | 1 Pet. 2:9.

MAR.
21

"Wake up, and strengthen what remains and is about to die."

The end of all things is at hand; therefore be self-controlled and sober-minded for the sake of your prayers. ❖ Be sober-minded; be watchful. Your adversary the devil prowls around like a roaring lion, seeking someone to devour. ❖ "Only take care, and keep your soul diligently, lest you forget the things that your eyes have seen, and lest they depart from your heart all the days of your life." ❖ "But my righteous one shall live by faith, and if he shrinks back, my soul has no pleasure in him." But we are not of those who shrink back and are destroyed, but of those who have faith and preserve their souls. ❖ "And what I say to you I say to all: Stay awake."

Fear not, for I am with you; be not dismayed, for I am your God; I will strengthen you, I will help you, I will uphold you with my righteous right hand. For I, the LORD your God, hold your right hand.

Rev. 3:2. | 1 Pet. 4:7. | 1 Pet. 5:8. | Deut. 4:9.
Heb. 10:38, 39. | Mark 13:37. | Isa. 41:10, 13.

MAR. 22

And Lot lifted up his eyes and saw that the Jordan Valley was well watered everywhere like the garden of the Lord, like the land of Egypt, in the direction of Zoar. (This was before the Lord destroyed Sodom and Gomorrah.) So Lot chose for himself all the Jordan Valley.

Lot … that righteous man.

Do not be deceived: God is not mocked, for whatever one sows, that will he also reap. ❖ "Remember Lot's wife."

Do not be unequally yoked with unbelievers. For what partnership has righteousness with lawlessness? Or what fellowship has light with darkness? … "Therefore go out from their midst, and be separate from them, says the Lord, and touch no unclean thing." ❖ Therefore do not associate with them; for at one time you were darkness, but now you are light in the Lord. Walk as children of light … and try to discern what is pleasing to the Lord. Take no part in the unfruitful works of darkness, but instead expose them.

Gen. 13:10, 11. | 2 Pet. 2:7, 8. | Gal. 6:7.
Luke 17:32. | 2 Cor. 6:14, 17. | Eph. 5:7, 8, 10, 11.

MAR. 23

"Holy, holy, holy, is the Lord God Almighty, who was and is and is to come!"

Yet you are holy, enthroned on the praises of Israel. ❖ "Do not come near; take your sandals off your feet, for the place on which you are standing is holy ground. … I am the God of your father, the God of Abraham, the God of Isaac, and the God of Jacob." And Moses hid his face, for he was afraid to look at God. ❖ To whom then will you compare me, that I should be like him? says the Holy One. ❖ For I am the LORD your God, the Holy One of Israel, your Savior. … I, I am the LORD, and besides me there is no savior.

But as he who called you is holy, you also be holy in all your conduct, since it is written, "You shall be holy, for I am holy." ❖ Or do you not know that your body is a temple of the Holy Spirit within you, whom you have from God? You are not your own. ❖ For we are the temple of the living God; as God said, "I will make my dwelling among them and walk among them, and I will be their God, and they shall be my people." ❖ "Do two walk together, unless they have agreed to meet?"

Rev. 4:8. | Ps. 22:3. | Exod. 3:5, 6.
Isa. 40:25. | Isa. 43:3, 11. | 1 Pet. 1:15, 16.
1 Cor. 6:19. | 2 Cor. 6:16. | Amos 3:3.

MAR. 24

And [Abraham] believed the LORD and he counted it to him as righteousness.

No distrust made him waver concerning the promise of God, but he grew strong in his faith as he gave glory to God, fully convinced that God was able to do what he had promised. That is why his faith was "counted to him as righteousness." But the words "it was counted to him" were not written for his sake alone, but for ours also. It will be counted to us who believe in him who raised from the dead Jesus our Lord.

For the promise to Abraham and his offspring that he would be heir of the world did not come through the law but through the righteousness of faith. ❖ "The righteous shall live by faith." ❖ Let us hold fast the confession of our hope without wavering, for he who promised is faithful. ❖ Our God is in the heavens; he does all that he pleases. ❖ "For nothing will be impossible with God." ... "And blessed is she who believed that there would be a fulfillment of what was spoken to her from the Lord."

Gen. 15:6. | Rom. 4:20-24. | Rom. 4:13. | Rom. 1:17.
Heb. 10:23. | Ps. 115:3. | Luke 1:37, 45.

MAR.
25

"I will never leave you nor forsake you."

So we can confidently say, "The Lord is my helper; I will not fear; what can man do to me?"

"Behold, I am with you and will keep you wherever you go, and will bring you back to this land. For I will not leave you until I have done what I have promised you." ❖ "Be strong and courageous. Do not fear or be in dread of them, for it is the LORD your God who goes with you. He will not leave you or forsake you."

For Demas, in love with this present world has deserted me. … At my first defense no one came to stand by me, but all deserted me. May it not be charged against them! But the Lord stood by me and strengthened me. ❖ For my father and my mother have forsaken me, but the LORD will take me in.

"And behold, I am with you always, to the end of the age." ❖ "[I am] the living one. I died, and behold I am alive forevermore." ❖ "I will not leave you as orphans; I will come to you." ❖ "My peace I give to you."

Heb. 13:5. | Heb. 13:6. | Gen. 28:15. | Deut. 31:6.
2 Tim. 4:10, 16, 17. | Ps. 27:10. | Matt. 28:20.
Rev. 1:18. | John 14:18. | John 14:27.

MAR.
26

"[The kingdom of heaven] will be like a man going on a journey, who called his servants and entrusted to them his property … to each according to his ability."

Do you not know that if you present yourselves to anyone as obedient slaves, you are slaves of the one whom you obey?

All these are empowered by one and the same Spirit, who apportions to each one individually as he wills. … To each is given the manifestation of the Spirit for the common good. ❖ As each has received a gift, use it to serve one another, as good stewards of God's varied grace. ❖ Moreover, it is required of stewards that they be found trustworthy. ❖ "Everyone to whom much was given, of him much will be required, and from him to whom they entrusted much, they will demand the more."

Who is sufficient for these things? ❖ I can do all things through him who strengthens me.

Matt. 25:14, 15. | Rom. 6:16. | 1 Cor. 12:11, 7.
1 Pet. 4:10. | 1 Cor. 4:2. | Luke 12:48.
2 Cor. 2:16. | Phil. 4:13.

MAR.
27

One who sows righteousness gets a sure reward.

"Now after a long time the master of those servants came and settled accounts with them. And he who had received the five talents came forward, bringing five talents more, saying, 'Master, you delivered to me five talents; here I have made five talents more.' His master said to him, 'Well done, good and faithful servant. You have been faithful over a little; I will set you over much. Enter into the joy of your master.'"

For we must all appear before the judgment seat of Christ, so that each one may receive what is due for what he has done in the body, whether good or evil.

I have fought the good fight, I have finished the race, I have kept the faith. Henceforth there is laid up for me the crown of righteousness, which the Lord, the righteous judge, will award to me on that Day, and not only to me but also to all who have loved his appearing.

"I am coming soon. Hold fast what you have, so that no one may seize your crown."

Prov. 11:18. | Matt. 25:19-21. | 2 Cor. 5:10.
2 Tim. 4:7, 8. | Rev. 3:11.

MAR.
28

"Be strong and courageous."

The Lord is my light and my salvation; whom shall I fear? The Lord is the stronghold of my life; of whom shall I be afraid? ❖ He gives power to the faint, and to him who has no might he increases strength. Even youths shall faint and be weary, and young men shall fall exhausted; but they who wait for the Lord shall renew their strength; they shall mount up with wings like eagles; they shall run and not be weary; they shall walk and not faint. ❖ My flesh and my heart may fail, but God is the strength of my heart and my portion forever.

If God is for us, who can be against us? ❖ The Lord is on my side; I will not fear. What can man do to me? ❖ Through you we push down our foes; through your name we tread down those who rise up against us. ❖ We are more than conquerors through him who loved us.

"Arise and work! The Lord be with you!"

Josh. 1:18. | Ps. 27:1. | Isa. 40:29-31.
Ps. 73:26. | Rom. 8:31. | Ps. 118:6.
Ps. 44:5. | Rom. 8:37. | 1 Chron. 22:16.

MAR. 29

"Come, you who are blessed by my Father, inherit the kingdom prepared for you from the foundation of the world."

"Fear not, little flock, for it is your Father's good pleasure to give you the kingdom." ❖ Has not God chosen those who are poor in the world to be rich in faith and heirs of the kingdom, which he has promised to those who love him? ❖ Heirs of God and fellow heirs with Christ, provided we suffer with him in order that we may also be glorified with him. ❖ "For the Father himself loves you, because you have loved me." ❖ Therefore God is not ashamed to be called their God, for he has prepared for them a city.

"The one who conquers will have this heritage, and I will be his God and he will be my son." ❖ Henceforth there is laid up for me the crown of righteousness, which the Lord, the righteous judge, will award to me on that Day, and not only to me but also to all who have loved his appearing. ❖ He who began a good work in you will bring it to completion at the day of Jesus Christ.

Matt. 25:34. | Luke 12:32. | James 2:5.
Rom. 8:17. | John 16:27. | Heb. 11:16.
Rev. 21:7. | 2 Tim. 4:8. | Phil. 1:6.

MAR. 30

And Isaac went out to meditate
in the field toward evening.

Let the words of my mouth and the meditation of my heart be acceptable in your sight, O LORD, my rock and my redeemer.

When I look at your heavens, the work of your fingers, the moon and the stars, which you have set in place, what is man that you are mindful of him, and the son of man that you care for him? ❖ Great are the works of the LORD, studied by all who delight in them.

Blessed is the man who walks not in the counsel of the wicked, nor stands in the way of sinners, nor sits in the seat of scoffers; but his delight is in the law of the LORD, and on his law he meditates day and night. ❖ "This Book of the Law shall not depart from your mouth, but you shall meditate on it day and night." ❖ My soul will be satisfied as with fat and rich food, and my mouth will praise you with joyful lips, when I remember you upon my bed, and meditate on you in the watches of the night.

Gen. 24:63. | Ps. 19:14. | Ps. 8:3, 4. | Ps. 111:2.
Ps. 1:1, 2. | Josh. 1:8. | Ps. 63:5, 6.

MAR.
31

And my God will supply every need of yours according to his riches in glory in Christ Jesus.

"But seek first the kingdom of God and his righteousness, and all these things will be added to you." ❖ He who did not spare his own Son but gave him up for us all, how will he not also with him graciously give us all things? ❖ For all things are yours, whether Paul or Apollos or Cephas or the world or life or death or the present or the future – all are yours, and you are Christ's, and Christ is God's. ❖ As having nothing, yet possessing everything.

The Lord is my shepherd; I shall not want. ❖ For the Lord God is a sun and shield; the Lord bestows favor and honor. No good thing does he withhold from those who walk uprightly. ❖ God … richly provides us with everything to enjoy. ❖ And God is able to make all grace abound to you, so that having all sufficiency in all things at all times, you may abound in every good work.

Phil. 4:19. | Matt. 6:33. | Rom. 8:32.
1 Cor. 3:21-23. | 2 Cor. 6:10. | Ps. 23:1.
Ps. 84:11. | 1 Tim. 6:17. | 2 Cor. 9:8.

April

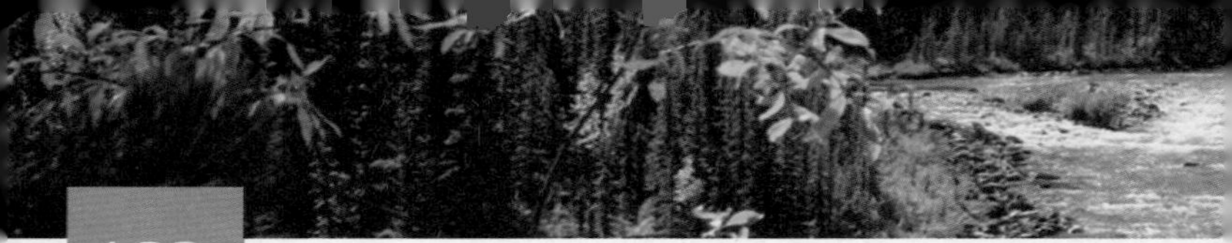

APR.
1

But the fruit of the Spirit is ... joy.

Joy in the Holy Spirit. ❖ Joy that is inexpressible and filled with glory.

As sorrowful, yet always rejoicing. ❖ In all our affliction, I am overflowing with joy. ❖ We rejoice in our sufferings.

Jesus, the founder and perfecter of our faith ... for the joy that was set before him endured the cross, despising the shame. ❖ "These things I have spoken to you, that my joy may be in you, and that your joy may be full." ❖ For as we share abundantly in Christ's sufferings, so through Christ we share abundantly in comfort too. ❖ Rejoice in the Lord always; again I will say, Rejoice. ❖ "The joy of the LORD is your strength."

In your presence there is fullness of joy; at your right hand are pleasures forevermore. ❖ "For the Lamb in the midst of the throne will be their shepherd, and he will guide them to springs of living water, and God will wipe away every tear from their eyes."

Gal. 5:22. | Rom. 14:17. | 1 Pet. 1:8. | 2 Cor. 6:10; 7:4.
Rom. 5:3. | Heb. 12:2. | John 15:11. | 2 Cor. 1:5.
Phil. 4:4. | Neh. 8:10. | Ps. 16:11. | Rev. 7:17.

APR. 2

"If you are returning to the LORD with all your heart, then put away the foreign gods and the Ashtaroth from among you and direct your heart to the LORD and serve him only."

Little children, keep yourselves from idols. ❖ "Therefore go out from their midst, and be separate from them, says the Lord, and touch no unclean thing; then I will welcome you, and I will be a father to you, and you shall be sons and daughters to me, says the Lord Almighty." ❖ "You cannot serve God and money."

"You shall worship no other god, for the LORD, whose name is Jealous, is a jealous God." ❖ "Serve him with a whole heart and with a willing mind, for the LORD searches all hearts and understands every plan and thought."

Behold, you delight in truth in the inward being, and you teach me wisdom in the secret heart. ❖ "Man looks on the outward appearance, but the LORD looks on the heart." ❖ Beloved, if our heart does not condemn us, we have confidence before God.

1 Sam. 7:3. | 1 John 5:21. | 2 Cor. 6:17, 18.
Matt. 6:24. | Exod. 34:14. | 1 Chron. 28:9.
Ps. 51:6. | 1 Sam. 16:7. | 1 John 3:21.

APR. 3

But do not overlook this one fact, beloved, that with the Lord one day is as a thousand years, and a thousand years as one day. The Lord is not slow to fulfill his promise as some count slowness.

For my thoughts are not your thoughts, neither are your ways my ways, declares the LORD. For as the heavens are higher than the earth, so are my ways higher than your ways and my thoughts than your thoughts. "For as the rain and the snow come down from heaven and do not return there but water the earth … so shall my word be that goes out from my mouth; it shall not return to me empty, but it shall accomplish that which I purpose, and shall succeed in the thing for which I sent it."

For God has consigned all to disobedience, that he may have mercy on all. Oh, the depth of the riches and wisdom and knowledge of God! How unsearchable are his judgments and how inscrutable his ways!

2 Pet. 3:8, 9. | Isa. 55:8-11. | Rom. 11:32, 33.

APR. 4

"Fear not, I am the first and the last."

For you have not come to what may be touched, a blazing fire and darkness and gloom and a tempest. … But you have come to Mount Zion … and to God, the judge of all, and to the spirits of the righteous made perfect, and to Jesus, the mediator of a new covenant. ❖ Jesus, the founder and perfecter of our faith. ❖ For we do not have a high priest who is unable to sympathize with our weaknesses, but one who in every respect has been tempted as we are, yet without sin. Let us then with confidence draw near to the throne of grace, that we may receive mercy and find grace to help in time of need.

Thus says the LORD, the King of Israel and his Redeemer, the LORD of hosts: "I am the first and I am the last; besides me there is no god." ❖ Mighty God, Everlasting Father, Prince of Peace.

Are you not from everlasting, O LORD my God, my Holy One? ❖ "For who is God, but the LORD? And who is a rock, except our God?"

Rev. 1:17. | Heb.12:18, 22-24. | Heb. 12:2.
Heb. 4:15, 16. | Isa. 44:6. | Isa. 9:6.
Hab. 1:12. | 2 Sam. 22:32.

APR.
5

"I will not let you go unless you bless me."

"Let them lay hold of my protection, let them make peace with me, let them make peace with me."

"O woman, great is your faith! Be it done for you as you desire." ❖ "According to your faith be it done to you." ❖ But let him ask in faith, with no doubting, for the one who doubts is like a wave of the sea that is driven and tossed by the wind. For that person must not suppose that he will receive anything from the Lord.

So they drew near to the village to which they were going. He acted as if he were going farther, but they urged him strongly, saying, "Stay with us ..." ... And he vanished from their sight. They said to each other, "Did not our hearts burn within us while he talked to us on the road, while he opened to us the Scriptures?" ❖ "Now therefore, if I have found favor in your sight, please show me now your ways, that I may know you in order to find favor in your sight." "My presence will go with you, and I will give you rest."

Gen. 32:26. | Isa. 27:5. | Matt. 15:28.
Matt. 9:29. | James 1:6, 7.
Luke 24:28, 29, 31, 32. | Exod. 33:13, 14.

He always lives to make intercession for them.

Who is to condemn? Christ Jesus is the one who died … , who indeed is interceding for us. ❖ For Christ has entered, not into holy places made with hands, which are copies of the true things, but into heaven itself, now to appear in the presence of God on our behalf. ❖ But if anyone does sin, we have an advocate with the Father, Jesus Christ the righteous. ❖ There is one mediator between God and men, the man Christ Jesus.

Since then we have a great high priest who has passed through the heavens, Jesus, the Son of God, let us hold fast our confession. For we do not have a high priest who is unable to sympathize with our weaknesses, but one who in every respect has been tempted as we are, yet without sin. Let us then with confidence draw near to the throne of grace, that we may receive mercy and find grace to help in time of need. ❖ For through him we both have access in one Spirit to the Father.

Heb. 7:25. | Rom. 8:34. | Heb. 9:24. | 1 John 2:1.
1 Tim. 2:5. | Heb. 4:14-16. | Eph. 2:18.

APR.
7

As sorrowful, yet always rejoicing; as poor, yet making many rich; as having nothing, yet possessing everything.

We rejoice in hope of the glory of God. More than that, we rejoice in our sufferings. ❖ I am filled with comfort. In all our affliction, I am overflowing with joy. ❖ You believe in him and rejoice with joy that is inexpressible and filled with glory.

In a severe test of affliction, their abundance of joy and their extreme poverty have overflowed in a wealth of generosity on their part. ❖ To me, though I am the very least of all the saints, this grace was given, to preach to the Gentiles the unsearchable riches of Christ, and to bring to light for everyone what is the plan of the mystery hidden for ages in God who created all things. ❖ Has not God chosen those who are poor in the world to be rich in faith and heirs of the kingdom, which he has promised to those who love him? ❖ And God is able to make all grace abound to you, so that having all sufficiency in all things at all times, you may abound in every good work.

2 Cor. 6:10. | Rom. 5:2, 3. | 2 Cor. 7:4. | 1 Pet. 1:8.
2 Cor. 8:2. | Eph. 3:8, 9. | James 2:5. | 2 Cor. 9:8.

APR. 8

In every way you were enriched in him.

For while we were still weak, at the right time Christ died for the ungodly. ❖ He who did not spare his own Son but gave him up for us all, how will he not also with him graciously give us all things?

For in him the whole fullness of deity dwells bodily, and you have been filled in him, who is the head of all rule and authority.

"Abide in me, and I in you. As the branch cannot bear fruit by itself, unless it abides in the vine, neither can you, unless you abide in me. I am the vine; you are the branches. Whoever abides in me and I in him, he it is that bears much fruit, for apart from me you can do nothing." ❖ For I have the desire to do what is right, but not the ability to carry it out. ❖ But grace was given to each one of us according to the measure of Christ's gift.

"If you abide in me, and my words abide in you, ask whatever you wish, and it will be done for you." ❖ Let the word of Christ dwell in you richly … in all wisdom.

1 Cor. 1:5. | Rom. 5:6. | Rom. 8:32.
Col. 2:9, 10. | John 15:4, 5. | Rom. 7:18.
Eph. 4:7. | John 15:7. | Col. 3:16.

APR.
9

"Fear not, for I have redeemed you."

"Fear not, for you will not be ashamed; be not confounded, for you will not be disgraced; for you will forget the shame of your youth, and the reproach of your widowhood you will remember no more. For your Maker is your husband, the LORD of hosts is his name; and the Holy One of Israel is your Redeemer." ❖ I have blotted out your transgressions like a cloud and your sins like mist; return to me, for I have redeemed you. ❖ But with the precious blood of Christ, like that of a lamb without blemish or spot.

"Their Redeemer is strong; the LORD of hosts is his name. He will surely plead their cause." ❖ "My Father, who has given them to me, is greater than all, and no one is able to snatch them out of the Father's hand."

Grace to you and peace from God our Father and the Lord Jesus Christ, who gave himself for our sins to deliver us from the present evil age, according to the will of our God and Father, to whom be the glory forever and ever. Amen.

Isa. 43:1. | Isa. 54:4, 5. | Isa. 44:22. | 1 Pet. 1:19.
Jer. 50:34. | John 10:29. | Gal. 1:3-5.

APR.
10

I am very dark, but lovely.

Behold, I was brought forth in iniquity, and in sin did my mother conceive me. ❖ "And your renown went forth among the nations because of your beauty, for it was perfect through the splendor that I had bestowed on you, declares the Lord God." ❖ "I am a sinful man, O Lord." ❖ Behold, you are beautiful, my love, behold, you are beautiful! ❖ "I despise myself, and repent in dust and ashes." ❖ You are altogether beautiful, my love; there is no flaw in you." ❖ When I want to do right, evil lies close at hand. ❖ "Take heart, my son; your sins are forgiven." ❖ For I know that nothing good dwells in me, that is, in my flesh. ❖ And you have been filled in him. ❖ Mature in Christ.

You were washed, you were sanctified, you were justified in the name of the Lord Jesus Christ and by the Spirit of our God. ❖ That you may proclaim the excellencies of him who called you out of darkness into his marvelous light.

Song of Songs 1:5. | Ps. 51:5. | Ezek. 16:14. | Luke 5:8.
Song of Songs 4:1. | Job 42:6. | Song of Songs 4:7.
Rom. 7:21. | Matt. 9:2. | Rom. 7:18. | Col. 2:10.
Col. 1:28. | 1 Cor. 6:11. | 1 Pet. 2:9.

APR.
11

When words are many, transgression is not lacking,
but whoever restrains his lips is prudent.

Know this, my beloved brothers: let every person be quick to hear, slow to speak, slow to anger. ❖ Whoever is slow to anger is better than the mighty, and he who rules his spirit than he who takes a city. ❖ If anyone does not stumble in what he says, he is a perfect man, able also to bridle his whole body. ❖ "By your words you will be justified, and by your words you will be condemned." ❖ Set a guard, O LORD over my mouth; keep watch over the door of my lips! ❖ Christ also suffered for you, leaving you an example, so that you might follow in his steps. He committed no sin, neither was deceit found in his mouth. When he was reviled, he did not revile in return; when he suffered, he did not threaten, but continued entrusting himself to him who judges justly. ❖ Consider him who endured from sinners such hostility against himself, so that you may not grow weary or fainthearted.

And in their mouth no lie was found, for they are blameless.

Prov. 10:19. | James 1:19. | Prov. 16:32.
James 3:2. | Matt. 12:37. | Ps. 141:3.
1 Pet. 2:21-23. | Heb. 12:3. | Rev. 14:5.

APR.
12

For God has done what the law, weakened by the flesh, could not do. By sending his own Son in the likeness of sinful flesh and for sin, he condemned sin in the flesh.

For since the law has but a shadow of the good things to come instead of the true form of these realities, it can never, by the same sacrifices that are continually offered every year, make perfect those who draw near. Otherwise, would they not have ceased to be offered? ❖ "By him everyone who believes is freed from everything from which you could not be freed by the law of Moses."

Since therefore the children share in flesh and blood, he himself likewise partook of the same things, that through death he might destroy the one who has the power of death, that is, the devil, and deliver all those who through fear of death were subject to lifelong slavery. For surely it is not angels that he helps, but he helps the offspring of Abraham. Therefore he had to be made like his brothers in every respect.

Rom. 8:3. | Heb. 10:1, 2. | Acts 13:38, 39. | Heb. 2:14-17.

APR.
13

Honor the Lord with your wealth and
with the firstfruits of all your produce.

Whoever sows sparingly will also reap sparingly, and whoever sows bountifully will also reap bountifully. ❖ On the first day of every week, each of you is to put something aside and store it up, as he may prosper.

For God is not so unjust as to overlook your work and the love that you showed for his sake in serving the saints, as you still do.

I appeal to you therefore, brothers, by the mercies of God, to present your bodies as a living sacrifice, holy and acceptable to God, which is your spiritual worship. ❖ For the love of Christ controls us, because we have concluded this: that one has died for all, therefore all have died; and he died for all, that those who live might no longer live for themselves but for him who for their sake died and was raised. ❖ So, whether you eat or drink, or whatever you do, do all to the glory of God.

Prov. 3:9. | 2 Cor. 9:6. | 1 Cor. 16:2. | Heb. 6:10.
Rom. 12:1. | 2 Cor. 5:14, 15. | 1 Cor. 10:31.

APR.
14

My soul will be satisfied as with fat and rich food, and my mouth will praise you with joyful lips, when I remember you upon my bed, and meditate on you in the watches of the night.

How precious to me are your thoughts, O God! How vast is the sum of them! If I would count them, they are more than the sand. I awake, and I am still with you. ❖ How sweet are your words to my taste, sweeter than honey to my mouth! ❖ Your love is better than wine.

Whom have I in heaven but you? And there is nothing on earth that I desire besides you. ❖ You are the most handsome of the sons of men; grace is poured upon your lips; therefore God has blessed you forever.

As an apple tree among the trees of the forest, so is my beloved among the young men. With great delight I sat in his shadow, and his fruit was sweet to my taste, he brought me to the banqueting house, and his banner over me was love. ❖ His appearance is like Lebanon, choice as the cedars. His mouth is most sweet, and he is altogether desirable. This is my beloved and this is my friend.

Ps. 63:5, 6. | Ps. 139:17, 18. | Ps. 119:103.
Song of Songs 1:2. | Ps. 73:25. | Ps. 45:2.
Song of Songs 2:3, 4. | Song of Songs 5:15, 16.

APR.
15

"Their Redeemer is strong."

For I know how many are your transgressions and how great are your sins. ❖ "I have granted help to one who is mighty." ❖ "Lord your Savior, and your Redeemer, the Mighty One of Jacob." ❖ "Mighty to save." ❖ Able to keep you from stumbling. ❖ Where sin increased, grace abounded all the more.

"Whoever believes in him is not condemned, but whoever does not believe is condemned already, because he has not believed in the name of the only Son of God." ❖ He is able to save to the uttermost those who draw near to God through him.

"Is my hand shortened, that it cannot redeem?" ❖ Who shall separate us from the love of Christ? … For I am sure that neither death nor life, nor angels nor rulers, nor things present nor things to come, nor powers, nor height nor depth, nor anything else in all creation, will be able to separate us from the love of God in Christ Jesus our Lord.

Jer. 50:34. | Amos 5:12. | Ps. 89:19. | Isa. 49:26.
Isa. 63:1. | Jude 24. | Rom. 5:20. | John 3:18.
Heb. 7:25. | Isa. 50:2. | Rom. 8:35, 38, 39.

APR.
16

I had said in my alarm, "I am cut off from your sight." But you heard the voice of my pleas for mercy when I cried to you for help.

I sink in deep mire, where there is no foothold; I have come into deep waters, and the flood sweeps over me. ❖ "Water closed over my head; I said, 'I am lost.' I called on your name, O LORD, from the depths of the pit; you heard my plea, 'Do not close your ear to my cry for help!' You came near when I called on you; you said, 'Do not fear!'"

"Will the Lord spurn forever, and never again be favorable? Has his steadfast love forever ceased? Are his promises at an end for all time? Has God forgotten to be gracious? Has he in anger shut up his compassion?" Then I said, "I will appeal to this, to the years of the right hand of the Most High." I will remember the deeds of the LORD; yes, I will remember your wonders of old. ❖ I believe that I shall look upon the goodness of the LORD in the land of the living!

Ps. 31:22. | Ps. 69:2. | Lam. 3:54-57.
Ps. 77:7-11. | Ps. 27:13.

APR.
17

"The one who offers thanksgiving as his sacrifice glories me."

Let the word of Christ dwell in you richly, teaching and admonishing one another in all wisdom, singing psalms and hymns and spiritual songs, with thankfulness in your hearts to God. And whatever you do, in word or deed, do everything in the name of the Lord Jesus, giving thanks to God the Father through him. ❖ Glorify God in your body.

But you are a … a royal priesthood … that you may proclaim the excellencies of him who called you out of darkness into his marvelous light. ❖ You yourselves like living stones are being built up as a spiritual house, to be a holy priesthood, to offer spiritual sacrifices acceptable to God through Jesus Christ ❖ Through him then let us continually offer up a sacrifice of praise to God, that is, the fruit of lips that acknowledge his name.

My soul makes its boast in the LORD; let the humble hear and be glad. Oh, magnify the LORD with me, and let us exalt his name together!

Ps. 50:23. | Col. 3:16, 17. | 1 Cor. 6:20. | 1 Pet. 2:9.
1 Pet. 2:5. | Heb. 13:15. | Ps. 34:2, 3.

APR.
18

"I will raise up for them a prophet
like you from among their brothers."

"[Moses] stood between the Lord and you at that time, to declare to you the word of the Lord. For you were afraid." ❖ There is one God, and there is one mediator between God and men, the man Christ Jesus.

Now the man Moses was very meek, more than all people who were on the face of the earth. ❖ "Take my yoke upon you, and learn from me, for I am gentle and lowly in heart, and you will find rest for your souls." ❖ Have this mind among yourselves, which is yours in Christ Jesus, who, though he was in the form of God, did not count equality with God a thing to be grasped, but made himself nothing, taking the form of a servant, being born in the likeness of men.

Now Moses was faithful in all God's house as a servant, to testify to the things that were to be spoken later, but Christ is faithful over God's house as a son. And we are his house if indeed we hold fast our confidence and our boasting in our hope.

Deut. 18:18. | Deut. 5:5. | 1 Tim. 2:5. | Num. 12:3.
Matt. 11:29. | Phil. 2:5-7. | Heb. 3:5, 6.

APR.
19

"Truly, truly, I say to you,
I am the door of the sheep."

And behold, the curtain of the temple was torn in two, from top to bottom. And the earth shook, and the rocks were split. ❖ For Christ also suffered once for sins, the righteous for the unrighteous, that he might bring us to God. ❖ By this the Holy Spirit indicates that the way into the holy places is not yet opened as long as the first section is still standing.

"I am the door. If anyone enters by me, he will be saved and will go in and out and find pasture."

"No one comes to the Father except through me." ❖ For through him we … have access in one Spirit to the Father. So then you are no longer strangers and aliens, but you are fellow citizens with the saints and members of the household of God. ❖ Therefore, brothers, since we have confidence to enter the holy places by the blood of Jesus, by the new and living way that he opened for us through the curtain, that is, through his flesh … ❖ We have peace with God through our Lord Jesus Christ. Through him we have also obtained access by faith into this grace in which we stand, and we rejoice in hope of the glory of God.

John 10:7. | Matt. 27:51. | 1 Pet. 3:18. | Heb. 9:8.
John 10:9. | John 14:6. | Eph. 2:18, 19.
Heb. 10:19, 20. | Rom. 5:1, 2.

APR.
20

"None of the devoted things
shall stick to your hand."

"Therefore go out from their midst, and be separate from them, says the Lord, and touch no unclean thing." ❖ Beloved, I urge you as sojourners and exiles to abstain from the passions of the flesh, which wage war against your soul. ❖ Hating even the garment stained by the flesh.

Beloved, we are God's children now, and what we will be has not yet appeared; but we know that when he appears we shall be like him, because we shall see him as he is. And everyone who thus hopes in him purifies himself as he is pure. ❖ For the grace of God has appeared, bringing salvation for all people, training us to renounce ungodliness and worldly passions, and to live self-controlled, upright, and godly lives in the present age, waiting for our blessed hope, the appearing of the glory of our great God and Savior Jesus Christ, who gave himself for us to redeem us from all lawlessness and to purify for himself a people for his own possession who are zealous for good works.

Deut. 13:17. | 2 Cor. 6:17. | 1 Pet. 2:11.
Jude 23. | 1 John 3:2, 3. | Titus 2:11-14.

APR.
21

Stand firm thus in the Lord.

"My foot has held fast to his steps; I have kept his way and have not turned aside."

For the LORD loves justice; he will not forsake his saints. They are preserved forever. ❖ The LORD will keep you from all evil; he will keep your life.

"My righteous one shall live by faith, and if he shrinks back, my soul has no pleasure in him." But we are not of those who shrink back and are destroyed, but of those who have faith and preserve their souls. ❖ If they had been of us, they would have continued with us. But they went out, that it might become plain that they all are not of us.

"If you abide in my word, you are truly my disciples." ❖ "The one who endures to the end will be saved." ❖ Be watchful, stand firm in the faith, act like men, be strong. ❖ "Hold fast what you have, so that no one may seize your crown." ❖ "The one who conquers will be clothed thus in white garments, and I will never blot his name out of the book of life."

Phil. 4:1. | Job 23:11. | Ps. 37:28. | Ps. 121:7.
Heb. 10:38, 39. | 1 John 2:19. | John 8:31.
Matt. 24:13. | 1 Cor. 16:13. | Rev. 3:11. | Rev. 3:5.

APR. 22

"If his offering is a burnt offering from the herd, he shall offer a male without blemish. He shall bring it to the entrance of the tent of meeting, that he may be accepted before the LORD. He shall lay his hand on the head of the burnt offering, and it shall be accepted for him to make atonement for him."

"God will provide for himself the lamb for a burnt offering." ❖ "Behold, the Lamb of God, who takes away the sin of the world!" ❖ And by that will we have been sanctified through the offering of the body of Jesus Christ once for all. ❖ "A ransom for many."

"No one takes it from me, but I lay it down of my own accord. I have authority to lay it down, and I have authority to take it up again." ❖ I will love them freely. ❖ The Son of God ... loved me and gave himself for me.

For our sake he made him to be sin who knew no sin, so that in him we might become the righteousness of God. ❖ He has blessed us in the Beloved.

Lev. 1:3, 4. | Gen. 22:8. | John 1:29.
Heb. 10:10. | Matt. 20:28. | John 10:18.
Hosea 14:4. | Gal. 2:20. | 2 Cor. 5:21. | Eph. 1:6.

APR.
23

The Lord *was my support.*

"Truly the hills are a delusion, the orgies on the mountains. Truly in the Lord our God is the salvation of Israel." ❖ The Lord is my rock and my fortress and my deliverer, my God, my rock, in whom I take refuge, my shield, and the horn of my salvation, my stronghold. ❖ "Shout, and sing for joy, O inhabitant of Zion, for great in your midst is the Holy One of Israel."

The angel of the Lord encamps around those who fear him, and delivers them. … When the righteous cry for help, the Lord hears and delivers them out of all their troubles. ❖ "The eternal God is your dwelling place, and underneath are the everlasting arms." ❖ So we can confidently say, "The Lord is my helper; I will not fear; what can man do to me?" ❖ For who is God, but the Lord? And who is a rock, except our God? – the God who equipped me with strength and made my way blameless.

But by the grace of God I am what I am.

Ps. 18:18. | Jer. 3:23. | Ps. 18:2. | Isa. 12:6.
Ps. 34:7, 17. | Deut. 33:27. | Heb. 13:6.
Ps. 18:31, 32. | 1 Cor. 15:10.

APR.
24

The Lord visited Sarah as he had said, and the Lord did to Sarah as he had promised.

Trust in him at all times, O people; pour out your heart before him; God is a refuge for us. ❖ David strengthened himself in the Lord his God. ❖ "God will visit you and bring you up out of this land to the land that he swore to Abraham, to Isaac, and to Jacob." ❖ "'I have surely seen the affliction of my people who are in Egypt, and have heard their groaning, and I have come down to deliver them.' This man led them out, performing wonders and signs in Egypt and at the Red Sea and in the wilderness for forty years." ❖ Not one word of all the good promises that the Lord had made to the house of Israel had failed; all came to pass.

He who promised is faithful. ❖ Has he said, and will he not do it? Or has he spoken, and will he not fulfill it? ❖ "Heaven and earth will pass away, but my words will not pass away." ❖ The grass withers, the flower fades, but the word of our God will stand forever.

Gen. 21:1. | Ps. 62:8. | 1 Sam. 30:6. | Gen. 50:24. Acts 7:34, 36. | Josh. 21:45. | Heb. 10:23. Num. 23:19. | Matt. 24:35. | Isa. 40:8.

APR.
25

"You shall call his name Jesus,
for he will save his people from their sins."

You know that he appeared to take away sins. ❖ That we might die to sin and live to righteousness. ❖ Consequently, he is able to save to the uttermost those who draw near to God through him.

But he was wounded for our transgressions; he was crushed for our iniquities; upon him was the chastisement that brought us peace, and with his stripes we are healed. … The Lord has laid on him the iniquity of us all. ❖ "Thus it is written, that the Christ should suffer … and that repentance and forgiveness of sins should be proclaimed in his name to all nations." ❖ He has appeared … to put away sin by the sacrifice of himself.

"God exalted him at his right hand as Leader and Savior, to give repentance." ❖ "Through this man forgiveness of sins is proclaimed to you, and by him everyone who believes is freed from everything from which you could not be freed by the law of Moses." ❖ Your sins are forgiven for his name's sake.

Matt. 1:21. | 1 John 3:5. | 1 Pet. 2:24. | Heb. 7:25.
Isa. 53:5, 6. | Luke 24:46, 47. | Heb. 9:26.
Acts 5:31. | Acts 13:38, 39. | 1 John 2:12.

APR.
26

His left hand is under my head,
and his right hand embraces me!

"Underneath are the everlasting arms." ❖ But when he saw the wind, he was afraid, and beginning to sink he cried out, "Lord, save me." Jesus immediately reached out his hand and took hold of him, saying to him, "O you of little faith, why did you doubt?" ❖ The steps of a man are established by the Lord, when he delights in his way; though he fall, he shall not be cast headlong, for the Lord upholds his hand.

"The beloved of the Lord dwells in safety. The High God surrounds him all day long, and dwells between his shoulders." ❖ Casting all your anxieties on him, because he cares for you. ❖ He who touches you touches the apple of his eye.

"They will never perish, and no one will snatch them out of my hand. My Father, who has given them to me, is greater than all."

Song of Songs 2:6. | Deut. 33:27.
Matt. 14:30, 31. | Ps. 37:23, 24. | Deut. 33:12.
1 Pet. 5:7. | Zech. 2:8. | John 10:28, 29.

APR.
27

This is what I mean, brothers:
the appointed time has grown very short.

"Man who is born of a woman is few of days and full of trouble. He comes out like a flower and withers; he flees like a shadow and continues not." ❖ And the world is passing away along with its desires, but whoever does the will of God abides forever. ❖ For as in Adam all die, so also in Christ shall all be made alive. ... "Death is swallowed up in victory." ❖ If we live, we live to the Lord, and if we die, we die to the Lord. So then, whether we live or whether we die, we are the Lord's. ❖ For to me to live is Christ, and to die is gain.

Therefore do not throw away your confidence, which has a great reward. For you have need of endurance, so that when you have done the will of God you may receive what is promised. For, "Yet a little while, and the coming one will come and will not delay." ❖ The night is far gone; the day is at hand. So then let us cast off the works of darkness and put on the armor of light. ❖ The end of all things is at hand; therefore be self-controlled and sober-minded for the sake of your prayers.

1 Cor. 7:29. | Job 14:1, 2. | 1 John 2:17.
1 Cor. 15:22, 54. | Rom. 14:8. | Phil. 1:21.
Heb. 10:35-37. | Rom. 13:12. | 1 Pet. 4:7.

APR.
28

"Behold, the Lamb of God."

For it is impossible for the blood of bulls and goats to take away sins. Consequently, when Christ came into the world, he said, "Sacrifices and offerings you have not desired, but a body have you prepared for me; in burnt offerings and sin offerings you have taken no pleasure. Then I said, 'Behold, I have come to do your will, O God.'" ❖ He was oppressed, and he was afflicted, yet he opened not his mouth; like a lamb that is led to the slaughter, and like a sheep that before its shearers is silent, so he opened not his mouth.

You were ransomed ... not with perishable things such as silver or gold, but with the precious blood of Christ, like that of a lamb without blemish or spot. He was ... made manifest in the last times for your sake, ... so that your faith and hope are in God.

"Worthy is the Lamb who was slain, to receive power and wealth and wisdom and might and honor and glory and blessing!"

John 1:29. | Heb. 10:4-7. | Isa. 53:7.
1 Pet. 1:18-21. | Rev. 5:12.

APR.
29

"Consider what great things he has done for you."

"And you shall remember the whole way that the Lord your God has led you these forty years in the wilderness, that he might humble you, testing you to know what was in your heart, whether you would keep his commandments or not. Know then in your heart that, as a man disciplines his son, the Lord your God disciplines you."

I know, O Lord, that your rules are righteous, and that in faithfulness you have afflicted me. ... It is good for me that I was afflicted, that I might learn your statutes. ... Before I was afflicted I went astray, but now I keep your word. ❖ The Lord has disciplined me severely, but he has not given me over to death. ❖ He does not deal with us according to our sins, nor repay us according to our iniquities. For as high as the heavens are above the earth, so great is his steadfast love toward those who fear him. For he knows our frame; he remembers that we are dust.

1 Sam. 12:24. | Deut. 8:2, 5. | Ps. 119:75, 71, 67.
Ps. 118:18. | Ps. 103:10, 11, 14.

APR. 30

Whoever keeps his word, in him truly the love of God is perfected.

Now may the God of peace who brought again from the dead our Lord Jesus, the great shepherd of the sheep, by the blood of the eternal covenant, equip you with everything good that you may do his will, working in us that which is pleasing in his sight, through Jesus Christ, to whom be glory forever and ever. Amen.

And by this we know that we have come to know him, if we keep his commandments. ❖ "If anyone loves me, he will keep my word, and my Father will love him, and we will come to him and make our home with him." ❖ No one who abides in him keeps on sinning; no one who keeps on sinning has either seen him or known him. Little children, let no one deceive you. Whoever practices righteousness is righteous, as he is righteous. ❖ By this is love perfected with us, so that we may have confidence for the day of judgment, because as he is so also are we in this world.

1 John 2:5. | Heb. 13:20, 21. | 1 John 2:3. John 14:23. | 1 John 3:6, 7. | 1 John 4:17.

May

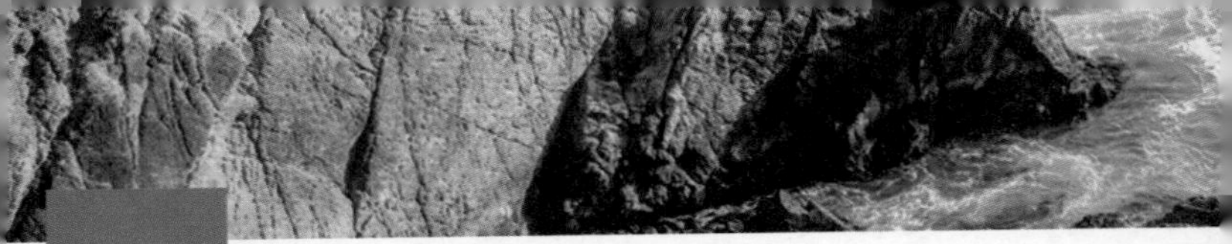

MAY
1

But the fruit of the Spirit is … peace.

To set the mind on the Spirit is life and peace.

God has called you to peace. ❖ "Peace I leave with you; my peace I give to you. Not as the world gives do I give to you." ❖ May the God of hope fill you with all joy and peace in believing, so that by the power of the Holy Spirit you may abound in hope.

I know whom I have believed, and I am convinced that he is able to guard until that Day what has been entrusted to me. ❖ You keep him in perfect peace whose mind is stayed on you, because he trusts in you.

And the effect of righteousness will be peace, and the result of righteousness, quietness and trust forever. My people will abide in a peaceful habitation, in secure dwellings, and in quiet resting places. ❖ "Whoever listens to me will dwell secure and will be at ease, without dread of disaster."

Great peace have those who love your law.

Gal. 5:22. | Rom. 8:6. | 1 Cor. 7:15.
John 14:27. | Rom. 15:13. | 2 Tim. 1:12. | Isa. 26:3.
Isa. 32:17, 18. | Prov. 1:33. | Ps. 119:165.

"Surely the Lord is in this place,
and I did not know it."

"For where two or three are gathered in my name, there am I among them." ❖ "And behold, I am with you always, to the end of the age." ❖ "My presence will go with you, and I will give you rest."

Where shall I go from your Spirit? Or where shall I flee from your presence? If I ascend to heaven, you are there! If I make my bed in Sheol, you are there! ❖ "Am I a God at hand, declares the Lord, and not a God afar off? Can a man hide himself in secret places so that I cannot see him? declares the Lord. Do I not fill heaven and earth? declares the Lord."

"Behold, heaven and the highest heaven cannot contain you; how much less this house that I have built!" ❖ For thus says the One who is high and lifted up, who inhabits eternity, whose name is Holy: "I dwell in the high and holy place, and also with him who is of a contrite and lowly spirit, to revive the spirit of the lowly, and to revive the heart of the contrite." ❖ We are the temple of the living God.

Gen. 28:16. | Matt. 18:20. | Matt. 28:20. | Exod. 33:14.
Ps. 139:7, 8. | Jer. 23:23, 24. | 1 Kings 8:27.
Isa. 57:15. | 2 Cor. 6:16.

MAY 3

"You therefore must be perfect,
as your heavenly Father is perfect."

"I am God Almighty; walk before me, and be blameless." ❖ "You shall be holy to me, for I the LORD am holy and have separated you from the peoples, that you should be mine."

You were bought with a price. So glorify God in your body.

You have been filled in him, who is the head of all rule and authority. ❖ Who gave himself for us to redeem us from all lawlessness. ❖ Be diligent to be found by him without spot or blemish, and at peace.

Blessed are those whose way is blameless, who walk in the law of the LORD! ❖ But the one who looks into the perfect law, the law of liberty, and perseveres, being no hearer who forgets but a doer who acts, he will be blessed in his doing. ❖ Search me, O God, and know my heart! Try me and know my thoughts! And see if there be any grievous way in me, and lead me in the way everlasting!

Matt. 5:48. | Gen. 17:1. | Lev. 20:26. | 1 Cor. 6:20.
Col. 2:10. | Titus 2:14. | 2 Pet. 3:14. | Ps. 119:1.
James 1:25. | Ps. 139:23, 24.

MAY
4

Behold, the LORD's hand is not shortened, that it cannot save, or his ear dull, that it cannot hear.

On the day I called, you answered me; my strength of soul you increased. ❖ While I was speaking in prayer, the man Gabriel, whom I had seen in the vision at the first, came to me in swift flight at the time of the evening sacrifice. ❖ Hide not your face from me. Turn not your servant away in anger, O you who have been my help. Cast me not off; forsake me not, O God of my salvation! ❖ But you, O LORD, do not be far off! O you my help, come quickly to my aid!

"Ah, Lord God! It is you who has made the heavens and the earth by your great power and by your outstretched arm! Nothing is too hard for you." ❖ He delivered us from such a deadly peril, and he will deliver us. On him we have set our hope that he will deliver us again. ❖ "And will not God give justice to his elect, who cry to him day and night? Will he delay long over them? I tell you, he will give justice to them speedily."

Isa. 59:1. | Ps. 138:2. | Dan. 9:21. | Ps. 27:9. | Ps. 22:19.
Jer. 32:17. | 2 Cor. 1:10. | Luke 18:7, 8.

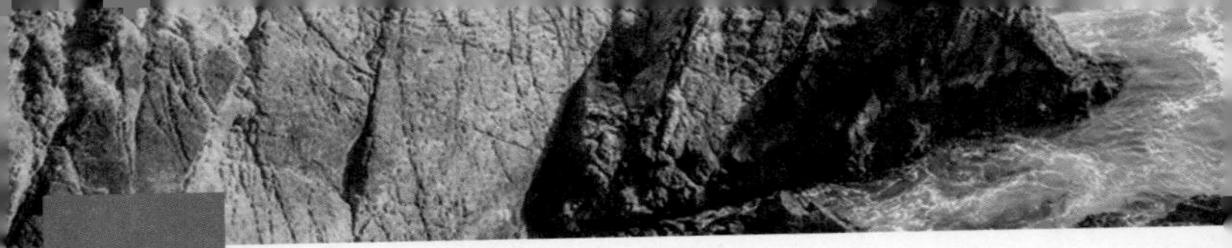

MAY 5

"Therefore do not be anxious, saying, 'What shall we eat?' or 'What shall we drink?' or 'What shall we wear?' For … your heavenly Father knows that you need them all."

Oh, fear the LORD, you his saints, for those who fear him have no lack! The young lions suffer want and hunger; but those who seek the LORD lack no good thing. ❖ No good thing does he withhold from those who walk uprightly. O LORD of hosts, blessed is the one who trusts in you!

I want you to be free from anxieties. ❖ Do not be anxious about anything, but in everything by prayer and supplication with thanksgiving let your requests be made known to God.

"Are not two sparrows sold for a penny? And not one of them will fall to the ground apart from your Father. But even the hairs of your head are all numbered. Fear not, therefore; you are of more value than many sparrows." ❖ "Why are you so afraid? Have you still no faith?" ❖ "Have faith in God."

Matt. 6:31, 32. | Ps. 34:9, 10. | Ps. 84:11, 12. | 1 Cor. 7:32. Phil. 4:6. | Matt.10:29-31. | Mark 4:40. | Mark 11:22.

MAY 6

Steadfast love and faithfulness meet;
righteousness and peace kiss each other.

"A righteous God and a Savior." ❖ The LORD was pleased, for his righteousness' sake, to magnify his law and make it glorious.

In Christ God was reconciling the world to himself, not counting their trespasses against them. ❖ Whom God put forward as a propitiation by his blood, to be received by faith. This was to show God's righteousness, because in his divine forbearance he had passed over former sins. It was to show his righteousness at the present time, so that he might be just and the justifier of the one who has faith in Jesus. ❖ But he was wounded for our transgressions; he was crushed for our iniquities; upon him was the chastisement that brought us peace, and with his stripes we are healed. ❖ Who shall bring any charge against God's elect? It is God who justifies. ❖ And to the one who does not work but trusts him who justifies the ungodly, his faith is counted as righteousness.

Ps. 85:10. | Isa. 45:21. | Isa. 42:21.
2 Cor. 5:19. | Rom. 3:25, 26. | Isa. 53:5.
Rom. 8:33. | Rom. 4:5.

MAY
7

"And you will hear of wars and rumors of wars. See that you are not alarmed."

God is our refuge and strength, a very present help in trouble. Therefore we will not fear though the earth gives way, though the mountains be moved into the heart of the sea, though its waters roar and foam, though the mountains tremble at its swelling. ❖ Come, my people, enter your chambers, and shut your doors behind you; hide yourselves for a little while until the fury has passed by. For behold, the LORD is coming out from his place to punish the inhabitants of the earth for their iniquity. ❖ In the shadow of your wings I will take refuge, till the storms of destruction pass by. ❖ Your life is hidden with Christ in God.

He is not afraid of bad news; his heart is firm, trusting in the LORD.

"I have said these things to you, that in me you may have peace. In the world you will have tribulation. But take heart; I have overcome the world."

Matt. 24:6. | Ps. 46:1-3. | Isa. 26:20, 21. | Ps. 57:1.
Col. 3:3. | Ps. 112:7. | John 16:33.

MAY
8

Yet it was the will of the LORD
to crush him; he has put him to grief.

"Now is my soul troubled. And what shall I say? 'Father, save me from this hour'? But for this purpose I have come to this hour. Father, glorify your name." Then a voice came from heaven: "I have glorified it, and I will glorify it again." ❖ "Father, if you are willing, remove this cup from me. Nevertheless, not my will, but yours, be done." And there appeared to him an angel from heaven, strengthening him.

And being found in human form, he humbled himself by becoming obedient to the point of death, even death on a cross. ❖ "For this reason the Father loves me, because I lay down my life that I may take it up again." ❖ "For I have come down from heaven, not to do my own will but the will of him who sent me." ❖ "Shall I not drink the cup that the Father has given me?" ❖ "He has not left me alone, for I always do the things that are pleasing to him." ❖ "My beloved Son, with whom I am well pleased." ❖ My chosen, in whom my soul delights.

Isa. 53:10. | John 12:27, 28. | Luke 22:42, 43.
Phil. 2:8. | John 10:17. | John 6:38. | John 18:11.
John 8:29. | Matt. 3:17. | Isa. 42:1.

MAY
9

Now faith is the assurance of things hoped for,
the conviction of things not seen.

If in this life only we have hoped in Christ, we are of all people most to be pitied.

"What no eye has seen, nor ear heard, nor the heart of man imagined, what God has prepared for those who love him" – these things God has revealed to us through the Spirit. ❖ When you … believed in him, [you] were sealed with the promised Holy Spirit, who is the guarantee of our inheritance until we acquire possession of it.

Jesus said to him, "Have you believed because you have seen me? Blessed are those who have not seen and yet have believed." ❖ Though you have not seen him, you love him. Though you do not now see him, you believe in him and rejoice with joy that is inexpressible and filled with glory, obtaining the outcome of your faith, the salvation of your souls.

We walk by faith, not by sight. ❖ Therefore do not throw away your confidence, which has a great reward.

Heb. 11:1. | 1 Cor. 15:19. | 1 Cor. 2:9, 10. | Eph. 1:13, 14.
John 20:29. | 1 Pet. 1:8, 9. | 2 Cor. 5:7. | Heb. 10:35.

MAY
10

The reason the Son of God appeared was to destroy the works of the devil.

For we do not wrestle against flesh and blood, but against the rulers, against the authorities, against the cosmic powers over this present darkness, against the spiritual forces of evil in the heavenly places. ❖ Since therefore the children share in flesh and blood, he himself likewise partook of the same things, that through death he might destroy the one who has the power of death, that is, the devil. ❖ He disarmed the rulers and authorities and put them to open shame, by triumphing over them in him. ❖ And I heard a loud voice in heaven, saying, "Now the salvation and the power and the kingdom of our God and the authority of his Christ have come, for the accuser of our brothers has been thrown down, who accuses them day and night before our God. And they have conquered him by the blood of the Lamb and by the word of their testimony, for they loved not their lives even unto death. ❖ But thanks be to God, who gives us the victory through our Lord Jesus Christ.

1 John 3:8. | Eph. 6:12. | Heb. 2:14. | Col. 2:15.
Rev. 12:10, 11. | 1 Cor. 15:57.

MAY
11

*Wake up from your drunken stupor,
as is right, and do not go on sinning.*

For you are all children of light, children of the day. We are not of the night or of the darkness. So then let us not sleep, as others do, but let us keep awake and be sober.

Besides this you know the time, that the hour has come for you to wake from sleep. For salvation is nearer to us now than when we first believed. The night is far gone; the day is at hand. So then let us cast off the works of darkness and put on the armor of light. ❖ Therefore take up the whole armor of God, that you may be able to withstand in the evil day, and having done all, to stand firm. ❖ Cast away from you all the transgressions that you have committed, and make yourselves a new heart and a new spirit! ❖ Therefore put away all filthiness and rampant wickedness and receive with meekness the implanted word, which is able to save your souls. ❖ And now, little children, abide in him, so that when he appears we may have confidence and not shrink from him in shame at his coming. If you know that he is righteous, you may be sure that everyone who practices righteousness has been born of him.

1 Cor. 15:34. | 1 Thess. 5:5, 6. | Rom. 13:11, 12.
Eph. 6:13. | Ezek. 18:31. | James 1:21. | 1 John 2:28, 29.

MAY
12

Beloved, let us love one another, for love is from God, and whoever loves has been born of God and knows God.

God's love has been poured into our hearts through the Holy Spirit who has been given to us. ❖ For you did not receive the spirit of slavery to fall back into fear, but you have received the Spirit of adoption as sons, by whom we cry, "Abba! Father!" The Spirit himself bears witness with our spirit that we are children of God. ❖ Whoever believes in the Son of God has the testimony in himself.

In this the love of God was made manifest among us, that God sent his only Son into the world, so that we might live through him. ❖ In him we have redemption through his blood, the forgiveness of our trespasses, according to the riches of his grace. ❖ So that in the coming ages he might show the immeasurable riches of his grace in kindness toward us in Christ Jesus.

Beloved, if God so loved us, we also ought to love one another.

1 John 4:7. | Rom. 5:5. | Rom. 8:15, 16. | 1 John 5:10.
1 John 4:9. | Eph. 1:7. | Eph. 2:7. | 1 John 4:11.

MAY
13

I desire then that in every place the men should pray, lifting holy hands without anger or quarreling.

"The true worshipers will worship the Father in spirit and truth, for the Father is seeking such people to worship him. God is spirit, and those who worship him must worship in spirit and truth." ❖ "Then you shall call, and the Lord will answer; you shall cry, and he will say, 'Here I am.'" ❖ "And whenever you stand praying, forgive, if you have anything against anyone." ❖ And without faith it is impossible to please him, for whoever would draw near to God must believe that he exists and that he rewards those who seek him. ❖ But let him ask in faith, with no doubting, for the one who doubts is like a wave of the sea that is driven and tossed by the wind. For that person must not suppose that he will receive anything from the Lord.

If I had cherished iniquity in my heart, the Lord would not have listened. ❖ My little children, I am writing these things to you so that you may not sin. But if anyone does sin, we have an advocate with the Father, Jesus Christ the righteous. He is the propitiation for our sins.

1 Tim. 2:8. | John 4:23, 24. | Isa. 58:9. | Mark 11:25.
Heb. 11:6. | James 1:6, 7. | Ps. 66:18. | 1 John 2:1, 2.

MAY 14

Share his sufferings.

"It is enough for the disciple to be like his teacher, and the servant like his master."

He was despised and rejected by men; a man of sorrows, and acquainted with grief; and as one from whom men hide their faces he was despised, and we esteemed him not. ❖ "In the world you will have tribulation." ❖ "Because you are not of the world, but I chose you out of the world, therefore the world hates you."

I looked for pity, but there was none. ❖ At my first defense no one came to stand by me, but all deserted me.

"Foxes have holes, and birds of the air have nests, but the Son of Man has nowhere to lay his head." ❖ For here we have no lasting city, but we seek the city that is to come.

Let us run with endurance the race that is set before us, looking to Jesus, the founder and perfecter of our faith, who for the joy that was set before him endured the cross, despising the shame, and is seated at the right hand of the throne of God.

Phil. 3:10. | Matt. 10:25. | Isa. 53:3.
John 16:33. | John 15:19. | Ps. 69:20. | 2 Tim. 4:16.
Matt. 8:20. | Heb. 13:14. | Heb. 12:1, 2.

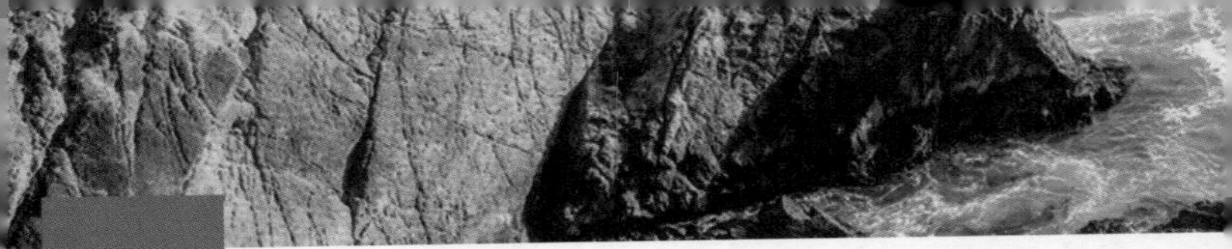

MAY
15

"He will wipe away every tear … and death shall be no more, neither … mourning … for the former things have passed away."

He will swallow up death forever; and the Lord God will wipe away tears from all faces, and the reproach of his people he will take away from all the earth, for the Lord has spoken. ❖ Your sun shall no more go down, nor your moon withdraw itself; for the Lord will be your everlasting light, and your days of mourning shall be ended. ❖ And no inhabitant will say, "I am sick"; the people who dwell there will be forgiven their iniquity. ❖ "No more shall be heard in it the sound of weeping and the cry of distress." ❖ And sorrow and sighing shall flee away.

Shall I ransom them from the power of Sheol? Shall I redeem them from Death? O Death, where are your plagues? O Sheol, where is your sting? ❖ The last enemy to be destroyed is death. … Then shall come to pass the saying that is written: "Death is swallowed up in victory."

The things that are unseen are eternal.

Rev. 21:4. | Isa. 25:8. | Isa. 60:20. | Isa. 33:24.
Isa. 65:19. | Isa. 35:10. | Hosea 13:14.
1 Cor. 15:26, 54. | 2 Cor. 4:18.

A servant of Christ Jesus.

"You call me Teacher and Lord, and you are right, for so I am." ❖ "If anyone serves me, he must follow me; and where I am, there will my servant be also. If anyone serves me, the Father will honor him." ❖ "Take my yoke upon you, and learn from me, for I am gentle and lowly in heart, and you will find rest for your souls. For my yoke is easy, and my burden is light."

But whatever gain I had, I counted as loss for the sake of Christ. ❖ But now that you have been set free from sin and have become slaves of God, the fruit you get leads to sanctification and its end, eternal life.

"No longer do I call you servants, for the servant does not know what his master is doing; but I have called you friends, for all that I have heard from my Father I have made known to you." ❖ So you are no longer a slave, but a son. ❖ Stand firm therefore, and do not submit again to a yoke of slavery. … For you were called to freedom, brothers. Only do not use your freedom as an opportunity for the flesh.

Rom. 1:1. | John 13:13. | John 12:26.
Matt. 11:29, 30. | Phil. 3:7. | Rom. 6:22.
John 15:15. | Gal. 4:7. | Gal. 5:1, 13.

MAY
17

"I am the Lord *your God; walk in my statutes, and be careful to obey my rules."*

But as he who called you is holy, you also be holy in all your conduct. ❖ Whoever says he abides in him ought to walk in the same way in which he walked. ... If you know that he is righteous, you may be sure that everyone who practices righteousness has been born of him. ❖ For neither circumcision counts for anything nor uncircumcision, but keeping the commandments of God. ❖ For whoever keeps the whole law but fails in one point has become accountable for all of it.

Not that we are sufficient in ourselves to claim anything as coming from us, but our sufficiency is from God. ❖ Teach me, O Lord, the way of your statutes.

Work out your own salvation with fear and trembling, for it is God who works in you, both to will and to work for his good pleasure. ❖ Now may the God of peace ... equip you with everything good that you may do his will, working in us that which is pleasing in his sight, through Jesus Christ.

Ezek. 20:19. | 1 Pet. 1:15. | 1 John 2:6, 29.
1 Cor. 7:19. | James 2:10. | 2 Cor. 3:5.
Ps. 119:33. | Phil. 2:12, 13. | Heb. 13:20, 21.

MAY
18

"For as the Father has life in himself, so he has granted the Son also to have life in himself."

Our Savior Christ Jesus … abolished death and brought life and immortality to light through the gospel. ❖ "I am the resurrection and the life." ❖ "Because I live, you also will live." ❖ We share in Christ. ❖ Those … who have shared in the Holy Spirit. ❖ Partakers of the divine nature. ❖ "The first man Adam became a living being"; the last Adam became a life-giving spirit. … Behold! I tell you a mystery. We shall not all sleep, but we shall all be changed, in a moment, in the twinkling of an eye, at the last trumpet. For the trumpet will sound, and the dead will be raised imperishable, and we shall be changed.

"Holy, holy, holy, is the Lord God Almighty, who was and is and is to come!" … who lives forever and ever. ❖ He who is the blessed and only Sovereign, the King of kings and Lord of lords, who alone has immortality. ❖ To the King of ages, immortal, be honor and glory forever and ever. Amen.

John 5:26. | 2 Tim. 1:10. | John 11:25. | John 14:19. Heb. 3:14. | Heb. 6:4. | 2 Pet. 1:4. | 1 Cor. 15:45, 51, 52. Rev. 4:8, 9. | 1 Tim. 6:15, 16. | 1 Tim. 1:17.

MAY
19

Wash me thoroughly from my iniquity.

"I will cleanse them from all the guilt of their sin against me, and I will forgive all the guilt of their sin and rebellion against me." ❖ "I will sprinkle clean water on you, and you shall be clean from all your uncleannesses, and from all your idols I will cleanse you."

"Unless one is born of water and the Spirit, he cannot enter the kingdom of God." ❖ If the sprinkling of defiled persons with the blood of goats and bulls and with the ashes of a heifer sanctifies for the purification of the flesh, how much more will the blood of Christ, who through the eternal Spirit offered himself without blemish to God, purify our conscience from dead works to serve the living God.

Yet he saved them for his name's sake, that he might make known his mighty power. ❖ Not to us, O Lord, not to us, but to your name give glory, for the sake of your steadfast love and your faithfulness!

Ps. 51:2. | Jer. 33:8. | Ezek. 36:25. | John 3:5.
Heb. 9:13, 14. | Ps. 106:8. | Ps. 115:1.

MAY
20

Keep a close watch on yourself.

Every athlete exercises self-control in all things. They do it to receive a perishable wreath, but we an imperishable. So I do not run aimlessly; I do not box as one beating the air. But I discipline my body and keep it under control, lest after preaching to others I myself should be disqualified. ❖ Put on the whole armor of God, that you may be able to stand against the schemes of the devil. For we do not wrestle against flesh and blood, but against the rulers, against the authorities, against the cosmic powers over this present darkness, against the spiritual forces of evil in the heavenly places.

And those who belong to Christ Jesus have crucified the flesh with its passions and desires. If we live by the Spirit, let us also walk by the Spirit. ❖ For all who are led by the Spirit of God are sons of God. ❖ Practice these things, devote yourself to them, so that all may see your progress.

1 Tim. 4:16. | 1 Cor. 9:25-27. | Eph. 6:11, 12.
Gal. 5:24, 25. | Rom. 8:14. | 1 Tim. 4:15.

MAY 21

Finally, be strong in the Lord and in the strength of his might.

"My grace is sufficient for you, for my power is made perfect in weakness." Therefore I will boast all the more gladly of my weaknesses, so that the power of Christ may rest upon me. For the sake of Christ, then, I am content with weaknesses, insults, hardships, persecutions, and calamities. For when I am weak, then I am strong. ❖ With the mighty deeds of the Lord GOD I will come; I will remind them of your righteousness, yours alone. ❖ The gospel … is the power of God for salvation.

I can do all things through him who strengthens me. ❖ I toil, struggling with all his energy that he powerfully works within me. ❖ But we have this treasure in jars of clay, to show that the surpassing power belongs to God and not to us.

"The joy of the LORD is your strength." ❖ May you be strengthened with all power, according to his glorious might, for all endurance and patience with joy.

Eph. 6:10. | 2 Cor. 12:9, 10. | Ps. 71:16.
Rom. 1:16. | Phil. 4:13. | Col. 1:29.
2 Cor. 4:7. | Neh. 8:10. | Col. 1:11.

MAY
22

"Peace I leave with you; my peace I give to you.
Not as the world gives do I give to you."

And the world is passing away along with its desires. ❖ Surely a man goes about as a shadow! Surely for nothing they are in turmoil; man heaps up wealth and does not know who will gather! ❖ But what fruit were you getting at that time from the things of which you are now ashamed? The end of those things is death.

"Martha, Martha, you are anxious and troubled about many things, but one thing is necessary. Mary has chosen the good portion, which will not be taken away from her." ❖ I want you to be free from anxieties.

"I have said these things to you, that in me you may have peace. In the world you will have tribulation. But take heart; I have overcome the world." ❖ Now may the Lord of peace himself give you peace at all times in every way. ❖ The LORD bless you and keep you; the LORD make his face to shine upon you and be gracious to you; the LORD lift up his countenance upon you and give you peace.

John 14:27. | 1 John 2:17. | Ps. 39:6.
Rom. 6:21. | Luke 10:41, 42. | 1 Cor. 7:32.
John 16:33. | 2 Thess. 3:16. | Num. 6:24-26.

MAY 23

"And you shall set the two stones on the shoulder pieces of the ephod, as stones of remembrance for the sons of Israel. And Aaron shall bear their names before the LORD."

[Jesus] holds his priesthood permanently, because he continues forever. Consequently, he is able to save to the uttermost those who draw near to God through him, since he always lives to make intercession for them. ❖ Him who is able to keep you from stumbling and to present you blameless before the presence of his glory.

Since then we have a great high priest who has passed through the heavens, Jesus, the Son of God, let us hold fast our confession. For we do not have a high priest who is unable to sympathize with our weaknesses, but one who in every respect has been tempted as we are, yet without sin. Let us then with confidence draw near to the throne of grace.

"The beloved of the LORD dwells in safety. The High God surrounds him all day long, and dwells between his shoulders."

Exod. 28:12. | Heb. 7:24, 25. | Jude 24.
Heb. 4:14-16. | Deut. 33:12.

MAY
24

And do not grieve the Holy Spirit of God,
by whom you were sealed for the day of redemption.

The love of the Spirit. ❖ "The Helper, the Holy Spirit." ❖ In all their affliction he was afflicted, and the angel of his presence saved them; in his love and in his pity he redeemed them; he lifted them up and carried them all the days of old. But they rebelled and grieved his Holy Spirit; therefore he turned to be their enemy, and himself fought against them.

By this we know that we abide in him and he in us, because he has given us of his Spirit. ❖ When you … believed in him, [you] were sealed with the promised Holy Spirit, who is the guarantee of our inheritance until we acquire possession of it. ❖ But I say, walk by the Spirit, and you will not gratify the desires of the flesh. For the desires of the flesh are against the Spirit, and the desires of the Spirit are against the flesh, for these are opposed to each other, to keep you from doing the things you want to do.

The Spirit helps us in our weakness.

Eph. 4:30. | Rom. 15:30. | John 14:26.
Isa. 63:9, 10. | 1 John 4:13. | Eph. 1:13, 14.
Gal. 5:16, 17. | Rom. 8:26.

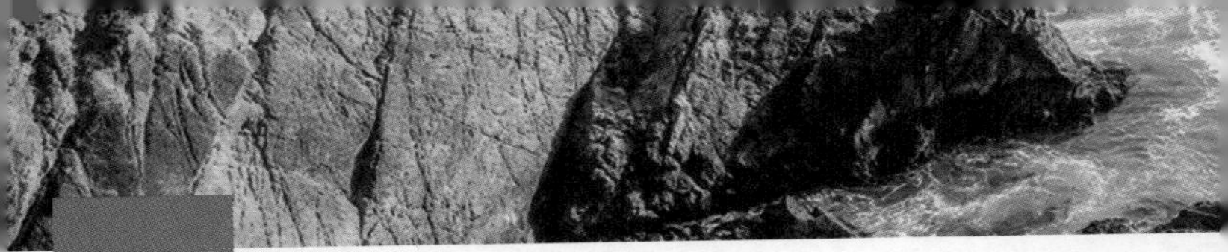

MAY
25

Oh, how abundant is your goodness, which you have stored up for those who fear you.

From of old no one has heard or perceived by the ear, no eye has seen a God besides you, who acts for those who wait for him. ❖ "What no eye has seen, nor ear heard, nor the heart of man imagined, what God has prepared for those who love him" – these things God has revealed to us through the Spirit. ❖ You make known to me the path of life; in your presence there is fullness of joy; at your right hand are pleasures forevermore.

How precious is your steadfast love, O God! The children of mankind take refuge in the shadow of your wings. They feast on the abundance of your house, and you give them drink from the river of your delights. For with you is the fountain of life; in your light do we see light.

Godliness is of value in every way, as it holds promise for the present life and also for the life to come.

Ps. 31:19. | Isa. 64:4. | 1 Cor. 2:9, 10.
Ps. 16:11. | Ps. 36:7-9. | 1 Tim. 4:8.

MAY 26

Our Lord Jesus, the great shepherd of the sheep.

The chief Shepherd. ❖ "I am the good shepherd. I know my own and my own know me. … My sheep hear my voice, and I know them, and they follow me. I give them eternal life, and they will never perish, and no one will snatch them out of my hand."

The Lord is my shepherd; I shall not want. He makes me lie down in green pastures. He leads me beside still waters. He restores my soul. He leads me in paths of righteousness for his name's sake.

All we like sheep have gone astray; we have turned every one to his own way; and the Lord has laid on him the iniquity of us all. ❖ "I am the good shepherd. The good shepherd lays down his life for the sheep." ❖ "I will seek the lost, and I will bring back the strayed, and I will bind up the injured, and I will strengthen the weak." ❖ For you were straying like sheep, but have now returned to the Shepherd and Overseer of your souls.

Heb. 13:20. | 1 Pet. 5:4. | John 10:14, 27, 28.
Ps. 23:1-3. | Isa. 53:6. | John 10:11.
Ezek. 34:16. | 1 Pet. 2:25.

MAY 27

The LORD is good, a stronghold in the day of trouble; he knows those who take refuge in him.

"Give thanks to the LORD of hosts, for the LORD is good, for his steadfast love endures forever!" ❖ God is our refuge and strength, a very present help in trouble. ❖ I will say to the LORD, "My refuge and my fortress, my God, in whom I trust." ❖ "Who is like you, a people saved by the LORD, the shield of your help, and the sword of your triumph!" ❖ This God – his way is perfect; the word of the LORD proves true; he is a shield for all those who take refuge in him. "For who is God, but the LORD? And who is a rock, except our God?"

But if anyone loves God, he is known by God. ❖ But God's firm foundation stands, bearing this seal: "The Lord knows those who are his," and, "Let everyone who names the name of the Lord depart from iniquity." ❖ The LORD knows the way of the righteous, but the way of the wicked will perish. ❖ "You have found favor in my sight, and I know you by name."

Nah. 1:7. | Jer. 33:11. | Ps. 46:1. | Ps. 91:2.
Deut. 33:29. | 2 Sam. 22:31, 32. | 1 Cor. 8:3.
2 Tim. 2:19. | Ps. 1:6. | Exod. 33:17.

MAY
28

We await a Savior.

For the grace of God has appeared, bringing salvation for all people, training us to renounce ungodliness and worldly passions, and to live self-controlled, upright, and godly lives in the present age, waiting for our blessed hope, the appearing of the glory of our great God and Savior Jesus Christ, who gave himself for us to redeem us from all lawlessness and to purify for himself a people for his own possession who are zealous for good works. ❖ But according to his promise we are waiting for new heavens and a new earth in which righteousness dwells. Therefore, beloved, since you are waiting for these, be diligent to be found by him without spot or blemish, and at peace.

Christ, having been offered once to bear the sins of many, will appear a second time, not to deal with sin but to save those who are eagerly waiting for him. ❖ It will be said on that day, "Behold, this is our God; we have waited for him, that he might save us. This is the LORD; we have waited for him; let us be glad and rejoice in his salvation."

Phil. 3:20. | Titus 2:11-14. | 2 Pet. 3:13, 14.
Heb. 9:28. | Isa. 25:9.

MAY
29

"For the life of the flesh is in the blood,
and I have given it for you on the altar
to make atonement for your souls, for it is
the blood that makes atonement by the life."

"Behold, the Lamb of God, who takes away the sin of the world!" ❖ The blood of the Lamb. ❖ The precious blood of Christ, like that of a lamb without blemish or spot. ❖ Without the shedding of blood there is no forgiveness of sins. ❖ The blood of Jesus his Son cleanses us from all sin.

He entered once for all into the holy places, not by means of the blood of goats and calves but by means of his own blood, thus securing an eternal redemption. ❖ Therefore, brothers, since we have confidence to enter the holy places by the blood of Jesus, by the new and living way that he opened for us through the curtain, that is, through his flesh ... let us draw near with a true heart in full assurance of faith.

You were bought with a price. So glorify God in your body.

Lev. 17:11. | John 1:29. | Rev. 7:14. | 1 Pet. 1:19.
Heb. 9:22. | 1 John 1:7. | Heb. 9:12.
Heb. 10:19, 20, 22. | 1 Cor. 6:20.

MAY 30

Let us therefore strive to enter that rest.

"Enter by the narrow gate. For the gate is wide and the way is easy that leads to destruction. … For the gate is narrow and the way is hard that leads to life, and those who find it are few." ❖ "The kingdom of heaven has suffered violence, and the violent take it by force." ❖ "Do not labor for the food that perishes, but for the food that endures to eternal life, which the Son of Man will give to you." ❖ Therefore, brothers, be all the more diligent to make your calling and election sure. … For in this way there will be richly provided for you an entrance into the eternal kingdom of our Lord and Savior Jesus Christ. ❖ So run that you may obtain it. Every athlete exercises self-control in all things. They do it to receive a perishable wreath, but we an imperishable.

Whoever has entered God's rest has also rested from his works as God did from his. ❖ The Lord will be your everlasting light, and your God will be your glory.

Heb. 4:11. | Matt. 7:13, 14. | Matt. 11:12. | John 6:27.
2 Pet. 1:10, 11. | 1 Cor. 9:24, 25. | Heb. 4:10. | Isa. 60:19.

MAY
31

"Your name shall ... be called ... Israel, for you have striven with God and with men, and have prevailed."

In his manhood he strove with God. He strove with the angel and prevailed; he wept and sought his favor. ❖ No distrust made [Abraham] waver concerning the promise of God, but he grew strong in his faith as he gave glory to God.

"Have faith in God. Truly, I say to you, whoever says to this mountain, 'Be taken up and thrown into the sea,' and does not doubt in his heart, but believes that what he says will come to pass, it will be done for him. Therefore I tell you, whatever you ask in prayer, believe that you have received it, and it will be yours." ❖ "If you can! All things are possible for one who believes." ❖ "And blessed is she who believed that there would be a fulfillment of what was spoken to her from the Lord."

"Increase our faith!"

Gen. 32:28. | Hosea 12:3, 4. | Rom. 4:20.
Mark 11:22-24. | Mark 9:23. | Luke 1:45. | Luke 17:5.

June

JUN. 1

But the fruit of the Spirit is …
patience … gentleness.

"The LORD, the LORD, a God merciful and gracious, slow to anger, and abounding in steadfast love and faithfulness."

Walk in a manner worthy of the calling to which you have been called, with all humility and gentleness, with patience, bearing with one another in love. ❖ Be kind to one another, tenderhearted, forgiving one another, as God in Christ forgave you. ❖ But the wisdom from above is first pure, then peaceable, gentle, open to reason, full of mercy and good fruits, impartial and sincere. ❖ Love is patient and kind.

In due season we will reap, if we do not give up. ❖ Be patient, therefore, brothers, until the coming of the Lord. See how the farmer waits for the precious fruit of the earth, being patient about it, until it receives the early and the late rains. You also, be patient. Establish your hearts, for the coming of the Lord is at hand.

Gal. 5:22, 23. | Exod. 34:6. | Eph. 4:1, 2. | Eph. 4:32.
James 3:17. | 1 Cor. 13:4. | Gal. 6:9. | James 5:7, 8.

JUN. 2

"In this manner you shall eat it: with your belt fastened. … And you shall eat it in haste. It is the LORD's Passover."

Arise and go, for this is no place to rest. ❖ For here we have no lasting city, but we seek the city that is to come. ❖ So then, there remains a Sabbath rest for the people of God.

"Stay dressed for action and keep your lamps burning, and be like men who are waiting for their master to come home from the wedding feast, so that they may open the door to him at once when he comes and knocks. Blessed are those servants whom the master finds awake when he comes." ❖ Therefore, preparing your minds for action, and being sober-minded, set your hope fully on the grace that will be brought to you at the revelation of Jesus Christ. ❖ But one thing I do: forgetting what lies behind, … I press on toward the goal for the prize of the upward call of God in Christ Jesus. Let those of us who are mature think this way.

Exod. 12:11. | Mic. 2:10. | Heb. 13:14. | Heb. 4:9.
Luke 12:35-37. | 1 Pet. 1:13. | Phil. 3:13-15.

JUN.
3

"Watch therefore, for you know neither the day nor the hour."

"But watch yourselves lest your hearts be weighed down with dissipation and drunkenness and cares of this life, and that day come upon you suddenly like a trap. For it will come upon all who dwell on the face of the whole earth. But stay awake at all times, praying that you may have strength to escape all these things that are going to take place, and to stand before the Son of Man."

The Lord will come like a thief in the night. While people are saying, "There is peace and security," then sudden destruction will come upon them as labor pains come upon a pregnant woman, and they will not escape. But you are not in darkness, brothers, for that day to surprise you like a thief. For you are all children of light, children of the day. We are not of the night or of the darkness. So then let us not sleep, as others do, but let us keep awake and be sober.

Matt. 25:13. | Luke 21:34-36. | 1 Thess. 5:2-6.

"The latter glory of this house shall be greater than the former. … And in this place I will give peace."

"The house that is to be built for the Lord must be exceedingly magnificent, of fame and glory throughout all lands." ❖ The glory of the Lord filled the Lord's house.

"Destroy this temple, and in three days I will raise it up." … But he was speaking about the temple of his body. ❖ Indeed, in this case, what once had glory has come to have no glory at all, because of the glory that surpasses it. ❖ And the Word became flesh and dwelt among us, and we have seen his glory, glory as of the only Son from the Father, full of grace and truth. ❖ In these last days [God] has spoken to us by his Son, whom he appointed the heir of all things, through whom also he created the world.

"Glory to God in the highest, and on earth peace among those with whom he is pleased!" ❖ Prince of Peace. ❖ For he himself is our peace. ❖ And the peace of God, which surpasses all understanding, will guard your hearts and your minds in Christ Jesus.

Hag. 2:9. | 1 Chron. 22:5. | 2 Chron. 7:2.
John 2:19, 21. | 2 Cor. 3:10. | John 1:14. | Heb. 1:2.
Luke 2:14. | Isa. 9:6. | Eph. 2:14. | Phil. 4:7.

JUN.
5

"So you also, when you have done all that you were commanded, say, 'We are unworthy servants.'"

Then what becomes of our boasting? It is excluded. By what kind of law? By a law of works? No, but by the law of faith. ❖ What do you have that you did not receive? If then you received it, why do you boast as if you did not receive it? ❖ For by grace you have been saved through faith. And this is not your own doing; it is the gift of God, not a result of works, so that no one may boast. For we are his workmanship, created in Christ Jesus for good works, which God prepared beforehand, that we should walk in them.

But by the grace of God I am what I am, and his grace toward me was not in vain. On the contrary, I worked harder than any of them, though it was not I, but the grace of God that is with me. ❖ For from him and through him and to him are all things. ❖ "For all things come from you, and of your own have we given you." ❖ Enter not into judgment with your servant, for no one living is righteous before you.

Luke 17:10. | Rom. 3:27. | 1 Cor. 4:7. | Eph. 2:8-10.
1 Cor. 15:10. | Rom. 11:36. | 1 Chron. 29:14. | Ps. 143:2.

JUN.
6

He will quiet you by his love.

"It was not because you were more in number than any other people that the LORD set his love on you and chose you, for you were the fewest of all peoples, but it is because the LORD loves you." ❖ We love because he first loved us. ❖ And you … he has now reconciled in his body of flesh by his death, in order to present you holy and blameless and above reproach before him.

In this is love, not that we have loved God but that he loved us and sent his Son to be the propitiation for our sins. ❖ But God shows his love for us in that while we were still sinners, Christ died for us. ❖ And behold, a voice from heaven said, "This is my beloved Son, with whom I am well pleased." ❖ "For this reason the Father loves me, because I lay down my life that I may take it up again." ❖ His Son … He is the radiance of the glory of God and the exact imprint of his nature, and he upholds the universe by the word of his power. After making purification for sins, he sat down at the right hand of the Majesty on high.

Zeph. 3:17. | Deut. 7:7, 8. | 1 John 4:19.
Col. 1:21, 22. | 1 John 4:10. | Rom. 5:8.
Matt. 3:17. | John 10:17. | Heb. 1:2, 3.

JUN.
7

They ought always to pray and not lose heart.

And he said to them, "Which of you who has a friend will go to him at midnight and say to him, 'Friend, lend me three loaves, for a friend of mine has arrived on a journey, and I have nothing to set before him'; and he will answer from within, 'Do not bother me; the door is now shut, and my children are with me in bed. I cannot get up and give you anything'? I tell you, though he will not get up and give him anything because he is his friend, yet because of his impudence he will rise and give him whatever he needs." ❖ Praying at all times in the Spirit, with all prayer and supplication. To that end keep alert with all perseverance, making supplication for all the saints.

"I will not let you go unless you bless me." … "You have striven with God and with men." ❖ Continue steadfastly in prayer, being watchful in it with thanksgiving.

[Jesus] went out to the mountain to pray, and all night he continued in prayer to God.

Luke 18:1. | Luke 11:5-8. | Eph. 6:18.
Gen. 32:26, 28. | Col. 4:2. | Luke 6:12.

JUN.
8

The LORD caused all that he did
to succeed in his hands.

Blessed is everyone who fears the LORD, who walks in his ways! You shall eat the fruit of the labor of your hands; you shall be blessed, and it shall be well with you. ❖ Trust in the LORD, and do good; dwell in the land and befriend faithfulness. Delight yourself in the LORD, and he will give you the desires of your heart. ❖ "Do not be frightened, and do not be dismayed, for the LORD your God is with you wherever you go." ❖ "But seek first the kingdom of God and his righteousness, and all these things will be added to you."

As long as he sought the LORD, God made him prosper. ❖ "Take care lest you forget the LORD your God by not keeping his commandments and his rules and his statutes, which I command you today. … Lest you say in your heart, 'My power and the might of my hand have gotten me this wealth.'" ❖ "Is not the LORD your God with you? And has he not given you peace on every side?"

Gen. 39:3. | Ps. 128:1, 2. | Ps. 37:3, 4. | Josh. 1:9. | Matt. 6:33.
2 Chron. 26:5. | Deut. 8:11, 17. | 1 Chron. 22:18.

JUN. 9

"No one ever spoke like this man!"

You are the most handsome of the sons of men; grace is poured upon your lips; therefore God has blessed you forever. ❖ The Lord GOD has given me the tongue of those who are taught, that I may know how to sustain with a word him who is weary. ❖ His mouth is most sweet, and he is altogether desirable. This is my beloved and this is my friend.

And all spoke well of him and marveled at the gracious words that were coming from his mouth. ❖ He was teaching them as one who had authority, and not as their scribes.

Let the word of Christ dwell in you richly … in all wisdom. ❖ The sword of the Spirit … is the word of God. ❖ For the word of God is living and active, sharper than any two-edged sword. ❖ For the weapons of our warfare are not of the flesh but have divine power to destroy strongholds. We destroy arguments and every lofty opinion raised against the knowledge of God, and take every thought captive to obey Christ.

John 7:46. | Ps. 45:2. | Isa. 50:4. | Song of Songs 5:16. Luke 4:22. | Matt. 7:29. | Col. 3:16. | Eph. 6:17. Heb. 4:12. | 2 Cor. 10:4, 5.

JUN.
10

"The younger son gathered all he had and took a journey into a far country, and there he squandered his property in reckless living."

And such were some of you. But you were washed, you were sanctified, you were justified in the name of the Lord Jesus Christ and by the Spirit of our God. ❖ We ... were by nature children of wrath, like the rest of mankind. But God, being rich in mercy, because of the great love with which he loved us, even when we were dead in our trespasses, made us alive together with Christ – by grace you have been saved – and raised us up with him and seated us with him in the heavenly places in Christ Jesus. ❖ In this is love, not that we have loved God but that he loved us and sent his Son to be the propitiation for our sins.

God shows his love for us in that while we were still sinners, Christ died for us. For if while we were enemies we were reconciled to God by the death of his Son, much more, now that we are reconciled, shall we be saved by his life.

Luke 15:13. | 1 Cor. 6:11. | Eph. 2:3-6.
1 John 4:10. | Rom. 5:8, 10.

JUN.
11

And he arose and came to his father. But while he was still a long way off, his father saw him and felt compassion, and ran and embraced him and kissed him.

The LORD is merciful and gracious, slow to anger and abounding in steadfast love. He will not always chide, nor will he keep his anger forever. He does not deal with us according to our sins, nor repay us according to our iniquities. For as high as the heavens are above the earth, so great is his steadfast love toward those who fear him; as far as the east is from the west, so far does he remove our transgressions from us. As a father shows compassion to his children, so the LORD shows compassion to those who fear him.

You have received the Spirit of adoption as sons, by whom we cry, "Abba! Father!" The Spirit himself bears witness with our spirit that we are children of God. ❖ But now in Christ Jesus you who once were far off have been brought near by the blood of Christ. ... So then you are no longer strangers and aliens, but you are fellow citizens with the saints and members of the household of God.

Luke 15:20. | Ps. 103:8-13. | Rom. 8:15, 16. | Eph. 2:13, 19.

JUN.
12

"Everything that can stand the fire, you shall pass through the fire, and it shall be clean."

"The LORD your God is testing you, to know whether you love the LORD your God with all your heart and with all your soul." ❖ "He will sit as a refiner and purifier of silver, and he will purify the sons of Levi and refine them like gold and silver, and they will bring offerings in righteousness to the LORD." ❖ Each one's work will become manifest, for the Day will disclose it, because it will be revealed by fire, and the fire will test what sort of work each one has done.

"I will turn my hand against you and will smelt away your dross as with lye and remove all your alloy." ❖ "I will refine them and test them."

You, O God, have tested us; you have tried us as silver is tried. ... We went through fire and through water; yet you have brought us out to a place of abundance.

"When you walk through fire you shall not be burned, and the flame shall not consume you."

Num. 31:23. | Deut. 13:3. | Mal. 3:3. | 1 Cor. 3:13.
Isa. 1:25. | Jer. 9:7. | Ps. 66:10, 12. | Isa. 43:2.

JUN. 13

"Abide in me, and I in you."

I have been crucified with Christ. It is no longer I who live, but Christ who lives in me. And the life I now live in the flesh I live by faith in the Son of God, who loved me and gave himself for me.

I know that nothing good dwells in me, that is, in my flesh. For I have the desire to do what is right, but not the ability to carry it out. ... Wretched man that I am! Who will deliver me from this body of death? Thanks be to God through Jesus Christ our Lord! ❖ But if Christ is in you, although the body is dead because of sin, the Spirit is life because of righteousness. ❖ If indeed you continue in the faith, stable and steadfast, not shifting from the hope of the gospel that you heard.

And now, little children, abide in him, so that when he appears we may have confidence and not shrink from him in shame at his coming. ❖ Whoever says he abides in him ought to walk in the same way in which he walked.

John 15:4. | Gal. 2:20. | Rom. 7:18, 24, 25. | Rom. 8:10. Col. 1:23. | 1 John 2:28. | 1 John 2:6.

JUN. 14

As we share abundantly in Christ's sufferings, so through Christ we share abundantly in comfort too.

Share his sufferings. ❖ But rejoice insofar as you share Christ's sufferings, that you may also rejoice and be glad when his glory is revealed. ❖ If we have died with him, we will also live with him. ❖ If children, then heirs – heirs of God and fellow heirs with Christ, provided we suffer with him in order that we may also be glorified with him.

So when God desired to show more convincingly to the heirs of the promise the unchangeable character of his purpose, he guaranteed it with an oath, so that by two unchangeable things, in which it is impossible for God to lie, we who have fled for refuge might have strong encouragement to hold fast to the hope set before us. ❖ Now may our Lord Jesus Christ himself, and God our Father, who loved us and gave us eternal comfort and good hope through grace, comfort your hearts and establish them in every good work and word.

2 Cor. 1:5. | Phil. 3:10. | 1 Pet. 4:13. | 2 Tim. 2:11.
Rom. 8:17. | Heb. 6:17, 18. | 2 Thess. 2:16, 17.

JUN.
15

"The secret things belong to the LORD our God,
but the things that are revealed belong to us."

O LORD, my heart is not lifted up; my eyes are not raised too high; I do not occupy myself with things too great and too marvelous for me. But I have calmed and quieted my soul, like a weaned child with its mother; like a weaned child is my soul within me.

The friendship of the LORD is for those who fear him, and he makes known to them his covenant. ❖ "There is a God in heaven who reveals mysteries." ❖ "Behold, these are but the outskirts of his ways, and how small a whisper do we hear of him!"

"No longer do I call you servants, for the servant does not know what his master is doing; but I have called you friends, for all that I have heard from my Father I have made known to you." ❖ "If you love me, you will keep my commandments. And I will ask the Father, and he will give you another Helper, to be with you forever, even the Spirit of truth."

Deut. 29:29. | Ps. 131:1, 2. | Ps. 25:14. | Dan. 2:28.
Job 26:14. | John 15:15. | John 14:15-17.

JUN. 16

Look carefully then how you walk, not as unwise but as wise, making the best use of the time, because the days are evil.

"Only be very careful to observe the commandment and the law … to love the LORD your God, and to walk in all his ways and to keep his commandments and to cling to him and to serve him with all your heart and with all your soul." ❖ Conduct yourselves wisely toward outsiders, making the best use of the time. Let your speech always be gracious, seasoned with salt, so that you may know how you ought to answer each person. ❖ Abstain from every form of evil.

"As the bridegroom was delayed, they all became drowsy and slept. But at midnight there was a cry, 'Here is the bridegroom! Come out to meet him.' … Watch therefore, for you know neither the day nor the hour."

Therefore, brothers, be all the more diligent to make your calling and election sure, for if you practice these qualities you will never fall. ❖ "Blessed are those servants whom the master finds awake when he comes."

Eph. 5:15, 16. | Josh. 22:5. | Col. 4:5, 6. | 1 Thess. 5:22. Matt. 25:5, 6, 13. | 2 Pet. 1:10. | Luke 12:37.

JUN.
17

In everything by prayer and supplication with thanksgiving let your requests be made known to God.

I love the Lord, because he has heard my voice and my pleas for mercy. Because he inclined his ear to me, therefore I will call on him as long as I live. ❖ "And when you pray, do not heap up empty phrases as the Gentiles do, for they think that they will be heard for their many words." ❖ The Spirit helps us in our weakness. For we do not know what to pray for as we ought, but the Spirit himself intercedes for us with groanings too deep for words.

I desire then that in every place the men should pray, lifting holy hands without anger or quarreling. ❖ Praying at all times in the Spirit, with all prayer and supplication. To that end keep alert with all perseverance, making supplication for all the saints.

"If two of you agree on earth about anything they ask, it will be done for them by my Father in heaven."

Phil. 4:6. | Ps. 116:1, 2. | Matt. 6:7. | Rom. 8:26.
1 Tim. 2:8. | Eph. 6:18. | Matt. 18:19.

JUN.
18

"And you shall put the mercy seat on the top of the ark. … There I will meet with you."

The way into the holy places is not yet opened. ❖ And Jesus cried out again with a loud voice and yielded up his spirit. And behold, the curtain of the temple was torn in two, from top to bottom.

Therefore, brothers, since we have confidence to enter the holy places by the blood of Jesus, by the new and living way that he opened for us through the curtain, that is, through his flesh, … let us draw near with a true heart in full assurance of faith, with our hearts sprinkled clean from an evil conscience and our bodies washed with pure water. ❖ Let us then with confidence draw near to the throne of grace, that we may receive mercy and find grace to help in time of need.

… Christ Jesus, whom God put forward as a propitiation by his blood, to be received by faith. This was to show God's righteousness, because in his divine forbearance he had passed over former sins. ❖ Through him we … have access in one Spirit to the Father.

Exod. 25:21, 22. | Heb. 9:8. | Matt. 27:50, 51.
Heb. 10:19, 20, 22. | Heb. 4:16.
Rom. 3:24, 25. | Eph. 2:18.

JUN.
19

The holiness without which no one will see the Lord.

"Unless one is born again he cannot see the kingdom of God." ❖ But nothing unclean will ever enter it. ❖ There is no flaw in you.

"You shall be holy, for I the LORD your God am holy." ❖ As obedient children, do not be conformed to the passions of your former ignorance, but as he who called you is holy, you also be holy in all your conduct, since it is written, "You shall be holy, for I am holy." And if you call on him as Father who judges impartially according to each one's deeds, conduct yourselves with fear throughout the time of your exile. ❖ Put off your old self, which belongs to your former manner of life and is corrupt through deceitful desires, and … be renewed in the spirit of your minds, and … put on the new self, created after the likeness of God in true righteousness and holiness. ❖ He chose us in him before the foundation of the world, that we should be holy and blameless before him.

Heb. 12:14. | John 3:3. | Rev. 21:27. | Song of Songs 4:7.
Lev. 19:2. | 1 Pet. 1:14-17. | Eph. 4:22-24. | Eph. 1:4.

"Take this child away and nurse him for me, and I will give you your wages."

"You go into the vineyard too, and whatever is right I will give you." ❖ "For truly, I say to you, whoever gives you a cup of water to drink because you belong to Christ will by no means lose his reward." ❖ Whoever brings blessing will be enriched, and one who waters will himself be watered. ❖ God is not so unjust as to overlook your work and the love that you showed for his sake in serving the saints, as you still do. ❖ Each will receive his wages according to his labor.

"Then the righteous will answer him, saying, 'Lord, when did we see you hungry and feed you, or thirsty and give you drink? And when did we see you a stranger and welcome you, or naked and clothe you?' ... And the King will answer them, ... 'As you did it to one of the least of these my brothers, you did it to me. ... Come, you who are blessed by my Father, inherit the kingdom prepared for you from the foundation of the world.'"

Exod. 2:9. | Matt. 20:4. | Mark 9:41. | Prov. 11:25.
Heb. 6:10. | 1 Cor. 3:8. | Matt. 25:37, 38, 40, 34.

JUN.
21

Christ also suffered for you, leaving you an example, so that you might follow in his steps.

"Even the Son of Man came not to be served but to serve." ❖ "Whoever would be first among you must be slave of all."

Jesus of Nazareth … went about doing good. ❖ Bear one another's burdens, and so fulfill the law of Christ.

The meekness and gentleness of Christ. ❖ In humility count others more significant than yourselves.

"Father, forgive them, for they know not what they do." ❖ Be kind to one another, tenderhearted, forgiving one another, as God in Christ forgave you.

Whoever says he abides in him ought to walk in the same way in which he walked. ❖ Looking to Jesus, the founder and perfecter of our faith, who for the joy that was set before him endured the cross, despising the shame, and is seated at the right hand of the throne of God.

1 Pet. 2:21. | Mark 10:45. | Mark 10:44. | Acts 10:38.
Gal. 6:2. | 2 Cor. 10:1. | Phil. 2:3. | Luke 23:34.
Eph. 4:32. | 1 John 2:6. | Heb. 12:2.

JUN.
22

You have died, and your life is hidden with Christ in God.

How can we who died to sin still live in it? ❖ I have been crucified with Christ. It is no longer I who live, but Christ who lives in me. And the life I now live in the flesh I live by faith in the Son of God, who loved me and gave himself for me. ❖ He died for all, that those who live might no longer live for themselves but for him who for their sake died and was raised. ❖ Therefore, if anyone is in Christ, he is a new creation. The old has passed away; behold, the new has come.

We are in him who is true, in his Son Jesus Christ. ❖ "Just as you, Father, are in me, and I in you, that they also may be in us." ❖ Now you are the body of Christ and individually members of it. ❖ "Because I live, you also will live."

"To the one who conquers I will give some of the hidden manna, and I will give him a white stone, with a new name written on the stone that no one knows except the one who receives it."

Col. 3:3. | Rom. 6:2. | Gal. 2:20. | 2 Cor. 5:15.
2 Cor. 5:17. | 1 John 5:20. | John 17:21.
1 Cor. 12:27. | John 14:19. | Rev. 2:17.

JUN.
23

"I will ask the Father, and he will give you another Helper … even the Spirit of truth."

"It is to your advantage that I go away, for if I do not go away, the Helper will not come to you. But if I go, I will send him to you."

The Spirit himself bears witness with our spirit that we are children of God. ❖ You did not receive the spirit of slavery to fall back into fear, but you have received the Spirit of adoption as sons, by whom we cry, "Abba! Father!" ❖ The Spirit helps us in our weakness. For we do not know what to pray for as we ought, but the Spirit himself intercedes for us with groanings too deep for words.

May the God of hope fill you with all joy and peace in believing, so that by the power of the Holy Spirit you may abound in hope. ❖ Hope does not put us to shame, because God's love has been poured into our hearts through the Holy Spirit who has been given to us.

By this we know that we abide in him and he in us, because he has given us of his Spirit.

John 14:16, 17. | John 16:7. | Rom. 8:16. | Rom. 8:15.
Rom. 8:26. | Rom. 15:13. | Rom. 5:5. | 1 John 4:13.

JUN.
24

The ark of the covenant of the LORD went before them three days' journey, to seek out a resting place for them.

My times are in your hand. ❖ He chose our heritage for us. ❖ Lead me, O LORD, in your righteousness; … make your way straight before me. ❖ Commit your way to the LORD; trust in him, and he will act. ❖ In all your ways acknowledge him, and he will make straight your paths. ❖ Your ears shall hear a word behind you, saying, "This is the way, walk in it," when you turn to the right or when you turn to the left.

The LORD is my shepherd; I shall not want. He makes me lie down in green pastures. He leads me beside still waters. ❖ As a father shows compassion to his children, so the LORD shows compassion to those who fear him. For he knows our frame; he remembers that we are dust. ❖ "The Gentiles seek after all these things, and your heavenly Father knows that you need them all." ❖ Casting all your anxieties on him, because he cares for you.

Num. 10:33. | Ps. 31:15. | Ps. 47:4. | Ps. 5:8. | Ps. 37:5. Prov. 3:6. | Isa. 30:21. | Ps. 23:1, 2. | Ps. 103:13, 14. Matt. 6:32. | 1 Pet. 5:7.

JUN.
25

*When he appears we shall be like him,
because we shall see him as he is.*

To all who did receive him, who believed in his name, he gave the right to become children of God. ❖ By which he has granted to us his precious and very great promises, so that through them you may become partakers of the divine nature, having escaped from the corruption that is in the world because of sinful desire.

From of old no one has heard or perceived by the ear, no eye has seen a God besides you, who acts for those who wait for him.

For now we see in a mirror dimly, but then face to face. Now I know in part; then I shall know fully, even as I have been fully known. ❖ Christ … will transform our lowly body to be like his glorious body, by the power that enables him even to subject all things to himself. ❖ As for me, I shall behold your face in righteousness; when I awake, I shall be satisfied with your likeness.

1 John 3:2. | John 1:12. | 2 Pet. 1:4. | Isa. 64:4.
1 Cor. 13:12. | Phil. 3:20, 21. | Ps. 17:15.

JUN.
26

"Oh that you would bless me, … and
that you would keep me from harm. …"
And God granted what he asked.

The blessing of the LORD makes rich, and he adds no sorrow with it. ❖ "When he is quiet, who can condemn? When he hides his face, who can behold him?"

Salvation belongs to the LORD; your blessing be on your people! ❖ Oh, how abundant is your goodness, which you have stored up for those who fear you and worked for those who take refuge in you, in the sight of the children of mankind! ❖ "I do not ask that you take them out of the world, but that you keep them from the evil one."

"Ask, and it will be given to you; seek, and you will find; knock, and it will be opened to you. For everyone who asks receives, and the one who seeks finds, and to the one who knocks it will be opened." ❖ The LORD redeems the life of his servants; none of those who take refuge in him will be condemned.

1 Chron. 4:10. | Prov. 10:22. | Job 34:29. | Ps. 3:8. | Ps. 31:19. John 17:15. | Matt. 7:7, 8. | Ps. 34:22.

JUN.
27

"Who can stand?"

Who can endure the day of his coming, and who can stand when he appears? For he is like a refiner's fire and like fullers' soap.

I looked, and behold, a great multitude that no one could number, from every nation, from all tribes and peoples and languages, standing before the throne and before the Lamb, clothed in white robes, with palm branches in their hands. … "These are the ones coming out of the great tribulation. They have washed their robes and made them white in the blood of the Lamb. They shall hunger no more, neither thirst anymore; the sun shall not strike them, nor any scorching heat. For the Lamb in the midst of the throne will be their shepherd, and he will guide them to springs of living water, and God will wipe away every tear from their eyes."

There is therefore now no condemnation for those who are in Christ Jesus. ❖ For freedom Christ has set us free; stand firm therefore, and do not submit again to a yoke of slavery.

Rev. 6:17. | Mal. 3:2. | Rev. 7:9, 14-17. | Rom. 8:1. | Gal. 5:1.

JUN. 28

"I know that my Redeemer lives."

If while we were enemies we were reconciled to God by the death of his Son, much more, now that we are reconciled, shall we be saved by his life. ❖ He holds his priesthood permanently, because he continues forever. Consequently, he is able to save to the uttermost those who draw near to God through him, since he always lives to make intercession for them.

"Because I live, you also will live." ❖ If in this life only we have hoped in Christ, we are of all people most to be pitied. But in fact Christ has been raised from the dead, the firstfruits of those who have fallen asleep.

"And a Redeemer will come to Zion, to those in Jacob who turn from transgression," declares the LORD. ❖ We have redemption through his blood, the forgiveness of our trespasses, according to the riches of his grace. ❖ You were ransomed from the futile ways inherited from your forefathers, not with perishable things such as silver or gold, but with the precious blood of Christ, like that of a lamb without blemish or spot.

Job 19:25. | Rom. 5:10. | Heb. 7:24, 25.
John 14:19. | 1 Cor. 15:19, 20. | Isa. 59:20.
Eph. 1:7. | 1 Pet. 1:18, 19.

JUN. 29

His commandments are not burdensome.

"This is the will of my Father, that everyone who looks on the Son and believes in him should have eternal life." ❖ Whatever we ask we receive from him, because we keep his commandments and do what pleases him.

"My yoke is easy, and my burden is light." ❖ "If you love me, you will keep my commandments. … Whoever has my commandments and keeps them, he it is who loves me. And he who loves me will be loved by my Father, and I will love him and manifest myself to him."

Blessed is the one who finds wisdom, and the one who gets understanding. … Her ways are ways of pleasantness, and all her paths are peace. ❖ Great peace have those who love your law; nothing can make them stumble. ❖ I delight in the law of God, in my inner being.

This is his commandment, that we believe in the name of his Son Jesus Christ and love one another. ❖ Love does no wrong to a neighbor; therefore love is the fulfilling of the law.

1 John 5:3. | John 6:40. | 1 John 3:22. | Matt. 11:30. John 14:15, 21. | Prov. 3:13, 17. | Ps. 119:165. Rom. 7:22. | 1 John 3:23. | Rom. 13:10.

JUN.
30

"Those whom I love, I reprove and discipline."

"My son, do not regard lightly the discipline of the Lord, nor be weary when reproved by him. For the Lord disciplines the one he loves, and chastises every son whom he receives." ❖ As a father the son in whom he delights. ❖ He wounds, but he binds up; he shatters, but his hands heal. ❖ Humble yourselves, therefore, under the mighty hand of God so that at the proper time he may exalt you. ❖ "I have tried you in the furnace of affliction."

He does not willingly afflict or grieve the children of men. ❖ He does not deal with us according to our sins, nor repay us according to our iniquities. For as high as the heavens are above the earth, so great is his steadfast love toward those who fear him; as far as the east is from the west, so far does he remove our transgressions from us. As a father shows compassion to his children, so the LORD shows compassion to those who fear him. For he knows our frame; he remembers that we are dust.

Rev. 3:19. | Heb. 12:5, 6. | Prov. 3:12. | Job 5:18.
1 Pet. 5:6. | Isa. 48:10. | Lam. 3:33. | Ps. 103:10-14.

July

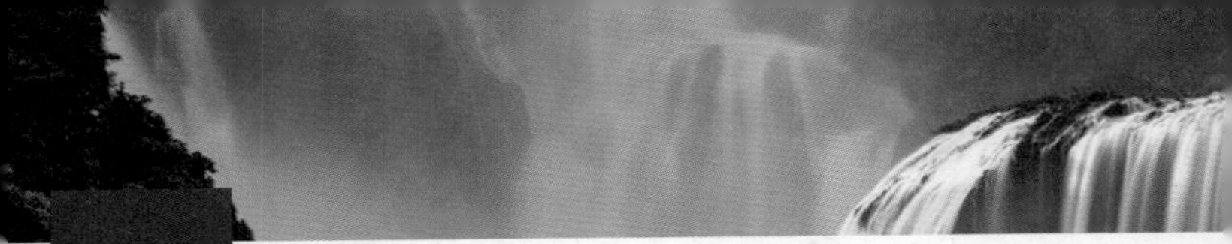

JUL.
1

But the fruit of the Spirit is … goodness.

Be imitators of God, as beloved children. ❖ "Love your enemies and pray for those who persecute you, so that you may be sons of your Father who is in heaven. For he makes his sun rise on the evil and on the good, and sends rain on the just and on the unjust." ❖ "Be merciful, even as your Father is merciful." ❖ The fruit of light is found in all that is good and right and true.

But when the goodness and loving kindness of God our Savior appeared, he saved us, not because of works done by us in righteousness, but according to his own mercy, by the washing of regeneration and renewal of the Holy Spirit, whom he poured out on us richly through Jesus Christ our Savior. ❖ The LORD is good to all, and his mercy is over all that he has made. ❖ He who did not spare his own Son but gave him up for us all, how will he not also with him graciously give us all things?

Gal. 5:22. | Eph. 5:1. | Matt. 5:44, 45. | Luke 6:36.
Eph. 5:9. | Titus 3:4-6. | Ps. 145:9. | Rom. 8:32.

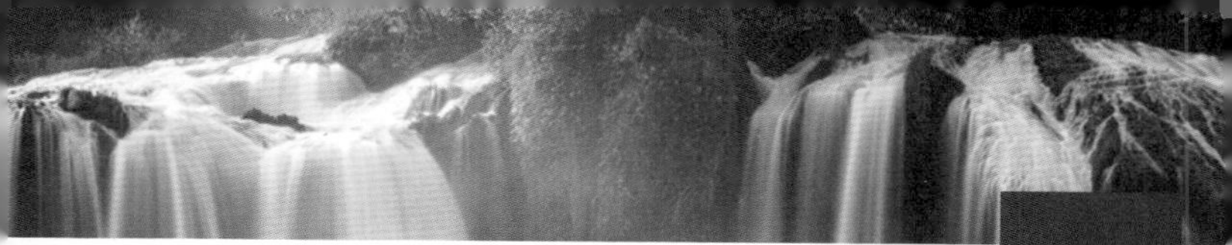

"This is the stature of the Passover:
no foreigner shall eat it."

We have an altar from which those who serve the tent have no right to eat. ❖ "Unless one is born again he cannot see the kingdom of God." ❖ You were at that time separated from Christ, alienated from the commonwealth of Israel and strangers to the covenants of promise. ... But now in Christ Jesus you who once were far off have been brought near by the blood of Christ.

For he himself is our peace, who has made us both one and has broken down in his flesh the dividing wall of hostility by abolishing the law of commandments and ordinances, that he might create in himself one new man in place of the two, so making peace.

So then you are no longer strangers and aliens, but you are fellow citizens with the saints and members of the household of God.

"Behold, I stand at the door and knock. If anyone hears my voice and opens the door, I will come in to him and eat with him, and he with me."

Exod. 12:43. | Heb. 13:10. | John 3:3. | Eph. 2:12, 13.
Eph. 2:14, 15. | Eph. 2:19. | Rev. 3:20.

JUL. 3

If children, then heirs – heirs of God and fellow heirs with Christ.

If you are Christ's, then you are Abraham's offspring, heirs according to promise.

See what kind of love the Father has given to us, that we should be called children of God. ❖ So you are no longer a slave, but a son, and if a son, then an heir through God. ❖ He predestined us for adoption through Jesus Christ, according to the purpose of his will.

"Father, I desire that they also, whom you have given me, may be with me where I am, to see my glory that you have given me."

"The one who conquers and who keeps my works until the end, to him I will give authority over the nations." ❖ "The one who conquers, I will grant him to sit with me on my throne, as I also conquered and sat down with my Father on his throne."

Rom. 8:17. | Gal. 3:29. | 1 John 3:1. | Gal. 4:7.
Eph. 1:5. | John 17:24. | Rev. 2:26. | Rev. 3:21.

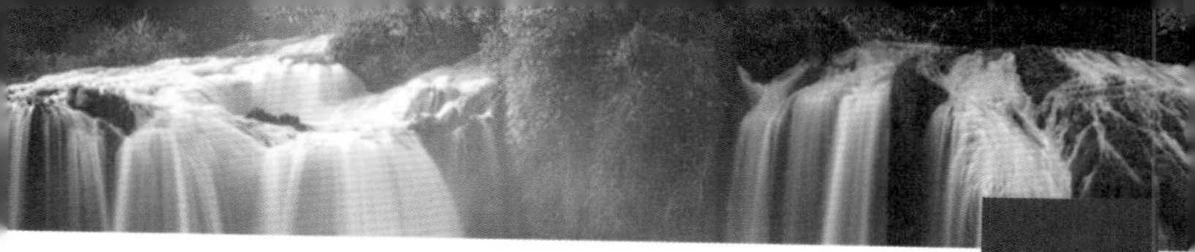

JUL.
4

Reclining at table close to Jesus.

"As one whom his mother comforts, so I will comfort you." ❖ They were bringing children to him that he might touch them. ... And he took them in his arms and blessed them, laying his hands on them. ❖ Jesus called his disciples to him and said, "I have compassion on the crowd because they have been with me now three days and have nothing to eat. And I am unwilling to send them away hungry, lest they faint on the way." ❖ For we do not have a high priest who is unable to sympathize with our weaknesses, but one who in every respect has been tempted as we are. ❖ In his love and in his pity he redeemed them.

"I will not leave you as orphans; I will come to you." ❖ "Can a woman forget her nursing child, that she should have no compassion on the son of her womb? Even these may forget, yet I will not forget you." ❖ "The Lamb in the midst of the throne will be their shepherd, and he will guide them to springs of living water, and God will wipe away every tear from their eyes."

John 13:23. | Isa. 66:13. | Mark 10:13, 16.
Matt. 15:32. | Heb. 4:15. | Isa. 63:9.
John 14:18. | Isa. 49:15. | Rev. 7:17.

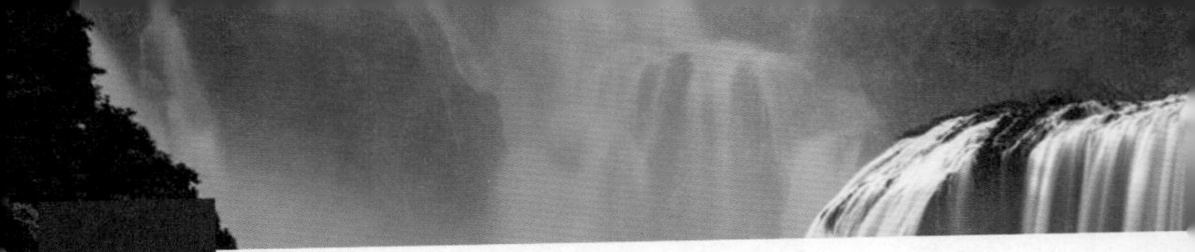

JUL.
5

We have come to know and to believe the love that God has for us.

But God, being rich in mercy, because of the great love with which he loved us, even when we were dead in our trespasses, made us alive together with Christ – by grace you have been saved – and raised us up with him and seated us with him in the heavenly places in Christ Jesus, so that in the coming ages he might show the immeasurable riches of his grace in kindness toward us in Christ Jesus.

"For God so loved the world, that he gave his only Son, that whoever believes in him should not perish but have eternal life." ❖ He who did not spare his own Son but gave him up for us all, how will he not also with him graciously give us all things? ❖ The LORD is good to all, and his mercy is over all that he has made.

We love because he first loved us.

"Blessed is she who believed that there would be a fulfillment of what was spoken to her from the Lord."

1 John 4:16. | Eph. 2:4-7. | John 3:16. | Rom. 8:32.
Ps. 145:9. | 1 John 4:19. | Luke 1:45.

JUL.
6

Let your speech always be gracious.

A word fitly spoken is like apples of gold in a setting of silver. Like a gold ring or an ornament of gold is a wise reprover to a listening ear. ❖ Let no corrupting talk come out of your mouths, but only such as is good for building up, as fits the occasion, that it may give grace to those who hear. ❖ "The good person out of his good treasure brings forth good, and the evil person out of his evil treasure brings forth evil. ... By your words you will be justified." ❖ The tongue of the wise brings healing.

Those who feared the LORD spoke with one another. The LORD paid attention and heard them, and a book of remembrance was written before him of those who feared the LORD and esteemed his name.

"If you utter what is precious, and not what is worthless, you shall be as my mouth." ❖ But as you excel in everything – in faith, in speech, in knowledge, in all earnestness, ... see that you excel in this act of grace also.

Col. 4:6. | Prov. 25:11, 12. | Eph. 4:29. | Matt. 12:35, 37.
Prov. 12:18. | Mal. 3:16. | Jer. 15:19. | 2 Cor. 8:7.

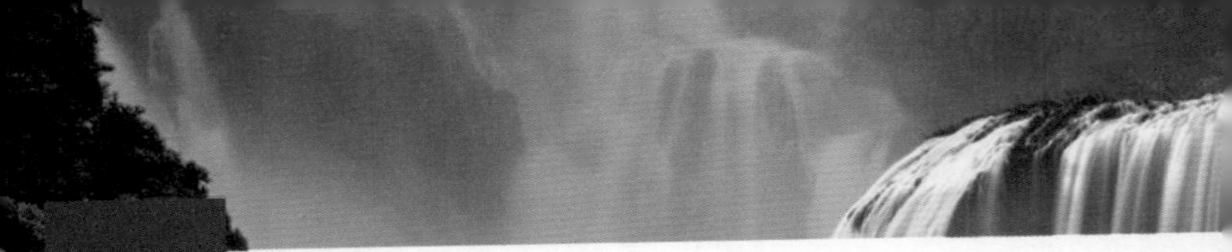

JUL.
7

Then Jesus was led up by the Spirit into the wilderness to be tempted by the devil.

In the days of his flesh, Jesus offered up prayers and supplications, with loud cries and tears, to him who was able to save him from death, and he was heard because of his reverence. Although he was a son, he learned obedience through what he suffered. And being made perfect, he became the source of eternal salvation to all who obey him. ❖ We do not have a high priest who is unable to sympathize with our weaknesses, but one who in every respect has been tempted as we are, yet without sin.

No temptation has overtaken you that is not common to man. God is faithful, and he will not let you be tempted beyond your ability, but with the temptation he will also provide the way of escape, that you may be able to endure it. ❖ "My grace is sufficient for you, for my power is made perfect in weakness."

Matt. 4:1. | Heb. 5:7-9. | Heb. 4:15.
1 Cor. 10:13. | 2 Cor. 12:9.

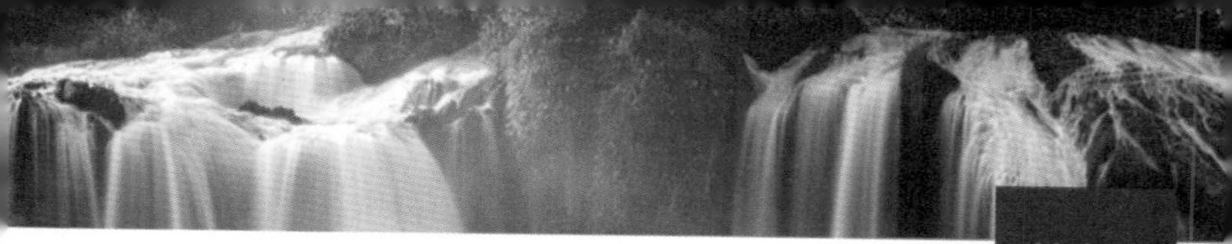

JUL.
8

If we confess our sins, he is faithful and just to forgive us our sins and to cleanse us from all unrighteousness.

I know my transgressions, and my sin is ever before me. Against you, you only, have I sinned and done what is evil in your sight.

"And he arose and came to his father. But while he was still a long way off, his father saw him and felt compassion, and ran and embraced him and kissed him." ❖ I have blotted out your transgressions like a cloud and your sins like mist; return to me, for I have redeemed you. ❖ Your sins are forgiven for his name's sake. ❖ God in Christ forgave you. ❖ So that he might be just and the justifier of the one who has faith in Jesus.

"I will sprinkle clean water on you, and you shall be clean." ❖ "They will walk with me in white, for they are worthy."

This is he who came by water and blood – Jesus Christ; not by the water only but by the water and the blood.

1 John 1:9. | Ps. 51:3, 4. | Luke 15:20. | Isa. 44:22.
1 John 2:12. | Eph. 4:32. | Rom. 3:26.
Ezek. 36:25. | Rev. 3:4. | 1 John 5:6.

JUL.
9

"I have taken your iniquity away from you, and I will clothe you with pure vestments."

Blessed is the one whose transgression is forgiven, whose sin is covered. ❖ We have all become like one who is unclean. ❖ I know that nothing good dwells in me, that is, in my flesh. For I have the desire to do what is right, but not the ability to carry it out.

For as many of you as were baptized into Christ have put on Christ. ❖ You have put off the old self with its practices and have put on the new self, which is being renewed in knowledge after the image of its creator. ❖ Not having a righteousness of my own that comes from the law, but … the righteousness from God that depends on faith.

"Bring quickly the best robe, and put it on him." ❖ The fine linen is the righteous deeds of the saints. ❖ I will greatly rejoice in the LORD; my soul shall exult in my God, for he has clothed me with the garments of salvation; he has covered me with the robe of righteousness.

Zech. 3:4. | Ps. 32:1. | Isa. 64:6. | Rom. 7:18.
Gal. 3:27. | Col. 3:9, 10. | Phil. 3:9.
Luke 15:22. | Rev. 19:8. | Isa. 61:10.

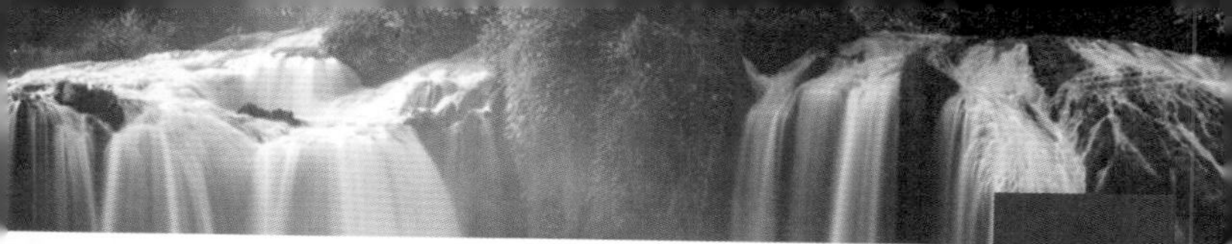

"A disciple is not above his teacher."

"You call me Teacher and Lord, and you are right, for so I am." "It is enough for the disciple to be like his teacher, and the servant like his master." ❖ "If they persecuted me, they will also persecute you. If they kept my word, they will also keep yours." ❖ "I have given them your word, and the world has hated them because they are not of the world, just as I am not of the world."

Consider him who endured from sinners such hostility against himself, so that you may not grow weary or fainthearted. In your struggle against sin you have not yet resisted to the point of shedding your blood.

Let us run with endurance the race that is set before us, looking to Jesus, the founder and perfecter of our faith, who for the joy that was set before him endured the cross, despising the shame, and is seated at the right hand of the throne of God. ❖ Since therefore Christ suffered in the flesh, arm yourselves with the same way of thinking.

Matt. 10:24. | John 13:13. | Matt. 10:25. | John 15:20. John 17:14. | Heb. 12:3, 4. | Heb. 12:1, 2. | 1 Pet. 4:1.

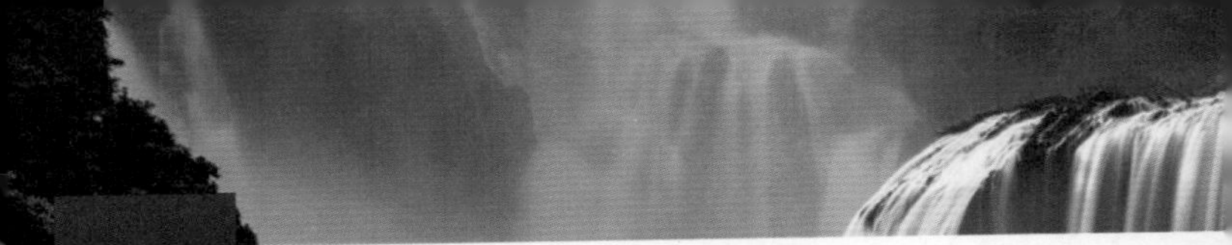

JUL.
11

"I am with you to save you."

Can the prey be taken from the mighty, or the captives of a tyrant be rescued? For thus says the Lord: "Even the captives of the mighty shall be taken, and the prey of the tyrant be rescued, for I will contend with those who contend with you. ... Then all flesh shall know that I am the Lord your Savior, and your Redeemer, the Mighty One of Jacob." ❖ Fear not, for I am with you; be not dismayed, for I am your God; I will strengthen you, I will help you, I will uphold you with my righteous right hand.

We do not have a high priest who is unable to sympathize with our weaknesses, but one who in every respect has been tempted as we are, yet without sin. ❖ Because he himself has suffered when tempted, he is able to help those who are being tempted. ❖ The steps of a man are established by the Lord, when he delights in his way; though he fall, he shall not be cast headlong, for the Lord upholds his hand.

Jer. 15:20. | Isa. 49:24-26. | Isa. 41:10.
Heb. 4:15. | Heb. 2:18. | Ps. 37:23, 24.

JUL.
12

"My presence will go with you,
and I will give you rest."

"Be strong and courageous. Do not fear or be in dread of them, for it is the LORD your God who goes with you. He will not leave you or forsake you. It is the LORD who goes before you. He will be with you; he will not leave you or forsake you. Do not fear or be dismayed." ❖ "Have I not commanded you? Be strong and courageous. Do not be frightened, and do not be dismayed, for the LORD your God is with you wherever you go." ❖ In all your ways acknowledge him, and he will make straight your paths.

He has said, "I will never leave you nor forsake you." So we can confidently say, "The Lord is my helper; I will not fear; what can man do to me?" ❖ Our sufficiency is from God.

"Lead us not into temptation." ❖ I know, O LORD, that the way of man is not in himself, that it is not in man who walks to direct his steps. ❖ My times are in your hand.

Exod. 33:14. | Deut. 31:6, 8. | Josh. 1:9.
Prov. 3:6. | Heb. 13:5, 6. | 2 Cor. 3:5.
Matt. 6:13. | Jer. 10:23. | Ps. 31:15.

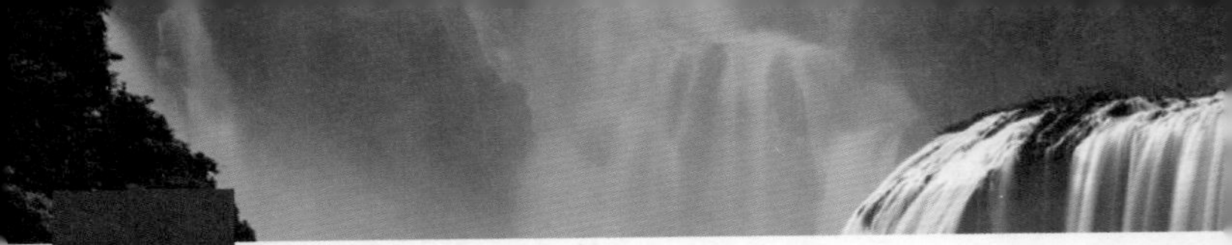

JUL.
13

I am my beloved's, and his desire is for me.

I know whom I have believed, and I am convinced that he is able to guard until that Day what has been entrusted to me. ❖ For I am sure that neither death nor life, nor angels nor rulers, nor things present nor things to come, nor powers, nor height nor depth, nor anything else in all creation, will be able to separate us from the love of God in Christ Jesus our Lord. ❖ "I kept them in your name, which you have given me. I have guarded them, and not one of them has been lost."

For the LORD takes pleasure in his people. ❖ "Delighting in the children of man." ❖ The great love with which he loved us. ❖ "Greater love has no one than this, that someone lays down his life for his friends."

You were bought with a price. So glorify God in your body. ❖ If we live, we live to the Lord, and if we die, we die to the Lord. So then, whether we live or whether we die, we are the Lord's.

Song of Songs 7:10. | 2 Tim. 1:12. | Rom. 8:38, 39.
John 17:12. | Ps. 149:4. | Prov. 8:31. | Eph. 2:4.
John 15:13. | 1 Cor. 6:20. | Rom. 14:8.

JUL.
14

"Out of the abundance of
the heart the mouth speaks."

Let the word of Christ dwell in you richly … in all wisdom.

Keep your heart with all vigilance, for from it flow the springs of life. ❖ Death and life are in the power of the tongue. ❖ The mouth of the righteous utters wisdom, and his tongue speaks justice. The law of his God is in his heart; his steps do not slip. ❖ Let no corrupting talk come out of your mouths, but only such as is good for building up, as fits the occasion, that it may give grace to those who hear.

"We cannot but speak of what we have seen and heard." ❖ I believed, even when I spoke.

"So everyone who acknowledges me before men, I also will acknowledge before my Father who is in heaven." ❖ With the heart one believes and is justified, and with the mouth one confesses and is saved.

Matt. 12:34. | Col. 3:16. | Prov. 4:23.
Prov. 18:21. | Ps. 37:30, 31. | Eph. 4:29. | Acts 4:20.
Ps. 116:10. | Matt. 10:32. | Rom. 10:10.

JUL.
15

"Your will be done, on earth as it is in heaven."

Bless the Lord, O you his angels, you mighty ones who do his word, obeying the voice of his word! Bless the Lord, all his hosts, his ministers, who do his will!

"I have come down from heaven, not to do my own will but the will of him who sent me." ❖ "I desire to do your will, O my God; your law is within my heart." ❖ "My Father, if this cannot pass unless I drink it, your will be done." ❖ "Not everyone who says to me, 'Lord, Lord,' will enter the kingdom of heaven, but the one who does the will of my Father who is in heaven." ❖ It is not the hearers of the law who are righteous before God, but the doers of the law who will be justified. ❖ "If you know these things, blessed are you if you do them." ❖ So whoever knows the right thing to do and fails to do it, for him it is sin.

Do not be conformed to this world, but be transformed by the renewal of your mind.

Matt. 6:10. | Ps. 103:20, 21. | John 6:38. | Ps. 40:8.
Matt. 26:42. | Matt. 7:21. | Rom. 2:13.
John 13:17. | James 4:17. | Rom. 12:2.

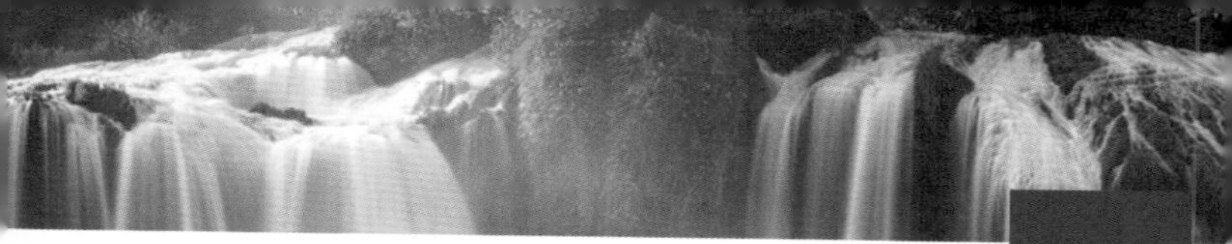

JUL.
16

"You shall be to me a kingdom of priests and a holy nation."

"You were slain, and by your blood you ransomed people for God from every tribe and language and people and nation, and you have made them a kingdom and priests to our God." ❖ But you are a chosen race, a royal priesthood, a holy nation, a people for his own possession, that you may proclaim the excellencies of him who called you out of darkness into his marvelous light.

You shall be called the priests of the LORD; they shall speak of you as the ministers of our God. ❖ Priests of God and of Christ.

Therefore, holy brothers, you who share in a heavenly calling, consider Jesus, the apostle and high priest of our confession. ❖ Through him then let us continually offer up a sacrifice of praise to God, that is, the fruit of lips that acknowledge his name.

For we are his workmanship, created in Christ Jesus for good works, which God prepared beforehand, that we should walk in them. ❖ God's temple is holy, and you are that temple.

Exod. 19:6. | Rev. 5:9, 10. | 1 Pet. 2:9. | Isa. 61:6. | Rev. 20:6.
Heb. 3:1. | Heb. 13:15. | Eph. 2:10. | 1 Cor. 3:17.

JUL.
17

"You are a gracious God and merciful,
slow to anger and abounding in steadfast love,
and relenting from disaster."

"Please let the power of the Lord be great as you have promised, saying, 'The LORD is slow to anger and abounding in steadfast love, forgiving iniquity and transgression, but he will by no means clear the guilty, visiting the iniquity of the fathers on the children, to the third and the fourth generation.'"

Do not remember against us our former iniquities; let your compassion come speedily to meet us. ... Help us, O God of our salvation, for the glory of your name; deliver us, and atone for our sins, for your name's sake! ❖ "Though our iniquities testify against us, act, O LORD, for your name's sake; for our backslidings are many; we have sinned against you." ... We acknowledge our wickedness, O LORD, and the iniquity of our fathers, for we have sinned against you.

If you, O LORD, should mark iniquities, O Lord, who could stand? But with you there is forgiveness, that you may be feared.

Jonah 4:2. | Num. 14:17, 18. | Ps. 79:8, 9.
Jer. 14:7, 20. | Ps. 130:3, 4.

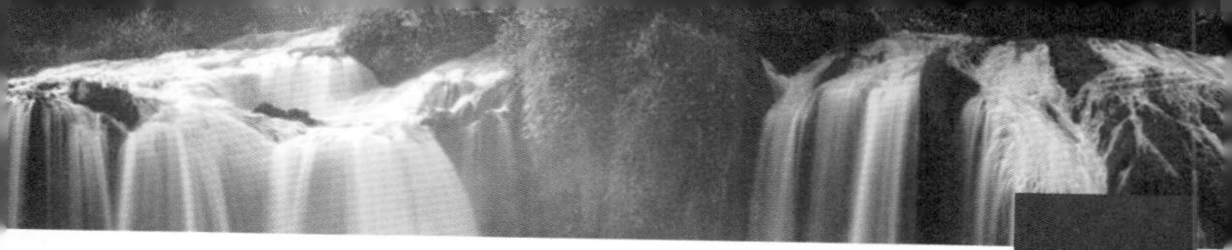

JUL.
18

"He calls his own sheep by name and leads them out."

God's firm foundation stands, bearing this seal: "The Lord knows those who are his," and, "Let everyone who names the name of the Lord depart from iniquity." ❖ "Many will say to me, 'Lord, Lord, did we not prophesy in your name, and cast out demons in your name, and do many mighty works in your name?' And then will I declare to them, 'I never knew you; depart from me, you workers of lawlessness.'" ❖ The LORD knows the way of the righteous, but the way of the wicked will perish.

"Behold, I have engraved you on the palms of my hands; your walls are continually before me." ❖ Set me as a seal upon your heart, as a seal upon your arm. ❖ The LORD is good, a stronghold in the day of trouble; he knows those who take refuge in him.

"In my Father's house are many rooms. If it were not so, would I have told you that I go to prepare a place for you? And if I go and prepare a place for you, I will come again and will take you to myself, that where I am you may be also."

John 10:3. | 2 Tim. 2:19. | Matt. 7:22, 23. | Ps. 1:6. | Isa. 49:16. Song of Songs 8:6. | Nah. 1:7. | John 14:2, 3.

JUL.
19

"He who is mighty has done great things for me, and holy is his name."

"Who is like you, O LORD, among the gods? Who is like you, majestic in holiness, awesome in glorious deeds, doing wonders?" ❖ There is none like you among the gods, O Lord, nor are there any works like yours. ❖ "Who will not fear, O Lord, and glorify your name? For you alone are holy." ❖ "Hallowed be your name."

"Blessed be the Lord God of Israel, for he has visited and redeemed his people."

Who is this who comes from Edom, in crimsoned garments from Bozrah, he who is splendid in his apparel, marching in the greatness of his strength? "It is I, speaking in righteousness, mighty to save." ❖ "I have granted help to one who is mighty; I have exalted one chosen from the people."

Now to him who is able to do far more abundantly than all that we ask or think, according to the power at work within us, to him be glory.

Luke 1:49. | Exod. 15:11. | Ps. 86:8.
Rev. 15:4. | Matt. 6:9. | Luke 1:68. | Isa. 63:1.
Ps. 89:19. | Eph. 3:20, 21.

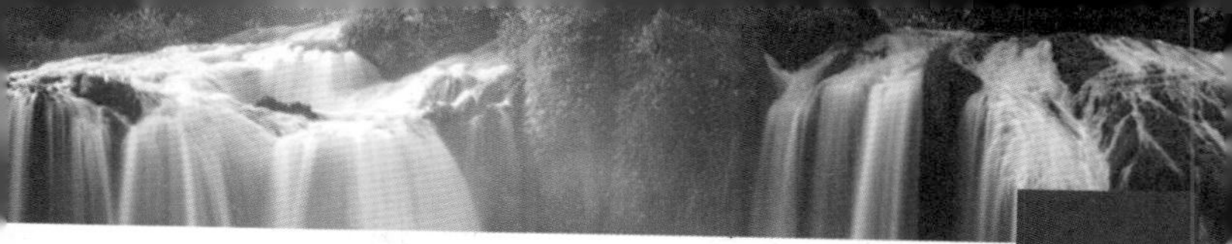

*"They are not of the world, just as
I am not of the world."*

He was despised and rejected by men; a man of sorrows, and acquainted with grief. ❖ "In the world you will have tribulation. But take heart; I have overcome the world."

It was indeed fitting that we should have such a high priest, holy, innocent, unstained, separated from sinners. ❖ That you may be blameless and innocent, children of God without blemish in the midst of a crooked and twisted generation.

"Jesus of Nazareth … went about doing good and healing all who were oppressed by the devil, for God was with him." ❖ So then, as we have opportunity, let us do good to everyone, and especially to those who are of the household of faith.

The true light, which enlightens everyone, was coming into the world. ❖ "You are the light of the world. A city set on a hill cannot be hidden. Let your light shine before others, so that they may see your good works and give glory to your Father who is in heaven."

John 17:16. | Isa. 53:3. | John 16:33. | Heb. 7:26. | Phil. 2:15.
Acts 10:38. | Gal. 6:10. | John 1:9. | Matt. 5:14, 16.

JUL.
21

What is the value of circumcision?

Much in every way. ❖ "Circumcise yourselves to the LORD; remove the foreskin of your hearts." ❖ "If then their uncircumcised heart is humbled and they make amends for their iniquity, then I will remember my covenant with Jacob, and I will remember my covenant with Isaac and my covenant with Abraham."

Christ became a servant to the circumcised to show God's truthfulness, in order to confirm the promises given to the patriarchs. ❖ In him also you were circumcised with a circumcision made without hands, by putting off the body of the flesh, by the circumcision of Christ. ❖ You, who were dead in your trespasses and the uncircumcision of your flesh, God made alive together with him, having forgiven us all our trespasses.

Put off your old self, which belongs to your former manner of life and is corrupt through deceitful desires, and … be renewed in the spirit of your minds, and … put on the new self, created after the likeness of God in true righteousness and holiness.

Rom. 3:1. | Rom. 3:2. | Jer. 4:4. | Lev. 26:41, 42.
Rom. 15:8. | Col. 2:11. | Col. 2:13. | Eph. 4:22-24.

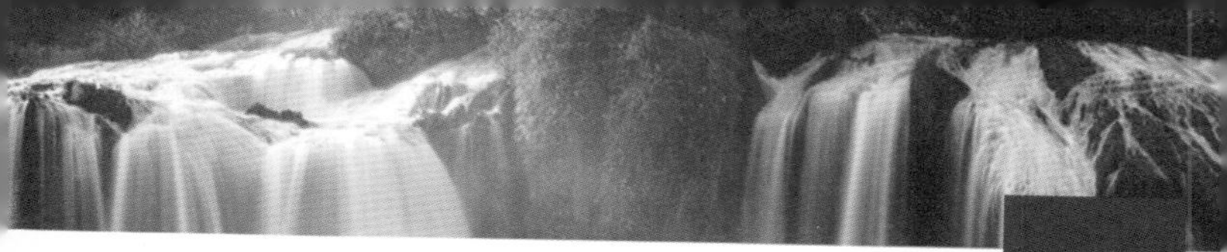

JUL.
22

The death he died he died to sin, once for all,
but the life he lives he lives to God.

He … was numbered with the transgressors. ❖ Christ, having been offered once to bear the sins of many. ❖ He himself bore our sins in his body on the tree, that we might die to sin and live to righteousness. By his wounds you have been healed. ❖ By a single offering he has perfected for all time those who are being sanctified. ❖ He holds his priesthood permanently, because he continues forever. Consequently, he is able to save to the uttermost those who draw near to God through him, since he always lives to make intercession for them. ❖ While we were still sinners, Christ died for us. Since, therefore, we have now been justified by his blood, much more shall we be saved by him from the wrath of God.

Since therefore Christ suffered in the flesh, arm yourselves with the same way of thinking, for whoever has suffered in the flesh has ceased from sin, so as to live for the rest of the time in the flesh no longer for human passions but for the will of God.

Rom. 6:10. | Isa. 53:12. | Heb. 9:28. | 1 Pet. 2:24.
Heb. 10:14. | Heb. 7:24, 25. | Rom. 5:8, 9. | 1 Pet. 4:1, 2.

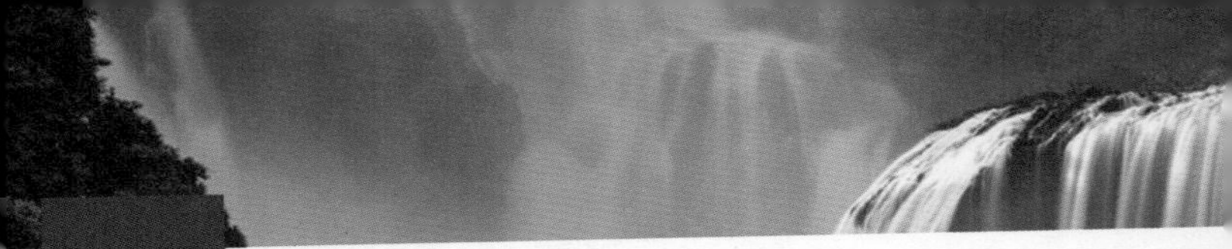

JUL.
23

Then comes the end.

"But concerning that day or that hour, no one knows, not even the angels in heaven, nor the Son, but only the Father. Be on guard, keep awake. For you do not know when the time will come. … And what I say to you I say to all: Stay awake." ❖ The Lord is not slow to fulfill his promise as some count slowness, but is patient toward you, not wishing that any should perish, but that all should reach repentance. ❖ The coming of the Lord is at hand. … Behold, the Judge is standing at the door. ❖ "Surely I am coming soon."

Since all these things are thus to be dissolved, what sort of people ought you to be in lives of holiness and godliness.

The end of all things is at hand; therefore be self-controlled and sober-minded for the sake of your prayers. ❖ "Stay dressed for action and keep your lamps burning, and be like men who are waiting for their master to come home from the wedding feast, so that they may open the door to him at once when he comes and knocks."

1 Cor. 15:24. | Mark 13:32, 33, 37. | 2 Pet. 3:9. | James 5:8, 9.
Rev. 22:20. | 2 Pet. 3:11. | 1 Pet. 4:7. | Luke 12:35, 36.

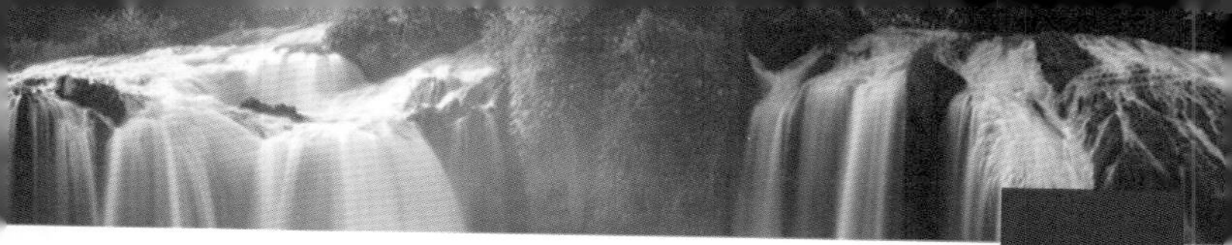

JUL.
24

Patient in tribulation.

"It is the LORD. Let him do what seems good to him." ❖ "Though I am in the right, I cannot answer him; I must appeal for mercy to my accuser." ❖ "The LORD gave, and the LORD has taken away; blessed be the name of the LORD." ❖ "Shall we receive good from God, and shall we not receive evil?"

Jesus wept. ❖ A man of sorrows, and acquainted with grief. … Surely he has borne our griefs and carried our sorrows.

"The Lord disciplines the one he loves, and chastises every son whom he receives." … For the moment all discipline seems painful rather than pleasant, but later it yields the peaceful fruit of righteousness to those who have been trained by it. ❖ May you be strengthened with all power, according to his glorious might, for all endurance and patience with joy. ❖ "In the world you will have tribulation. But take heart; I have overcome the world."

Rom. 12:12. | 1 Sam. 3:18. | Job 9:15. | Job 1:21.
Job 2:10. | John 11:35. | Isa. 53:3, 4.
Heb. 12:6, 11. | Col. 1:11. | John 16:33.

JUL.
25

We know that we have passed out of death into life.

"Whoever hears my word and believes him who sent me has eternal life. He does not come into judgment, but has passed from death to life." ❖ Whoever has the Son has life; whoever does not have the Son of God does not have life.

It is God who establishes us with you in Christ, and has anointed us, and who has also put his seal on us and given us his Spirit in our hearts as a guarantee. ❖ By this we shall know that we are of the truth and reassure our heart before him. … Beloved, if our heart does not condemn us, we have confidence before God. ❖ We know that we are from God, and the whole world lies in the power of the evil one.

You were dead in the trespasses and sins. … [God] made us alive together with Christ. ❖ He has delivered us from the domain of darkness and transferred us to the kingdom of his beloved Son.

1 John 3:14. | John 5:24. | 1 John 5:12. | 2 Cor. 1:21, 22. 1 John 3:19, 21. | 1 John 5:19. | Eph. 2:1, 5. | Col. 1:13.

JUL.
26

By faith Abraham obeyed when he was called to go out to a place that he was to receive as an inheritance.

He chose our heritage for us. ❖ "He encircled him, he cared for him, he kept him as the apple of his eye. Like an eagle that stirs up its nest, that flutters over its young, spreading out its wings, catching them, bearing them on its pinions, the LORD alone guided him, no foreign god was with him."

"I am the LORD your God, who teaches you to profit, who leads you in the way you should go." ❖ "Who is a teacher like him?"

We walk by faith, not by sight. ❖ Here we have no lasting city, but we seek the city that is to come. ❖ Beloved, I urge you as sojourners and exiles to abstain from the passions of the flesh, which wage war against your soul. ❖ "Arise and go, for this is no place to rest, because of uncleanness that destroys with a grievous destruction."

Heb. 11:8. | Ps. 47:4. | Deut. 32:10-12. | Isa. 48:17. Job 36:22. | 2 Cor. 5:7. | Heb. 13:14. | 1 Pet. 2:11. | Mic. 2:10.

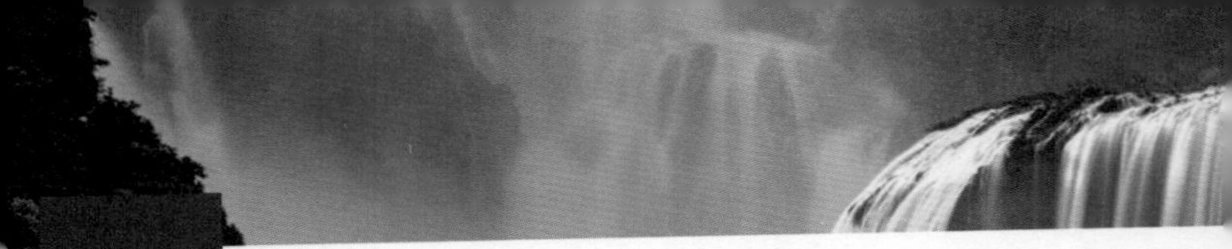

JUL.
27

Christ, who is the image of God.

"The glory of the LORD shall be revealed, and all flesh shall see it together." ❖ No one has ever seen God; the only God, who is at the Father's side, he has made him known. … And the Word became flesh and dwelt among us, and we have seen his glory, glory as of the only Son from the Father, full of grace and truth. ❖ "Whoever has seen me has seen the Father." ❖ He is the radiance of the glory of God and the exact imprint of his nature. ❖ He was manifested in the flesh.

In whom we have redemption, the forgiveness of sins. He is the image of the invisible God, the firstborn of all creation. ❖ Those whom he foreknew he also predestined to be conformed to the image of his Son, in order that he might be the firstborn among many brothers.

Just as we have borne the image of the man of dust, we shall also bear the image of the man of heaven.

2 Cor. 4:4. | Isa. 40:5. | John 1:18, 14. | John 14:9. | Heb. 1:3.
1 Tim. 3:16. | Col. 1:14, 15. | Rom. 8:29. | 1 Cor. 15:49.

JUL.
28

Walk in love.

"A new commandment I give to you, that you love one another: just as I have loved you, you also are to love one another." ❖ Above all, keep loving one another earnestly, since love covers a multitude of sins. ❖ Love covers all offenses.

"Whenever you stand praying, forgive, if you have anything against anyone, so that your Father also who is in heaven may forgive you your trespasses." ❖ "Love your enemies, and do good, and lend, expecting nothing in return." ❖ Do not rejoice when your enemy falls, and let not your heart be glad when he stumbles. ❖ Do not repay evil for evil or reviling for reviling, but on the contrary, bless, for to this you were called, that you may obtain a blessing. ❖ If possible, so far as it depends on you, live peaceably with all. ❖ Be kind to one another, tenderhearted, forgiving one another, as God in Christ forgave you.

Little children, let us not love in word or talk but in deed and in truth.

Eph. 5:2. | John 13:34. | 1 Pet. 4:8. | Prov. 10:12.
Mark 11:25. | Luke 6:35. | Prov. 24:17.
1 Pet. 3:9. | Rom. 12:18. | Eph. 4:32. | 1 John 3:18.

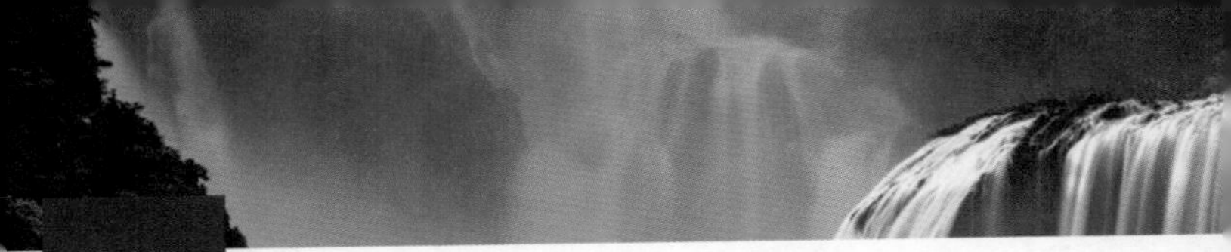

JUL.
29

Oh that you would rend the heavens and come down.

Make haste, my beloved, and be like a gazelle or a young stag on the mountains of spices. ❖ We ourselves … groan inwardly as we wait eagerly for adoption as sons, the redemption of our bodies. ❖ Bow your heavens, O LORD, and come down! Touch the mountains so that they smoke!

"This Jesus, who was taken up from you into heaven, will come in the same way as you saw him go into heaven." ❖ Christ … will appear a second time, not to deal with sin but to save those who are eagerly waiting for him. ❖ It will be said on that day, "Behold, this is our God; we have waited for him, that he might save us. This is the LORD; we have waited for him; let us be glad and rejoice in his salvation."

He who testifies to these things says, "Surely I am coming soon." Amen. Come, Lord Jesus! ❖ Our blessed hope, the appearing of the glory of our great God and Savior Jesus Christ. ❖ But our citizenship is in heaven.

Isa. 64:1. | Song of Songs 8:14. | Rom. 8:23.
Ps. 144:5. | Acts 1:11. | Heb. 9:28. | Isa. 25:9.
Rev. 22:20. | Titus 2:13. | Phil. 3:20.

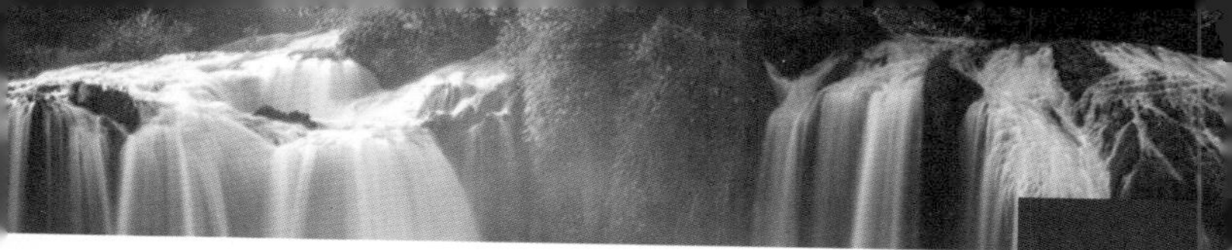

Seek the things that are above, where Christ is, seated at the right hand of God.

Get wisdom; get insight. ❖ The wisdom from above. ❖ "The deep says, 'It is not in me,' and the sea says, 'It is not with me.'" ❖ We were buried therefore with him by baptism into death, in order that, just as Christ was raised from the dead by the glory of the Father, we too might walk in newness of life. For if we have been united with him in a death like his, we shall certainly be united with him in a resurrection like his.

Let us also lay aside every weight, and sin which clings so closely, and let us run with endurance the race that is set before us. ❖ God … made us alive together with Christ … and raised us up with him and seated us with him in the heavenly places in Christ Jesus.

People who speak thus make it clear that they are seeking a homeland. ❖ Seek the LORD, all you humble of the land, who do his just commands; seek righteousness; seek humility.

Col. 3:1. | Prov. 4:5. | James 3:17. | Job 28:14. | Rom. 6:4, 5.
Heb. 12:1. | Eph. 2:4-6. | Heb. 11:14. | Zeph. 2:3.

JUL.
31

Share in suffering as a good soldier of Christ Jesus.

"I made him a witness to the peoples, a leader and commander for the peoples." ❖ It was fitting that he, for whom and by whom all things exist, in bringing many sons to glory, should make the founder of their salvation perfect through suffering. ❖ Through many tribulations we must enter the kingdom of God.

We do not wrestle against flesh and blood, but against the rulers, against the authorities, against the cosmic powers over this present darkness, against the spiritual forces of evil in the heavenly places. Therefore take up the whole armor of God. ❖ We are not waging war according to the flesh. For the weapons of our warfare are not of the flesh but have divine power to destroy strongholds.

After you have suffered a little while, the God of all grace, who has called you to his eternal glory in Christ, will himself restore, confirm, strengthen, and establish you.

2 Tim. 2:3. | Isa. 55:4. | Heb. 2:10. | Acts 14:22.
Eph. 6:12, 13. | 2 Cor. 10:3, 4. | 1 Pet. 5:10.

August

AUG.
1

The fruit of the Spirit is . . . faithfulness.

By grace you have been saved through faith. And this is not your own doing; it is the gift of God. ❖ Without faith it is impossible to please him. ❖ "Whoever believes in him is not condemned, but whoever does not believe is condemned already, because he has not believed in the name of the only Son of God." ❖ "I believe; help my unbelief!"

Whoever keeps his word, in him truly the love of God is perfected. By this we may be sure that we are in him. ❖ Faith working through love. ❖ Faith apart from works is useless. ❖ We walk by faith, not by sight. ❖ I have been crucified with Christ. It is no longer I who live, but Christ who lives in me. And the life I now live in the flesh I live by faith in the Son of God, who loved me and gave himself for me. ❖ Though you have not seen him, you love him. Though you do not now see him, you believe in him and rejoice with joy that is inexpressible and filled with glory, obtaining the outcome of your faith, the salvation of your souls.

Gal. 5:22. | Eph. 2:8. | Heb. 11:6. | John 3:18.
Mark 9:24. | 1 John 2:5. | Gal. 5:6. | James 2:20.
2 Cor. 5:7. | Gal. 2:20. | 1 Pet. 1:8, 9.

AUG.
2

The Lamb that was slain.

"Your lamb shall be without blemish … and … the whole assembly of the congregation of Israel shall kill their lambs at twilight. Then they shall take some of the blood and put it on the two doorposts and the lintel of the houses in which they eat it. … And when I see the blood, I will pass over you. ❖ The sprinkled blood. ❖ Christ, our Passover lamb, has been sacrificed. ❖ "Delivered up according to the definite plan and foreknowledge of God." ❖ Because of his own purpose and grace, which he gave us in Christ Jesus before the ages began.

In him we have redemption through his blood, the forgiveness of our trespasses. ❖ Since therefore Christ suffered in the flesh, arm yourselves with the same way of thinking, for whoever has suffered in the flesh has ceased from sin, so as to live for the rest of the time in the flesh no longer for human passions but for the will of God.

Rev. 13:8. | Exod. 12:5-7, 13. | Heb. 12:24. | 1 Cor. 5:7.
Acts 2:23. | 2 Tim. 1:9. | Eph. 1:7. | 1 Pet. 4:1, 2.

AUG.
3

His mercy is for those who fear him.

Oh, how abundant is your goodness, which you have stored up for those who fear you and worked for those who take refuge in you, in the sight of the children of mankind! In the cover of your presence you hide them from the plots of men; you store them in your shelter from the strife of tongues.

If you call on him as Father who judges impartially according to each one's deeds, conduct yourselves with fear throughout the time of your exile. ❖ The LORD is near to all who call on him … in truth. He fulfills the desire of those who fear him; he also hears their cry and saves them.

"Because your heart was penitent, and you humbled yourself before the LORD, … and you have torn your clothes and wept before me, I also have heard you, declares the LORD." ❖ "But this is the one to whom I will look: he who is humble and contrite in spirit and trembles at my word." ❖ The LORD is near to the brokenhearted and saves the crushed in spirit.

Luke 1:50. | Ps. 31:19, 20. | 1 Pet. 1:17. | Ps. 145:18, 19.
2 Kings 22:19. | Isa. 66:2. | Ps. 34:18.

AUG.
4

"It is finished," and he bowed his head and gave up his spirit.

Jesus, the founder and perfecter of our faith. ❖ "I glorified you on earth, having accomplished the work that you gave me to do." ❖ We have been sanctified through the offering of the body of Jesus Christ once for all. And every priest stands daily at his service, offering repeatedly the same sacrifices, which can never take away sins. But when Christ had offered for all time a single sacrifice for sins, he sat down at the right hand of God, waiting from that time until his enemies should be made a footstool for his feet. For by a single offering he has perfected for all time those who are being sanctified. ❖ Canceling the record of debt that stood against us with its legal demands. This he set aside, nailing it to the cross.

"I lay down my life that I may take it up again. No one takes it from me, but I lay it down of my own accord. I have authority to lay it down, and I have authority to take it up again." ❖ "Greater love has no one than this, that someone lays down his life for his friends."

John 19:30. | Heb. 12:2. | John 17:4. | Heb. 10:10-14.
Col. 2:14. | John 10:17, 18. | John 15:13.

AUG.
5

Walk in newness of life.

Just as you once presented your members as slaves to impurity and to lawlessness leading to more lawlessness, so now present your members as slaves to righteousness leading to sanctification. ❖ I appeal to you therefore, brothers, by the mercies of God, to present your bodies as a living sacrifice, holy and acceptable to God, which is your spiritual worship. Do not be conformed to this world, but be transformed by the renewal of your mind.

If anyone is in Christ, he is a new creation. The old has passed away; behold, the new has come. ❖ Neither circumcision counts for anything, nor uncircumcision, but a new creation. And as for all who walk by this rule, peace and mercy be upon them. ❖ Now this I say and testify in the Lord, that you must no longer walk as the Gentiles do, in the futility of their minds. ... But that is not the way you learned Christ! – assuming that you have heard about him and were taught in him, as the truth is in Jesus. ... Put on the new self, created after the likeness of God in true righteousness and holiness.

Rom. 6:4. | Rom. 6:19. | Rom. 12:1, 2. | 2 Cor. 5:17.
Gal. 6:15, 16. | Eph. 4:17, 20, 21, 24.

AUG.
6

The LORD reproves him whom he loves.

"See now that I, even I, am he, and there is no god beside me; I kill and I make alive; I wound and I heal; and there is none that can deliver out of my hand." ❖ "I know the plans I have for you, declares the LORD, plans for wholeness and not for evil, to give you a future and a hope." ❖ "My thoughts are not your thoughts, neither are your ways my ways, declares the LORD."

"Therefore, behold, I will allure her, and bring her into the wilderness, and speak tenderly to her." ❖ As a man disciplines his son, the LORD your God disciplines you. ❖ For the moment all discipline seems painful rather than pleasant, but later it yields the peaceful fruit of righteousness to those who have been trained by it. ❖ Humble yourselves, therefore, under the mighty hand of God so that at the proper time he may exalt you.

I know, O LORD, that your rules are righteous, and that in faithfulness you have afflicted me.

Prov. 3:12. | Deut. 32:39. | Jer. 29:11. | Isa. 55:8. | Hosea 2:14. Deut. 8:5. | Heb. 12:11. | 1 Pet. 5:6. | Ps. 119:75.

AUG.
7

"The Helper, the Holy Spirit,
whom the Father will send in my name."

"If you knew the gift of God, and who it is that is saying to you, 'Give me a drink,' you would have asked him, and he would have given you living water." ❖ "If you then, who are evil, know how to give good gifts to your children, how much more will the heavenly Father give the Holy Spirit to those who ask him!" ❖ "Truly, truly, I say to you, whatever you ask of the Father in my name, he will give it to you. Until now you have asked nothing in my name. Ask, and you will receive, that your joy may be full." ❖ You do not have, because you do not ask.

"When the Spirit of truth comes, he will guide you into all the truth, for he will not speak on his own authority, but whatever he hears he will speak, and he will declare to you the things that are to come. He will glorify me, for he will take what is mine and declare it to you."

They rebelled and grieved his Holy Spirit; therefore he turned to be their enemy, and himself fought against them.

John 14:26. | John 4:10. | Luke 11:13. | John 16:23, 24.
James 4:2. | John 16:13, 14. | Isa. 63:10.

AUG. 8

The path of the righteous is like the light of dawn, which shines brighter and brighter until full day.

Not that I have already obtained this or am already perfect, but I press on to make it my own, because Christ Jesus has made me his own. ❖ "Let us know; let us press on to know the LORD."

"Then the righteous will shine like the sun in the kingdom of their Father." ❖ We all, with unveiled face, beholding the glory of the Lord, are being transformed into the same image from one degree of glory to another. For this comes from the Lord who is the Spirit. ❖ When the perfect comes, the partial will pass away. … For now we see in a mirror dimly, but then face to face. Now I know in part; then I shall know fully, even as I have been fully known. ❖ Beloved, we are God's children now, and what we will be has not yet appeared; but we know that when he appears we shall be like him, because we shall see him as he is. And everyone who thus hopes in him purifies himself as he is pure.

Prov. 4:18. | Phil. 3:12. | Hosea 6:3. | Matt. 13:43.
2 Cor. 3:18. | 1 Cor. 13:10, 12. | 1 John 3:2, 3.

AUG. 9

You are altogether beautiful,
my love; there is no flaw in you.

The whole head is sick, and the whole heart faint. From the sole of the foot even to the head, there is no soundness in it, but bruises and sores and raw wounds; they are not pressed out or bound up or softened with oil. ❖ We have all become like one who is unclean, and all our righteous deeds are like a polluted garment. ❖ I know that nothing good dwells in me, that is, in my flesh. ❖ You were washed, you were sanctified, you were justified in the name of the Lord Jesus Christ and by the Spirit of our God. ❖ All glorious is the princess in her chamber. ❖ "Perfect through the splendor that I had bestowed on you, declares the Lord GOD." ❖ Let the favor of the Lord our God be upon us.

"They have washed their robes and made them white in the blood of the Lamb." ❖ So that he might present the church to himself in splendor, without spot or wrinkle or any such thing, that she might be holy and without blemish. ❖ You have been filled in him.

Song of Songs 4:7. | Isa. 1:5, 6. | Isa. 64:6. | Rom. 7:18.
1 Cor. 6:11. | Ps. 45:13. | Ezek. 16:14. | Ps. 90:17.
Rev. 7:14. | Eph. 5:27. | Col. 2:10.

AUG.
10

"I do not ask that you take them out of the world, but that you keep them from the evil one."

Blameless and innocent, children of God without blemish in the midst of a crooked and twisted generation, among whom you shine as lights in the world. ❖ "You are the salt of the earth, ... the light of the world. ... Let your light shine before others, so that they may see your good works and give glory to your Father who is in heaven."

"It was I who kept you from sinning against me."

But the Lord is faithful. He will establish you and guard you against the evil one. ❖ I did not do so, because of the fear of God. ❖ Who gave himself for our sins to deliver us from the present evil age, according to the will of our God and Father. ❖ Now to him who is able to keep you from stumbling and to present you blameless before the presence of his glory with great joy, to the only God, our Savior, through Jesus Christ our Lord, be glory, majesty, dominion, and authority, before all time and now and forever. Amen.

John 17:15. | Phil. 2:15. | Matt. 5:13, 14, 16. | Gen. 20:6.
2 Thess. 3:3. | Neh. 5:15. | Gal. 1:4. | Jude 24, 25.

AUG.
11

That through death he might destroy the one who has the power of death.

Our Savior Christ Jesus ... abolished death and brought life and immortality to light through the gospel. ❖ He will swallow up death forever; and the Lord GOD will wipe away tears from all faces, and the reproach of his people he will take away from all the earth, for the LORD has spoken. ❖ When the perishable puts on the imperishable, and the mortal puts on immortality, then shall come to pass the saying that is written: "Death is swallowed up in victory. O death, where is your victory? O death, where is your sting?" The sting of death is sin, and the power of sin is the law. But thanks be to God, who gives us the victory through our Lord Jesus Christ.

God gave us a spirit not of fear but of power and love and self-control. ❖ Even though I walk through the valley of the shadow of death, I will fear no evil, for you are with me; your rod and your staff, they comfort me.

Heb. 2:14. | 2 Tim. 1:10. | Isa. 25:8.
1 Cor. 15:54-57. | 2 Tim. 1:7. | Ps. 23:4.

AUG. 12

For the Lord will not cast off forever, but, though he cause grief, he will have compassion.

"Fear not, ... declares the LORD, for I am with you. ... Of you I will not make a full end. I will discipline you in just measure." ❖ "For a brief moment I deserted you, but with great compassion I will gather you. In overflowing anger for a moment I hid my face from you, but with everlasting love I will have compassion on you," says the LORD, your Redeemer. ... "For the mountains may depart and the hills be removed, but my steadfast love shall not depart from you, and my covenant of peace shall not be removed," says the LORD, who has compassion on you. "O afflicted one, storm-tossed and not comforted, behold, I will set your stones in antimony, and lay your foundations with sapphires."

I will bear the indignation of the LORD because I have sinned against him, until he pleads my cause and executes judgment for me. He will bring me out to the light; I shall look upon his vindication.

Lam. 3:31, 32. | Jer. 46:28. | Isa. 54:7, 8, 10, 11. | Mic. 7:9.

AUG.
13

He has prepared for them a city.

"And if I go and prepare a place for you, I will come again and will take you to myself, that where I am you may be also." ❖ An inheritance that is imperishable, undefiled, and unfading, kept in heaven for you. ❖ Here we have no lasting city, but we seek the city that is to come.

"This Jesus, who was taken up from you into heaven, will come in the same way as you saw him go into heaven." ❖ Be patient, therefore, brothers, until the coming of the Lord. See how the farmer waits for the precious fruit of the earth, being patient about it, until it receives the early and the late rains. You also, be patient. Establish your hearts, for the coming of the Lord is at hand. ❖ "Yet a little while, and the coming one will come and will not delay."

We who are alive, who are left, will be caught up together with them in the clouds to meet the Lord in the air, and so we will always be with the Lord. Therefore encourage one another with these words.

Heb. 11:16. | John 14:3. | 1 Pet. 1:4. | Heb. 13:14. | Acts 1:11. James 5:7, 8. | Heb. 10:37. | 1 Thess. 4:17, 18.

AUG.
14

"The joy of the Lord is your strength."

Sing for joy, O heavens, and exult, O earth; break forth, O mountains, into singing! for the Lord has comforted his people and will have compassion on his afflicted. ❖ "Behold, God is my salvation; I will trust, and will not be afraid; for the Lord God is my strength and my song, and he has become my salvation." ❖ The Lord is my strength and my shield; in him my heart trusts, and I am helped; my heart exults, and with my song I give thanks to him. ❖ My soul shall exult in my God, for he has clothed me with the garments of salvation; he has covered me with the robe of righteousness, as a bridegroom decks himself like a priest with a beautiful headdress, and as a bride adorns herself with her jewels.

In Christ Jesus, then, I have reason to be proud of my work for God. ❖ We also rejoice in God through our Lord Jesus Christ, through whom we have now received reconciliation. ❖ I will take joy in the God of my salvation.

Neh. 8:10. | Isa. 49:13. | Isa. 12:2. | Ps. 28:7. | Isa. 61:10.
Rom. 15:17. | Rom. 5:11. | Hab. 3:18.

AUG.
15

Now may the God of peace … equip you with everything good that you may do his will.

Finally, brothers, rejoice. Aim for restoration, comfort one another, agree with one another, live in peace; and the God of love and peace will be with you.

By grace you have been saved through faith. And this is not your own doing; it is the gift of God, not a result of works, so that no one may boast. ❖ Every good gift and every perfect gift is from above, coming down from the Father of lights with whom there is no variation or shadow due to change.

Work out your own salvation with fear and trembling, for it is God who works in you, both to will and to work for his good pleasure. ❖ Be transformed by the renewal of your mind, that by testing you may discern what is the will of God, what is good and acceptable and perfect. ❖ Filled with the fruit of righteousness that comes through Jesus Christ, to the glory and praise of God.

Not that we are sufficient in ourselves to claim anything as coming from us, but our sufficiency is from God.

Heb. 13:20, 21. | 2 Cor. 13:11. | Eph. 2:8, 9. | James 1:17.
Phil. 2:12, 13. | Rom. 12:2. | Phil. 1:11. | 2 Cor. 3:5.

AUG. 16

"The house that is to be built for the Lord must be exceedingly magnificent."

You yourselves like living stones are being built up as a spiritual house. ❖ Do you not know that you are God's temple and that God's Spirit dwells in you? If anyone destroys God's temple, God will destroy him. For God's temple is holy, and you are that temple. ❖ Do you not know that your body is a temple of the Holy Spirit within you, whom you have from God? You are not your own, for you were bought with a price. So glorify God in your body. ❖ What agreement has the temple of God with idols? For we are the temple of the living God; as God said, "I will make my dwelling among them and walk among them, and I will be their God, and they shall be my people." ❖ You are … built on the foundation of the apostles and prophets, Christ Jesus Himself being the cornerstone, in whom the whole structure, being joined together, grows into a holy temple in the Lord. In him you also are being built together into a dwelling place for God by the Spirit.

1 Chron. 22:5. | 1 Pet. 2:5. | 1 Cor. 3:16, 17.
1 Cor. 6:19, 20. | 2 Cor. 6:16. | Eph. 2:19-22.

AUG.
17

Pray for one another, that you may be healed.

Abraham answered and said, "Behold, I have undertaken to speak to the Lord, I who am but dust and ashes. Suppose five of the fifty righteous are lacking. Will you destroy the whole city for lack of five?" And he said, "I will not destroy it if I find forty-five there."

"Father, forgive them, for they know not what they do." ❖ "Pray for those who persecute you."

"I am praying for them. I am not praying for the world but for those whom you have given me, for they are yours. ... I do not ask for these only, but also for those who will believe in me through their word." ❖ Bear one another's burdens, and so fulfill the law of Christ.

The prayer of a righteous person has great power as it is working. Elijah was a man with a nature like ours, and he prayed fervently that it might not rain, and for three years and six months it did not rain on the earth.

James 5:16. | Gen. 18:27, 28. | Luke 23:34. | Matt. 5:44.
John 17:9, 20. | Gal. 6:2. | James 5:16, 17.

AUG.
18

*"What god is there in heaven or on earth
who can do such works and mighty acts as yours?"*

Who in the skies can be compared to the LORD? Who among the heavenly beings is like the LORD? ... O LORD God of hosts, who is mighty as you are, O LORD, with your faithfulness all around you? ❖ There is none like you among the gods, O Lord, nor are there any works like yours. ❖ "Because of your promise, and according to your own heart, you have brought about all this greatness, to make your servant know it. Therefore you are great, O LORD God. For there is none like you, and there is no God besides you, according to all that we have heard with our ears."

"What no eye has seen, nor ear heard, nor the heart of man imagined, what God has prepared for those who love him" – these things God has revealed to us through the Spirit. ❖ "The secret things belong to the LORD our God, but the things that are revealed belong to us and to our children."

Deut. 3:24. | Ps. 89:6, 8. | Ps. 86:8. | 2 Sam. 7:21, 22.
1 Cor. 2:9, 10. | Deut. 29:29.

AUG.
19

As he who called you is holy,
you also be holy in all your conduct.

You know how … we exhorted each one of you … and charged you to walk in a manner worthy of God, who calls you into his own kingdom and glory. ❖ That you may proclaim the excellencies of him who called you out of darkness into his marvelous light.

At one time you were darkness, but now you are light in the Lord. Walk as children of light (for the fruit of light is found in all that is good and right and true), and try to discern what is pleasing to the Lord. Take no part in the unfruitful works of darkness, but instead expose them. ❖ Filled with the fruit of righteousness that comes through Jesus Christ, to the glory and praise of God.

"Let your light shine before others, so that they may see your good works and give glory to your Father who is in heaven." ❖ Whether you eat or drink, or whatever you do, do all to the glory of God.

1 Pet. 1:15. | 1 Thess. 2:11, 12. | 1 Pet. 2:9. | Eph. 5:8-11.
Phil. 1:11. | Matt. 5:16. | 1 Cor. 10:31.

AUG.
20

"God is not man, that he should lie, or a son of man, that he should change his mind."

The Father of lights with whom there is no variation or shadow due to change. ❖ Jesus Christ is the same yesterday and today and forever.

His faithfulness is a shield and buckler.

When God desired to show more convincingly to the heirs of the promise the unchangeable character of his purpose, he guaranteed it with an oath, so that by two unchangeable things, in which it is impossible for God to lie, we who have fled for refuge might have strong encouragement to hold fast to the hope set before us.

"The faithful God who keeps covenant and steadfast love with those who love him and keep his commandments, to a thousand generations." ❖ All the paths of the LORD are steadfast love and faithfulness, for those who keep his covenant and his testimonies. ❖ Blessed is he whose help is the God of Jacob, whose hope is in the LORD his God ... who keeps faith forever.

Num. 23:19. | James 1:17. | Heb. 13:8. | Ps. 91:4.
Heb. 6:17, 18. | Deut. 7:9. | Ps. 25:10. | Ps. 146:5, 6.

AUG.
21

The LORD is my portion.

All things are yours, … and you are Christ's, and Christ is God's. ❖ Our … Savior Jesus Christ … gave himself for us. ❖ [God] put all things under his feet and gave him as head over all things to the church. ❖ Christ loved the church and gave himself up for her, … so that he might present the church to himself in splendor, without spot or wrinkle or any such thing, that she might be holy and without blemish.

My soul makes its boast in the LORD. ❖ I will greatly rejoice in the LORD; my soul shall exult in my God, for he has clothed me with the garments of salvation; he has covered me with the robe of righteousness.

Whom have I in heaven but you? And there is nothing on earth that I desire besides you. My flesh and my heart may fail, but God is the strength of my heart and my portion forever. ❖ I say to the LORD, "You are my Lord; I have no good apart from you." … The LORD is my chosen portion and my cup; you hold my lot. The lines have fallen for me in pleasant places; indeed, I have a beautiful inheritance.

Ps. 119:57. | 1 Cor. 3:21, 23. | Titus 2:13, 14.
Eph. 1:22. | Eph. 5:25, 27. | Ps. 34:2. | Isa. 61:10.
Ps. 73:25, 26. | Ps. 16:2, 5, 6.

AUG.
22

None of us lives to himself, and
none of us dies to himself.

If we live, we live to the Lord, and if we die, we die to the Lord. So then, whether we live or whether we die, we are the Lord's. ❖ Let no one seek his own good, but the good of his neighbor. ❖ You were bought with a price. So glorify God in your body.

Christ will be honored in my body, whether by life or by death. For to me to live is Christ, and to die is gain. If I am to live in the flesh, that means fruitful labor for me. Yet which I shall choose I cannot tell. I am hard pressed between the two. My desire is to depart and be with Christ, for that is far better.

Through the law I died to the law, so that I might live to God. I have been crucified with Christ. It is no longer I who live, but Christ who lives in me. And the life I now live in the flesh I live by faith in the Son of God, who loved me and gave himself for me.

Rom. 14:7. | Rom. 14:8. | 1 Cor. 10:24.
1 Cor. 6:20. | Phil. 1:20-23. | Gal. 2:19, 20.

AUG.
23

I have loved you with an everlasting love; therefore I have continued my faithfulness to you.

But we ought always to give thanks to God for you, brothers beloved by the Lord, because God chose you as the firstfruits to be saved, through sanctification by the Spirit and belief in the truth. To this he called you through our gospel, so that you may obtain the glory of our Lord Jesus Christ. ❖ [God] saved us and called us to a holy calling, not because of our works but because of his own purpose and grace, which he gave us in Christ Jesus before the ages began. ❖ Your eyes saw my unformed substance; in your book were written, every one of them, the days that were formed for me, when as yet there were none of them.

"For God so loved the world, that he gave his only Son, that whoever believes in him should not perish but have eternal life."

In this is love, not that we have loved God but that he loved us and sent his Son to be the propitiation for our sins.

Jer. 31:3. | 2 Thess. 2:13, 14. | 2 Tim. 1:9.
Ps. 139:16. | John 3:16. | 1 John 4:10.

AUG. 24

"I know their sufferings."

A man of sorrows, and acquainted with grief. ❖ We do not have a high priest who is unable to sympathize with our weaknesses.

"He took our illnesses and bore our diseases." ❖ Jesus, wearied as he was from his journey, was sitting beside the well.

When Jesus saw her weeping, and the Jews who had come with her also weeping, he was deeply moved in his spirit and greatly troubled. … Jesus wept. ❖ For because he himself has suffered when tempted, he is able to help those who are being tempted.

He looked down from his holy height; from heaven the Lord looked at the earth, to hear the groans of the prisoners, to set free those who were doomed to die. ❖ "He knows the way that I take; when he has tried me, I shall come out as gold." ❖ When my spirit faints within me, you know my way! ❖ He who touches you touches the apple of his eye. ❖ In all their affliction he was afflicted, and the angel of his presence saved them.

Exod. 3:7. | Isa. 53:3. | Heb. 4:15. | Matt. 8:17. | John 4:6. John 11:33, 35. | Heb. 2:18. | Ps. 102:19, 20. | Job 23:10. Ps. 142:3. | Zech. 2:8. | Isa. 63:9.

AUG.
25

"Look to the rock from which you were hewn, and to the quarry from which you were dug."

Behold, I was brought forth in iniquity. ❖ "No eye pitied you, ... but you were cast out on the open field, for you were abhorred, on the day that you were born. And when I passed by you and saw you wallowing in your blood, I said to you, ... 'Live!'"

He drew me up from the pit of destruction, out of the miry bog, and set my feet upon a rock, making my steps secure. He put a new song in my mouth, a song of praise to our God.

While we were still weak, at the right time Christ died for the ungodly. For one will scarcely die for a righteous person – though perhaps for a good person one would dare even to die – but God shows his love for us in that while we were still sinners, Christ died for us. ❖ But God, being rich in mercy, because of the great love with which he loved us, even when we were dead in our trespasses, made us alive together with Christ.

Isa. 51:1. | Ps. 51:5. | Ezek. 16:5, 6. | Ps. 40:2, 3.
Rom. 5:6-8. | Eph. 2:4, 5.

AUG.
26

"You shall make a plate of pure gold and engrave on it, like the engraving of a signet, 'Holy to the Lord.'"

The holiness without which no one will see the Lord. ❖ "God is spirit, and those who worship him must worship in spirit and truth." ❖ We have all become like one who is unclean, and all our righteous deeds are like a polluted garment. ❖ "Among those who are near me I will be sanctified, and before all the people I will be glorified."

"This is the law of the temple: the whole territory on the top of the mountain all around shall be most holy." ❖ Holiness befits your house, O Lord, forevermore.

"For their sake I consecrate myself, that they also may be sanctified in truth." ❖ Since then we have a great high priest who has passed through the heavens, Jesus, the Son of God, let us … with confidence draw near to the throne of grace, that we may receive mercy and find grace to help in time of need.

Exod. 28:36. | Heb. 12:14. | John 4:24. | Isa. 64:6. | Lev. 10:3. Ezek. 43:12. | Ps. 93:5. | John 17:19. | Heb. 4:14, 16.

AUG.
27

Your word is a lamp to my feet
and a light to my path.

By the word of your lips I have avoided the ways of the violent. My steps have held fast to your paths; my feet have not slipped. ❖ When you walk, they will lead you; when you lie down, they will watch over you; and when you awake, they will talk with you. For the commandment is a lamp and the teaching a light. ❖ Your ears shall hear a word behind you, saying, "This is the way, walk in it," when you turn to the right or when you turn to the left.

"I am the light of the world. Whoever follows me will not walk in darkness, but will have the light of life." ❖ We have something more sure, the prophetic word, to which you will do well to pay attention as to a lamp shining in a dark place. ❖ Now we see in a mirror dimly, but then face to face. Now I know in part; then I shall know fully, even as I have been fully known. ❖ They will need no light of lamp or sun, for the Lord God will be their light, and they will reign forever and ever.

Ps. 119:105. | Ps. 17:4, 5. | Prov. 6:22, 23. | Isa. 30:21.
John 8:12. | 2 Pet. 1:19. | 1 Cor. 13:12. | Rev. 22:5.

AUG.
28

"The accuser of our brothers has been thrown down, who accuses them day and night before our God."

They have conquered him by the blood of the Lamb and by the word of their testimony. ❖ Who shall bring any charge against God's elect? It is God who justifies. Who is to condemn? Christ Jesus is the one who died – more than that, who was raised – who is at the right hand of God, who indeed is interceding for us.

He disarmed the rulers and authorities and put them to open shame. ❖ That through death he might destroy the one who has the power of death, that is, the devil, and deliver all those who through fear of death were subject to lifelong slavery. ❖ In all these things we are more than conquerors through him who loved us. ❖ Put on the whole armor of God, that you may be able to stand against the schemes of the devil … And take … the sword of the Spirit, which is the word of God. ❖ Thanks be to God, who gives us the victory through our Lord Jesus Christ.

Rev. 12:10. | Rev. 12:11. | Rom. 8:33, 34. | Col. 2:15.
Heb. 2:14, 15. | Rom. 8:37. | Eph. 6:11, 17. | 1 Cor. 15:57.

AUG.
29

Blessed is he who trusts in the Lord.

No distrust made [Abraham] waver concerning the promise of God, but he grew strong in his faith as he gave glory to God, fully convinced that God was able to do what he had promised. ❖ The men of Judah prevailed, because they relied on the Lord, the God of their fathers.

God is our refuge and strength, a very present help in trouble. Therefore we will not fear though the earth gives way, though the mountains be moved into the heart of the sea. ❖ It is better to take refuge in the Lord than to trust in man. It is better to take refuge in the Lord than to trust in princes. ❖ The steps of a man are established by the Lord, when he delights in his way; though he fall, he shall not be cast headlong, for the Lord upholds his hand.

Oh, taste and see that the Lord is good! Blessed is the man who takes refuge in him! Oh, fear the Lord, you his saints, for those who fear him have no lack!

Prov. 16:20. | Rom. 4:20, 21. | 2 Chron. 13:18. | Ps. 46:1, 2. Ps. 118:8, 9. | Ps. 37:23, 24. | Ps. 34:8, 9.

AUG. 30

The king … held out to Esther the golden scepter. … Then Esther approached and touched the tip of the scepter.

"If he cries to me, I will hear, for I am compassionate."

So we have come to know and to believe the love that God has for us. God is love, and whoever abides in love abides in God, and God abides in him. By this is love perfected with us, so that we may have confidence for the day of judgment, because as he is so also are we in this world. There is no fear in love, but perfect love casts out fear. For fear has to do with punishment, and whoever fears has not been perfected in love. We love because he first loved us. ❖ Let us draw near with a true heart in full assurance of faith, with our hearts sprinkled clean from an evil conscience and our bodies washed with pure water. ❖ For through him we both have access in one Spirit to the Father. ❖ We have boldness and access with confidence through our faith in him. ❖ Let us then with confidence draw near to the throne of grace, that we may receive mercy and find grace to help in time of need.

Esther 5:2. | Exod. 22:27. | 1 John 4:16-19. | Heb. 10:22. Eph. 2:18. | Eph. 3:12. | Heb. 4:16.

AUG. 31

The free gift following many trespasses brought justification.

"Though your sins are like scarlet, they shall be as white as snow; though they are red like crimson, they shall become like wool." ❖ "I, I am he who blots out your transgressions for my own sake, and I will not remember your sins. Put me in remembrance; let us argue together; set forth your case, that you may be proved right." ❖ I have blotted out your transgressions like a cloud and your sins like mist; return to me, for I have redeemed you.

"For God so loved the world, that he gave his only Son, that whoever believes in him should not perish but have eternal life." ❖ But the free gift is not like the trespass. For if many died through one man's trespass, much more have the grace of God and the free gift by the grace of that one man Jesus Christ abounded for many. ❖ And such were some of you. But you were washed, you were sanctified, you were justified in the name of the Lord Jesus Christ and by the Spirit of our God.

Rom. 5:16. | Isa. 1:18. | Isa. 43:25, 26. | Isa. 44:22.
John 3:16. | Rom. 5:15. | 1 Cor. 6:11.

September

SEPT. 1

The fruit of the Spirit is … gentleness.

The meek shall obtain fresh joy in the LORD, and the poor among mankind shall exult in the Holy One of Israel. ❖ "Unless you turn and become like children, you will never enter the kingdom of heaven. Whoever humbles himself like this child is the greatest in the kingdom of heaven." ❖ The imperishable beauty of a gentle and quiet spirit … in God's sight is very precious. ❖ Love does not envy or boast; it is not arrogant.

Pursue … gentleness. ❖ "Take my yoke upon you, and learn from me, for I am gentle and lowly in heart." ❖ He was oppressed, and he was afflicted, yet he opened not his mouth; like a lamb that is led to the slaughter, and like a sheep that before its shearers is silent, so he opened not his mouth. ❖ Christ also suffered for you, leaving you an example, so that you might follow in his steps. He committed no sin, neither was deceit found in his mouth. When he was reviled, he did not revile in return … but continued entrusting himself to him who judges justly.

Gal. 5:22, 23. | Isa. 29:19. | Matt. 18:3, 4. | 1 Pet. 3:4.
1 Cor. 13:4. | 1 Tim. 6:11. | Matt. 11:29.
Isa. 53:7. | 1 Pet. 2:21-23.

SEPT. 2

Wait for the L*ORD*; *be strong,*
and let your heart take courage.

Have you not known? Have you not heard? The LORD is the everlasting God, the Creator of the ends of the earth. He does not faint or grow weary. ... He gives power to the faint, and to him who has no might he increases strength. ❖ Fear not, for I am with you; be not dismayed, for I am your God; I will strengthen you, I will help you, I will uphold you with my righteous right hand. ❖ You have been a stronghold to the poor, a stronghold to the needy in his distress, a shelter from the storm and a shade from the heat; for the breath of the ruthless is like a storm against a wall.

The testing of your faith produces steadfastness. And let steadfastness have its full effect, that you may be perfect and complete, lacking in nothing. ❖ Therefore do not throw away your confidence, which has a great reward. For you have need of endurance, so that when you have done the will of God you may receive what is promised.

Ps. 27:14. | Isa. 40:28, 29. | Isa. 41:10. | Isa. 25:4.
James 1:3, 4. | Heb. 10:35, 36.

SEPT.
3

*"No leaven shall be seen
with you in all your territory."*

The fear of the LORD is hatred of evil. ❖ Abhor what is evil. ❖ Abstain from every form of evil. ❖ See to it that no one fails to obtain the grace of God; that no "root of bitterness" springs up and causes trouble, and by it many become defiled.

If I had cherished iniquity in my heart, the Lord would not have listened. ❖ Do you not know that a little leaven leavens the whole lump? Cleanse out the old leaven that you may be a new lump, as you really are unleavened. For Christ, our Passover lamb, has been sacrificed. Let us therefore celebrate the festival, not with the old leaven, the leaven of malice and evil, but with the unleavened bread of sincerity and truth. ❖ Let a person examine himself, then, and so eat of the bread and drink of the cup. ❖ "Let everyone who names the name of the Lord depart from iniquity." ❖ It was indeed fitting that we should have such a high priest, holy, innocent, unstained, separated from sinners. ❖ In him there is no sin.

Exod. 13:7. | Prov. 8:13. | Rom. 12:9. | 1 Thess. 5:22.
Heb. 12:15. | Ps. 66:18. | 1 Cor. 5:6-8. | 1 Cor. 11:28.
2 Tim. 2:19. | Heb. 7:26. | 1 John 3:5.

SEPT.
4

"Wait, my daughter."

"Be careful, be quiet, do not fear, and do not let your heart be faint." ❖ "Be still, and know that I am God." ❖ "Did I not tell you that if you believed you would see the glory of God?" ❖ The haughtiness of man shall be humbled, and the lofty pride of men shall be brought low, and the LORD alone will be exalted in that day.

Mary ... sat at the Lord's feet and listened to his teaching ... "Mary has chosen the good portion, which will not be taken away from her." ❖ "In returning and rest you shall be saved; in quietness and in trust shall be your strength." ❖ Ponder in your own hearts on your beds, and be silent.

Be still before the LORD and wait patiently for him; fret not yourself over the one who prospers in his way, over the man who carries out evil devices!

He is not afraid of bad news; his heart is firm, trusting in the LORD. His heart is steady. ❖ "Whoever believes will not be in haste."

Ruth 3:18. | Isa. 7:4. | Ps. 46:10. | John 11:40.
Isa. 2:17. | Luke 10:39, 42. | Isa. 30:15. | Ps. 4:4.
Ps. 37:7. | Ps. 112:7, 8. | Isa. 28:16.

SEPT.
5

Just as the body is one and
has many members, … so it is with Christ.

He is the head of the body, the church. ❖ Head over all things to the church, which is his body, the fullness of him who fills all in all. ❖ We are members of his body.

"A body have you prepared for me." ❖ Your eyes saw my unformed substance; in your book were written, every one of them, the days that were formed for me, when as yet there were none of them.

"Yours they were, and you gave them to me." ❖ He chose us in him before the foundation of the world. ❖ Those whom he foreknew he also predestined to be conformed to the image of his Son.

We are to grow up in every way into him who is the head, into Christ, from whom the whole body, joined and held together by every joint with which it is equipped … makes the body grow so that it builds itself up in love.

1 Cor. 12:12. | Col. 1:18. | Eph. 1:22, 23.
Eph. 5:30. | Heb. 10:5. | Ps. 139:16. | John 17:6.
Eph. 1:4. | Rom. 8:29. | Eph. 4:15, 16.

SEPT.
6

Let us lift up our hearts and hands to God in heaven.

Who is like the Lord our God, who is seated on high, who looks far down on the heavens and the earth? ❖ To you, O Lord, I lift up my soul. ❖ I stretch out my hands to you; my soul thirsts for you like a parched land. … Hide not your face from me, lest I be like those who go down to the pit. Let me hear in the morning of your steadfast love, for in you I trust. Make me know the way I should go, for to you I lift up my soul.

Because your steadfast love is better than life, my lips will praise you. So I will bless you as long as I live; in your name I will lift up my hands. ❖ Gladden the soul of your servant, for to you, O Lord, do I lift up my soul. For you, O Lord, are good and forgiving, abounding in steadfast love to all who call upon you.

"Whatever you ask in my name, this I will do."

Lam. 3:41. | Ps. 113:5, 6. | Ps. 25:1. | Ps. 143:6-8.
Ps. 63:3, 4. | Ps. 86:4, 5. | John 14:13.

SEPT.
7

Rejoice in hope.

The hope laid up for you in heaven. ❖ If in this life only we have hoped in Christ, we are of all people most to be pitied. ❖ Through many tribulations we must enter the kingdom of God. ❖ "Whoever does not bear his own cross and come after me cannot be my disciple." ❖ That no one be moved by these afflictions. For you yourselves know that we are destined for this.

Rejoice in the Lord always; again I will say, Rejoice. ❖ May the God of hope fill you with all joy and peace in believing, so that by the power of the Holy Spirit you may abound in hope. ❖ Blessed be the God and Father of our Lord Jesus Christ! According to his great mercy, he has caused us to be born again to a living hope through the resurrection of Jesus Christ from the dead. ❖ Though you have not seen him, you love him. Though you do not now see him, you believe in him and rejoice with joy that is inexpressible and filled with glory. ❖ Through him we have also obtained access by faith into this grace in which we stand, and we rejoice in hope of the glory of God.

Rom. 12:12. | Col. 1:5. | 1 Cor. 15:19. | Acts 14:22. Luke 14:27. | 1 Thess. 3:3. | Phil. 4:4. | Rom. 15:13. 1 Pet. 1:3. | 1 Pet. 1:8. | Rom. 5:2.

SEPT. 8

"You have been weighed in the balances and found wanting."

The LORD is a God of knowledge, and by him actions are weighed. ❖ "For what is exalted among men is an abomination in the sight of God." ❖ "The LORD sees not as man sees: man looks on the outward appearance, but the LORD looks on the heart." ❖ Do not be deceived: God is not mocked, for whatever one sows, that will he also reap. For the one who sows to his own flesh will from the flesh reap corruption, but the one who sows to the Spirit will from the Spirit reap eternal life.

"What will it profit a man if he gains the whole world and forfeits his life? Or what shall a man give in return for his life?" ❖ But whatever gain I had, I counted as loss for the sake of Christ.

Behold, you delight in truth in the inward being. ❖ You have tried my heart, you have visited me by night, you have tested me, and you will find nothing.

Dan. 5:27. | 1 Sam. 2:3. | Luke 16:15. | 1 Sam. 16:7. Gal. 6:7, 8. | Matt. 16:26. | Phil. 3:7. | Ps. 51:6. | Ps. 17:3.

SEPT.
9

"He has filled the hungry with good things,
and the rich he has sent empty away."

"You say, I am rich, I have prospered, and I need nothing, not realizing that you are wretched, pitiable, poor, blind, and naked. I counsel you to buy from me gold refined by fire, so that you may be rich. … Those whom I love, I reprove and discipline, so be zealous and repent."

"Blessed are those who hunger and thirst for righteousness, for they shall be satisfied." ❖ When the poor and needy seek water, and there is none, and their tongue is parched with thirst, I the LORD will answer them; I the God of Israel will not forsake them. ❖ I am the LORD your God. … Open your mouth wide, and I will fill it.

"Why do you spend your money for that which is not bread, and your labor for that which does not satisfy? Listen diligently to me, and eat what is good, and delight yourselves in rich food." ❖ "I am the bread of life; whoever comes to me shall not hunger, and whoever believes in me shall never thirst."

Luke 1:53. | Rev. 3:17-19. | Matt. 5:6. | Isa. 41:17.
Ps. 81:10. | Isa. 55:2. | John 6:35.

SEPT. 10

"I will give them one heart and one way, that they may fear me forever, for their own good and the good of their children after them."

"I will give you a new heart, and a new spirit I will put within you." ❖ Good and upright is the LORD; therefore he instructs sinners in the way. He leads the humble in what is right, and teaches the humble his way. All the paths of the LORD are steadfast love and faithfulness, for those who keep his covenant and his testimonies. ❖ "That they may all be one, just as you, Father, are in me, and I in you, that they also may be in us, so that the world may believe that you have sent me."

I ... urge you to walk in a manner worthy of the calling to which you have been called, with all humility and gentleness, ... eager to maintain the unity of the Spirit in the bond of peace. There is one body and one Spirit – just as you were called to the one hope that belongs to your call – one Lord, one faith, one baptism, one God and Father of all, who is over all and through all and in all.

Jer. 32:39. | Ezek. 36:26. | Ps. 25:8-10.
John 17:21. | Eph. 4:1-6.

SEPT.
11

Do not be conformed to this world, but be transformed by the renewal of your mind.

"You shall not fall in with the many to do evil."

Do you not know that friendship with the world is enmity with God? Therefore whoever wishes to be a friend of the world makes himself an enemy of God. ❖ What partnership has righteousness with lawlessness? Or what fellowship has light with darkness? What accord has Christ with Belial? Or what portion does a believer share with an unbeliever? What agreement has the temple of God with idols? ❖ Do not love the world or the things in the world. If anyone loves the world, the love of the Father is not in him. And the world is passing away along with its desires, but whoever does the will of God abides forever.

In which you once walked, following the course of this world, following the prince of the power of the air, the spirit that is now at work in the sons of disobedience. ❖ That is not the way you learned Christ! – assuming that you have heard about him, … as the truth is in Jesus.

Rom. 12:2. | Exod. 23:2. | James 4:4. | 2 Cor. 6:14-16.
1 John 2:15, 17. | Eph. 2:2. | Eph. 4:20, 21.

SEPT.
12

"I have seen his ways, but I will heal him."

"I am the Lord, your healer."

O Lord, you have searched me and known me! You know when I sit down and when I rise up; you discern my thoughts from afar. You search out my path and my lying down and are acquainted with all my ways. ❖ You have set our iniquities before you, our secret sins in the light of your presence. ❖ All are naked and exposed to the eyes of him to whom we must give account.

"Come now, let us reason together, says the Lord: though your sins are like scarlet, they shall be as white as snow; though they are red like crimson, they shall become like wool." ❖ "He is merciful to him, and says, 'Deliver him from going down into the pit; I have found a ransom.'" ❖ But he was wounded for our transgressions; he was crushed for our iniquities; upon him was the chastisement that brought us peace, and with his stripes we are healed. ❖ He has sent me to bind up the brokenhearted. ❖ "Your faith has made you well; go in peace, and be healed of your disease."

Isa. 57:18. | Exod. 15:26. | Ps. 139:1-3. | Ps. 90:8. | Heb. 4:13.
Isa. 1:18. | Job 33:24. | Isa. 53:5. | Isa. 61:1. | Mark 5:34.

SEPT. 13

"If anyone thirsts, let him come to me and drink."

My soul longs, yes, faints for the courts of the Lord; my heart and flesh sing for joy to the living God. ❖ O God, you are my God; earnestly I seek you; my soul thirsts for you; my flesh faints for you, as in a dry and weary land where there is no water. So I have looked upon you in the sanctuary, beholding your power and glory.

"Come, everyone who thirsts, come to the waters; and he who has no money, come, buy and eat! Come, buy wine and milk without money and without price." ❖ The Spirit and the Bride say, "Come." And let the one who hears say, "Come." And let the one who is thirsty come; let the one who desires take the water of life without price. ❖ "Whoever drinks of the water that I will give him will never be thirsty forever. The water that I will give him will become in him a spring of water welling up to eternal life." ❖ "My blood is true drink."

Eat, friends, drink, and be drunk with love!

John 7:37. | Ps. 84:2. | Ps. 63:1, 2. | Isa. 55:1. | Rev. 22:17. John 4:14. | John 6:55. | Song of Songs 5:1.

SEPT.
14

"I, I am he who comforts you."

Blessed be the God and Father of our Lord Jesus Christ, the Father of mercies and God of all comfort, who comforts us in all our affliction, so that we may be able to comfort those who are in any affliction, with the comfort with which we ourselves are comforted by God. ❖ As a father shows compassion to his children, so the LORD shows compassion to those who fear him. For he knows our frame; he remembers that we are dust. ❖ "As one whom his mother comforts, so I will comfort you." ❖ Casting all your anxieties on him, because he cares for you.

You, O Lord, are a God merciful and gracious, slow to anger and abounding in steadfast love and faithfulness. ❖ "Another Helper, ... even the Spirit of truth." ❖ The Spirit helps us in our weakness.

"He will wipe away every tear from their eyes, and death shall be no more, neither shall there be mourning nor crying nor pain anymore, for the former things have passed away."

Isa. 51:12. | 2 Cor. 1:3, 4. | Ps. 103:13, 14.
Isa. 66:13. | 1 Pet. 5:7. | Ps. 86:15.
John 14:16, 17. | Rom. 8:26. | Rev. 21:4.

SEPT.
15

Sin will have no dominion over you,
since you are not under law but under grace.

What then? Are we to sin because we are not under law but under grace? By no means! ❖ Likewise, my brothers, you also have died to the law through the body of Christ, so that you may belong to another, to him who has been raised from the dead, in order that we may bear fruit for God. ❖ Not being outside the law of God but under the law of Christ. ❖ The sting of death is sin, and the power of sin is the law. But thanks be to God, who gives us the victory through our Lord Jesus Christ.

The law of the Spirit of life has set you free in Christ Jesus from the law of sin and death. ❖ "Everyone who commits sin is a slave to sin. … So if the Son sets you free, you will be free indeed."

Stand firm therefore, and do not submit again to a yoke of slavery.

Rom. 6:14. | Rom. 6:15. | Rom. 7:4. | 1 Cor. 9:21.
1 Cor. 15:56, 57. | Rom. 8:2. | John 8:34, 36. | Gal. 5:1.

SEPT.
16

The LORD weighs the heart.

The LORD knows the way of the righteous, but the way of the wicked will perish. ❖ "The LORD will show who is his, and who is holy." ❖ "Your Father who sees in secret will reward you."

Search me, O God, and know my heart! Try me and know my thoughts! And see if there be any grievous way in me, and lead me in the way everlasting! ❖ There is no fear in love, but perfect love casts out fear. ❖ O Lord, all my longing is before you; my sighing is not hidden from you. ❖ When my spirit faints within me, you know my way! ❖ He who searches hearts knows what is the mind of the Spirit, because the Spirit intercedes for the saints according to the will of God.

God's firm foundation stands, bearing this seal: "The Lord knows those who are his," and, "Let everyone who names the name of the Lord depart from iniquity."

Prov. 21:2. | Ps. 1:6. | Num. 16:5. | Matt. 6:4. | Ps. 139:23, 24.
1 John 4:18. | Ps. 38:9. | Ps. 142:3. | Rom. 8:27. | 2 Tim. 2:19.

SEPT.
17

"A bruised reed he will not break."

The sacrifices of God are a broken spirit; a broken and contrite heart, O God, you will not despise. ❖ He heals the brokenhearted and binds up their wounds. ❖ Thus says the One who is high and lifted up, who inhabits eternity, whose name is Holy: "I dwell in the high and holy place, and also with him who is of a contrite and lowly spirit, to revive the spirit of the lowly, and to revive the heart of the contrite. For I will not contend forever, nor will I always be angry; for the spirit would grow faint before me, and the breath of life that I made."

"I will seek the lost, and I will bring back the strayed, and I will bind up the injured, and I will strengthen the weak." ❖ Therefore lift your drooping hands and strengthen your weak knees, and make straight paths for your feet, so that what is lame may not be put out of joint but rather be healed. ❖ "Behold, your God. … He will come and save you."

Matt. 12:20. | Ps. 51:17. | Ps. 147:3. | Isa. 57:15, 16.
Ezek. 34:16. | Heb. 12:12, 13. | Isa. 35:4.

SEPT.
18

Open my eyes, that I may behold wondrous things out of your law.

Then he opened their minds to understand the Scriptures. ❖ "To you it has been given to know the secrets of the kingdom of heaven, but to them it has not been given." ❖ "I thank you, Father, Lord of heaven and earth, that you have hidden these things from the wise and understanding and revealed them to little children; yes, Father, for such was your gracious will." ❖ Now we have received not the spirit of the world, but the Spirit who is from God, that we might understand the things freely given us by God. ❖ How precious to me are your thoughts, O God! How vast is the sum of them! If I would count them, they are more than the sand. ❖ Oh, the depth of the riches and wisdom and knowledge of God! How unsearchable are his judgments and how inscrutable his ways! "For who has known the mind of the Lord, or who has been his counselor?" … For from him and through him and to him are all things. To him be glory forever. Amen.

Ps. 119:18. | Luke 24:45. | Matt. 13:11. | Matt. 11:25, 26.
1 Cor. 2:12. | Ps. 139:17, 18. | Rom. 11:33, 34, 36.

SEPT.
19

The God of all grace.

"I … will proclaim before you my name 'The LORD.' And I will be gracious to whom I will be gracious." ❖ "He is merciful to him, and says, 'Deliver him from going down into the pit; I have found a ransom.'" ❖ Are justified by his grace as a gift, through the redemption that is in Christ Jesus, whom God put forward as a propitiation by his blood, to be received by faith. This was to show God's righteousness, because in his divine forbearance he had passed over former sins. ❖ Grace and truth came through Jesus Christ.

By grace you have been saved through faith. And this is not your own doing; it is the gift of God. ❖ Grace, mercy, and peace from God the Father and Christ Jesus our Lord. ❖ Grace was given to each one of us according to the measure of Christ's gift. ❖ As each has received a gift, use it to serve one another, as good stewards of God's varied grace. ❖ He gives more grace.

Grow in the grace and knowledge of our Lord and Savior Jesus Christ. To him be the glory both now and to the day of eternity.

1 Pet. 5:10. | Exod. 33:19. | Job 33:24. | Rom. 3:24, 25.
John 1:17. | Eph. 2:8. | 1 Tim. 1:2. | Eph. 4:7.
1 Pet. 4:10. | James 4:6. | 2 Pet. 3:18.

*Blessed is the one who finds wisdom,
and the one who gets understanding.*

"Whoever finds me finds life and obtains favor from the Lord."

Thus says the Lord: "Let not the wise man boast in his wisdom, let not the mighty man boast in his might, … but let him who boasts boast in this, that he understands and knows me, that I am the Lord." ❖ The fear of the Lord is the beginning of wisdom.

Whatever gain I had, I counted as loss for the sake of Christ. Indeed, I count everything as loss because of the surpassing worth of knowing Christ Jesus my Lord. For his sake I have suffered the loss of all things and count them as rubbish, in order that I may gain Christ. ❖ In whom are hidden all the treasures of wisdom and knowledge. ❖ "I have counsel and sound wisdom; I have insight; I have strength."

Christ Jesus, whom God made our wisdom and our righteousness and sanctification and redemption.

Whoever captures souls is wise.

Prov. 3:13. | Prov. 8:35. | Jer. 9:23, 24. | Prov. 9:10.
Phil. 3:7, 8. | Col. 2:3. | Prov. 8:14. | 1 Cor. 1:30. | Prov. 11:30.

SEPT.
21

We know that for those who love God
all things work together for good.

Surely the wrath of man shall praise you; the remnant of wrath you will put on like a belt. ❖ "You meant evil against me, but God meant it for good."

All things are yours, whether … the world or life or death or the present or the future – all are yours, and you are Christ's, and Christ is God's. ❖ It is all for your sake, so that as grace extends to more and more people it may increase thanksgiving, to the glory of God. So we do not lose heart. Though our outer nature is wasting away, our inner nature is being renewed day by day. For this slight momentary affliction is preparing for us an eternal weight of glory beyond all comparison.

Count it all joy, my brothers, when you meet trials of various kinds, for you know that the testing of your faith produces steadfastness. And let steadfastness have its full effect, that you may be perfect and complete, lacking in nothing.

Rom. 8:28. | Ps. 76:10. | Gen. 50:20. | 1 Cor. 3:21-23.
2 Cor. 4:15-17. | James 1:2-4.

SEPT.
22

May my meditation be pleasing to him,
for I rejoice in the Lord.

As an apple tree among the trees of the forest, so is my beloved among the young men. With great delight I sat in his shadow, and his fruit was sweet to my taste. ❖ For who in the skies can be compared to the Lord? Who among the heavenly beings is like the Lord?

My beloved is radiant and ruddy, distinguished among ten thousand. ❖ "One pearl of great value." ❖ The ruler of kings on earth.

His head is the finest gold; his locks are wavy, black as a raven. ❖ Head over all things. ❖ He is the head of the body, the church.

His cheeks are like beds of spices, mounds of sweet-smelling herbs. ❖ He could not be hidden. ❖ His lips are lilies, dripping liquid myrrh. ❖ "No one ever spoke like this man!" ❖ His appearance is like Lebanon, choice as the cedars. ❖ Make your face shine on your servant. ❖ "Lift up the light of your face upon us, O Lord!"

Ps. 104:34. | Song 2:3. | Ps. 89:6. | Song 5:10. | Matt. 13:46.
Rev. 1:5. | Song 5:11. | Eph. 1:22. | Col. 1:18.
Song 5:13. | Mark 7:24. | Song 5:13. | John 7:46.
Song 5:15. | Ps. 31:16. | Ps. 4:6.

SEPT.
23

"Our God has not forsaken us."

Beloved, do not be surprised at the fiery trial when it comes upon you to test you, as though something strange were happening to you. ❖ It is for discipline that you have to endure. God is treating you as sons. For what son is there whom his father does not discipline? If you are left without discipline, in which all have participated, then you are illegitimate children and not sons.

"The LORD your God is testing you, to know whether you love the LORD your God with all your heart and with all your soul."

"The LORD will not forsake his people, for his great name's sake, because it has pleased the LORD to make you a people for himself." ❖ "Can a woman forget her nursing child, that she should have no compassion on the son of her womb? Even these may forget, yet I will not forget you." ❖ Blessed is he whose help is the God of Jacob, whose hope is in the LORD his God.

"And will not God give justice to his elect, who cry to him day and night? Will he delay long over them? I tell you, he will give justice to them speedily."

Ezra 9:9. | 1 Pet. 4:12. | Heb. 12:7, 8.
Deut. 13:3. | 1 Sam. 12:22.
Isa. 49:15. | Ps. 146:5. | Luke 18:7, 8.

SEPT.
24

For me it is good to be near God.

O LORD, I love the habitation of your house and the place where your glory dwells. ❖ For a day in your courts is better than a thousand elsewhere. I would rather be a doorkeeper in the house of my God than dwell in the tents of wickedness. ❖ Blessed is the one you choose and bring near, to dwell in your courts! We shall be satisfied with the goodness of your house, the holiness of your temple!

The LORD is good to those who wait for him, to the soul who seeks him. ❖ Therefore the LORD waits to be gracious to you, and therefore he exalts himself to show mercy to you. For the LORD is a God of justice; blessed are all those who wait for him.

Therefore, brothers, since we have confidence to enter the holy places by the blood of Jesus, by the new and living way that he opened for us, … let us draw near with a true heart in full assurance of faith, with our hearts sprinkled clean from an evil conscience.

Ps. 73:28. | Ps. 26:8. | Ps. 84:10. | Ps. 65:4. | Lam. 3:25.
Isa. 30:18. | Heb. 10:19, 20, 22.

SEPT. 25

And let steadfastness have its full effect, that you may be perfect and complete, lacking nothing.

Now for a little while, if necessary, you have been grieved by various trials, so that the tested genuineness of your faith – more precious than gold that perishes though it is tested by fire – may be found to result in praise and glory and honor at the revelation of Jesus Christ. ❖ More than that, we rejoice in our sufferings, knowing that suffering produces endurance, and endurance produces character, and character produces hope.

It is good that one should wait quietly for the salvation of the LORD. ❖ You knew that you yourselves had a better possession and an abiding one. Therefore do not throw away your confidence, which has a great reward. For you have need of endurance, so that when you have done the will of God you may receive what is promised. ❖ Now may our Lord Jesus Christ himself, and God our Father, who loved us and gave us eternal comfort and good hope through grace, comfort your hearts.

James 1:4. | 1 Pet. 1:6, 7. | Rom. 5:3, 4. | Lam. 3:26.
Heb. 10:34-36. | 2 Thess. 2:16, 17.

SEPT. 26

"A God of faithfulness and without iniquity, just and upright is he."

Him who judges justly. ❖ We must all appear before the judgment seat of Christ, so that each one may receive what is due for what he has done in the body, whether good or evil. ❖ Each of us will give an account of himself to God. ❖ "The soul who sins shall die."

"Awake, O sword, against my shepherd, against the man who stands next to me," declares the LORD of hosts. "Strike the shepherd." ❖ The LORD has laid on him the iniquity of us all. ❖ Steadfast love and faithfulness meet; righteousness and peace kiss each other. ❖ Mercy triumphs over judgment. ❖ The wages of sin is death, but the free gift of God is eternal life in Christ Jesus our Lord.

"A righteous God and a Savior; there is none besides me." ❖ Just and the justifier of the one who has faith in Jesus. ❖ Justified by his grace as a gift, through the redemption that is in Christ Jesus.

Deut. 32:4. | 1 Pet. 2:23. | 2 Cor. 5:10.
Rom. 14:12. | Ezek. 18:4. | Zech. 13:7. | Isa. 53:6.
Ps. 85:10. | James 2:13. | Rom. 6:23.
Isa. 45:21. | Rom. 3:26. | Rom. 3:24.

SEPT.
27

Humble yourselves, therefore, under the mighty hand of God so that at the proper time he may exalt you.

Everyone who is arrogant in heart is an abomination to the LORD; be assured, he will not go unpunished.

But now, O LORD, you are our Father; we are the clay, and you are our potter; we are all the work of your hand. Be not so terribly angry, O LORD, and remember not iniquity forever. Behold, please look, we are all your people. ❖ "You have disciplined me, and I was disciplined, like an untrained calf; bring me back that I may be restored, for you are the LORD my God. For after I had turned away, I relented, and after I was instructed, I slapped my thigh; I was ashamed, and I was confounded, because I bore the disgrace of my youth." ❖ It is good for a man that he bear the yoke in his youth.

"Affliction does not come from the dust, nor does trouble sprout from the ground, but man is born to trouble as the sparks fly upward."

1 Pet. 5:6. | Prov. 16:5. | Isa. 64:8, 9. | Jer. 31:18, 19. Lam. 3:27. | Job 5:6, 7.

SEPT.
28

"So shall they put my name upon the people of Israel, and I will bless them."

O LORD our God, other lords besides you have ruled over us, but your name alone we bring to remembrance. ❖ We have become like those over whom you have never ruled, like those who are not called by your name.

"All the peoples of the earth shall see that you are called by the name of the LORD, and they shall be afraid of you." ❖ The LORD will not forsake his people, for his great name's sake, because it has pleased the LORD to make you a people for himself.

"O Lord, hear; O Lord, forgive. O Lord, pay attention and act. Delay not, for your own sake, O my God, because your city and your people are called by your name." ❖ Help us, O God of our salvation, for the glory of your name; deliver us, and atone for our sins, for your name's sake! Why should the nations say, "Where is their God?" ❖ The name of the LORD is a strong tower; the righteous man runs into it and is safe.

Num. 6:27. | Isa. 26:13. | Isa. 63:19. | Deut. 28:10.
1 Sam. 12:22. | Dan. 9:19. | Ps. 79:9, 10. | Prov. 18:10.

SEPT.
29

By this we know love,
that he laid down his life for us.

The love of Christ that surpasses knowledge. ❖ "Greater love has no one than this, that someone lays down his life for his friends." ❖ You know the grace of our Lord Jesus Christ, that though he was rich, yet for your sake he became poor, so that you by his poverty might become rich. ❖ Beloved, if God so loved us, we also ought to love one another. ❖ Be kind to one another, tenderhearted, forgiving one another, as God in Christ forgave you. ❖ Bearing with one another and, if one has a complaint against another, forgiving each other; as the Lord has forgiven you, so you also must forgive. ❖ "For even the Son of Man came not to be served but to serve, and to give his life as a ransom for many." ❖ Christ also suffered for you, leaving you an example, so that you might follow in his steps.

"You also ought to wash one another's feet. For I have given you an example, that you also should do just as I have done to you." ❖ We ought to lay down our lives for the brothers.

1 John 3:16. | Eph. 3:19. | John 15:13. | 2 Cor. 8:9.
1 John 4:11. | Eph. 4:32. | Col. 3:13. | Mark 10:45.
1 Pet. 2:21. | John 13:14, 15. | 1 John 3:16.

SEPT. 30

"He knows the way that I take; when he has tried me, I shall come out as gold."

He knows our frame. ❖ He does not willingly afflict or grieve the children of men.

God's firm foundation stands, bearing this seal: "The Lord knows those who are his," and, "Let everyone who names the name of the Lord depart from iniquity." Now in a great house there are not only vessels of gold and silver but also of wood and clay, some for honorable use, some for dishonorable. Therefore, if anyone cleanses himself from what is dishonorable, he will be a vessel for honorable use, set apart as holy, useful to the master of the house, ready for every good work.

He will sit as a refiner and purifier of silver, and he will purify the sons of Levi and refine them like gold and silver, and they will bring offerings in righteousness to the LORD. ❖ "I will … refine them as one refines silver. … They will call upon my name, and I will answer them. I will say, 'They are my people'; and they will say, 'The LORD is my God.'"

Job 23:10. | Ps. 103:14. | Lam. 3:33.
2 Tim. 2:19-21. | Mal. 3:3. | Zech. 13:9.

October

OCT.
1

The fruit of the Spirit is … self-control.

Every athlete exercises self-control in all things. They do it to receive a perishable wreath, but we an imperishable. So I do not run aimlessly; I do not box as one beating the air. But I discipline my body and keep it under control, lest after preaching to others I myself should be disqualified. ❖ Do not get drunk with wine, for that is debauchery, but be filled with the Spirit.

"If anyone would come after me, let him deny himself and take up his cross and follow me."

So then let us not sleep, as others do, but let us keep awake and be sober. For those who sleep, sleep at night, and those who get drunk, are drunk at night. But since we belong to the day, let us be sober. ❖ To renounce ungodliness and worldly passions, and to live self-controlled, upright, and godly lives in the present age, waiting for our blessed hope, the appearing of the glory of our great God and Savior Jesus Christ.

Gal. 5:22, 23. | 1 Cor. 9:25-27. | Eph. 5:18. | Matt. 16:24.
1 Thess. 5:6-8. | Titus 2:12, 13.

OCT.
2

"The goat shall bear all their iniquities on itself to a remote area, and he shall let the goat go free in the wilderness."

As far as the east is from the west, so far does he remove our transgressions from us. ❖ "In those days and in that time," declares the Lord, "iniquity shall be sought in Israel, and there shall be none. And sin in Judah, and none shall be found, for I will pardon those whom I leave as a remnant." ❖ You will cast all our sins into the depths of the sea. … Who is a God like you, pardoning iniquity?

All we like sheep have gone astray; we have turned every one to his own way; and the Lord has laid on him the iniquity of us all. ❖ He shall bear their iniquities. Therefore I will divide him a portion with the many, and he shall divide the spoil with the strong, because he poured out his soul to death and was numbered with the transgressors; yet he bore the sin of many, and makes intercession for the transgressors. ❖ "The Lamb of God, who takes away the sin of the world!"

Lev. 16:22. | Ps. 103:12. | Jer. 50:20. | Mic. 7:19, 18.
Isa. 53:6. | Isa. 53:11, 12. | John 1:29.

OCT. 3

To him who loves us and has freed us from our sins by his blood.

Many waters cannot quench love, neither can floods drown it. … Love is strong as death. ❖ "Greater love has no one than this, that someone lays down his life for his friends."

He himself bore our sins in his body on the tree, that we might die to sin and live to righteousness. By his wounds you have been healed. ❖ In him we have redemption through his blood, the forgiveness of our trespasses, according to the riches of his grace.

You were washed, you were sanctified, you were justified in the name of the Lord Jesus Christ and by the Spirit of our God. ❖ You are a chosen race, a royal priesthood, a holy nation, a people for his own possession, that you may proclaim the excellencies of him who called you out of darkness into his marvelous light. ❖ I appeal to you therefore, brothers, by the mercies of God, to present your bodies as a living sacrifice, holy and acceptable to God, which is your spiritual worship.

Rev. 1:5. | Song of Songs 8:7, 6. | John 15:13. | 1 Pet. 2:24. Eph. 1:7. | 1 Cor. 6:11. | 1 Pet. 2:9. | Rom. 12:1.

OCT. 4

Moses did not know that the skin of his face shone because he had been talking with God.

Not to us, O LORD, not to us, but to your name give glory. ❖ "Lord, when did we see you hungry and feed you, or thirsty and give you drink?" ❖ In humility count others more significant than yourselves. ❖ Clothe yourselves … with humility.

[Jesus] was transfigured before them, and his face shone like the sun, and his clothes became white as light. ❖ Gazing at him, all who sat in the council saw that his face was like the face of an angel. ❖ "The glory that you have given me I have given to them." ❖ We all, with unveiled face, beholding the glory of the Lord, are being transformed into the same image from one degree of glory to another. For this comes from the Lord who is the Spirit. ❖ "You are the light of the world. A city set on a hill cannot be hidden. Nor do people light a lamp and put it under a basket, but on a stand, and it gives light to all in the house."

Exod. 34:29. | Ps. 115:1. | Matt. 25:37. | Phil. 2:3. | 1 Pet. 5:5.
Matt. 17:2. | Acts 6:15. | John 17:22.
2 Cor. 3:18. | Matt. 5:14, 15.

OCT. 5

"Call upon me in the day of trouble;
I will deliver you, and you shall glorify me."

Why are you cast down, O my soul, and why are you in turmoil within me? Hope in God; for I shall again praise him, my salvation and my God. ❖ O LORD, you hear the desire of the afflicted; you will strengthen their heart; you will incline your ear. ❖ For you, O Lord, are good and forgiving, abounding in steadfast love to all who call upon you.

So Jacob said to his household, … "Let us arise and go up to Bethel, so that I may make there an altar to the God who answers me in the day of my distress and has been with me wherever I have gone." ❖ Bless the LORD, O my soul, and forget not all his benefits.

I love the LORD, because he has heard my voice and my pleas for mercy. Because he inclined his ear to me, therefore I will call on him as long as I live. The snares of death encompassed me; the pangs of Sheol laid hold on me; I suffered distress and anguish. Then I called on the name of the LORD.

Ps. 50:15. | Ps. 42:11. | Ps. 10:17. | Ps. 86:5.
Gen. 35:2, 3. | Ps. 103:2. | Ps. 116:1-4.

OCT.
6

"The Lord our God the Almighty reigns."

"I know that you can do all things." ❖ "What is impossible with men is possible with God." ❖ He does according to his will among the host of heaven and among the inhabitants of the earth; and none can stay his hand or say to him, "What have you done?" ❖ "There is none who can deliver from my hand; I work, and who can turn it back?" ❖ "Abba, Father, all things are possible for you."

"Do you believe that I am able to do this?" They said to him, "Yes, Lord." Then he touched their eyes, saying, "According to your faith be it done to you." ❖ "Lord, if you will, you can make me clean." And Jesus stretched out his hand and touched him, saying, "I will; be clean." ❖ Mighty God. ❖ "All authority in heaven and on earth has been given to me."

Some trust in chariots and some in horses, but we trust in the name of the LORD our God. ❖ "Be strong and courageous. Do not be afraid or dismayed, … for there are more with us than with him."

Rev. 19:6. | Job 42:2. | Luke 18:27. | Dan. 4:35. | Isa. 43:13. Mark 14:36. | Matt. 9:28, 29. | Matt. 8:2, 3. | Isa. 9:6. Matt. 28:18. | Ps. 20:7. | 2 Chron. 32:7.

OCT.
7

He … teaches the humble his way.

"Blessed are the meek."

Again I saw that under the sun the race is not to the swift, nor the battle to the strong, nor bread to the wise, nor riches to the intelligent, nor favor to those with knowledge. ❖ The heart of man plans his way, but the LORD establishes his steps.

To you I lift up my eyes, O you who are enthroned in the heavens! Behold, as the eyes of servants look to the hand of their master, as the eyes of a maidservant to the hand of her mistress, so our eyes look to the LORD our God. ❖ Make me know the way I should go, for to you I lift up my soul.

"O our God, will you not execute judgment on them? For we are powerless against this great horde that is coming against us. We do not know what to do, but our eyes are on you."

If any of you lacks wisdom, let him ask God, who gives generously to all without reproach, and it will be given him.

"When the Spirit of truth comes, he will guide you into all the truth."

Ps. 25:9. | Matt. 5:5. | Eccl. 9:11. | Prov. 16:9. | Ps. 123:1, 2.
Ps. 143:8. | 2 Chron. 20:12. | James 1:5. | John 16:13.

OCT. 8

"I will not fear; what can man do to me?"

Who shall separate us from the love of Christ? Shall tribulation, or distress, or persecution, or famine, or nakedness, or danger, or sword? No, in all these things we are more than conquerors through him who loved us.

"Do not fear those who kill the body, and after that have nothing more that they can do. But I will warn you whom to fear: fear him who, after he has killed, has authority to cast into hell. Yes, I tell you, fear him!"

"Blessed are those who are persecuted for righteousness' sake, for theirs is the kingdom of heaven. Blessed are you when others revile you and persecute you and utter all kinds of evil against you falsely on my account. Rejoice and be glad, for your reward is great in heaven." ❖ "But I do not account my life of any value nor as precious to myself, if only I may finish my course." ❖ I will also speak of your testimonies before kings and shall not be put to shame.

Heb. 13:6. | Rom. 8:35, 37. | Luke 12:4, 5.
Matt. 5:10-12. | Acts 20:24. | Ps. 119:46.

OCT. 9

"You are a God ready to forgive, gracious and merciful."

The Lord is not slow to fulfill his promise as some count slowness, but is patient toward you, not wishing that any should perish, but that all should reach repentance. ❖ And count the patience of our Lord as salvation.

But I received mercy for this reason, that in me, as the foremost, Jesus Christ might display his perfect patience as an example to those who were to believe in him for eternal life. ❖ Whatever was written in former days was written for our instruction, that through endurance and through the encouragement of the Scriptures we might have hope.

Or do you presume on the riches of his kindness and forbearance and patience, not knowing that God's kindness is meant to lead you to repentance? ❖ "Rend your hearts and not your garments." Return to the LORD, your God, for he is gracious and merciful, slow to anger, and abounding in steadfast love; and he relents over disaster.

Neh. 9:17. | 2 Pet. 3:9. | 2 Pet. 3:15. | 1 Tim. 1:16.
Rom. 15:4. | Rom. 2:4. | Joel 2:13.

OCT.
10

Every family in heaven and on earth.

One God and Father of all, who is over all and through all and in all. ❖ In Christ Jesus you are all sons of God, through faith. ❖ As a plan for the fullness of time, to unite all things in him, things in heaven and things on earth.

He is not ashamed to call them brothers. ❖ "Here are my mother and my brothers! For whoever does the will of my Father in heaven is my brother and sister and mother." ❖ "Go to my brothers and say to them, 'I am ascending to my Father and your Father.'"

I saw under the altar the souls of those who had been slain for the word of God and for the witness they had borne. ... Then they were each given a white robe and told to rest a little longer, until the number of their fellow servants and their brothers should be complete, who were to be killed as they themselves had been. ❖ That apart from us they should not be made perfect.

Eph. 3:15. | Eph. 4:6. | Gal. 3:26. | Eph. 1:10. | Heb. 2:11. Matt. 12:49, 50. | John 20:17. | Rev. 6:9-11. | Heb. 11:40.

OCT. 11

Be not far from me, for trouble is near.

How long, O Lord? Will you forget me forever? How long will you hide your face from me? How long must I take counsel in my soul and have sorrow in my heart all the day? ❖ Hide not your face from me. Turn not your servant away in anger, O you who have been my help. Cast me not off; forsake me not, O God of my salvation!

When he calls to me, I will answer him; I will be with him in trouble; I will rescue him and honor him. ❖ The Lord is near to all who call on him, to all who call on him in truth. He fulfills the desire of those who fear him; he also hears their cry and saves them.

"I will not leave you as orphans; I will come to you." ❖ "Behold, I am with you always, to the end of the age."

God is our refuge and strength, a very present help in trouble. ❖ For God alone my soul waits in silence; from him comes my salvation. For God alone, O my soul, wait in silence, for my hope is from him.

Ps. 22:11. | Ps. 13:1, 2. | Ps. 27:9. | Ps. 91:15. | Ps. 145:18, 19.
John 14:18. | Matt. 28:20. | Ps. 46:1. | Ps. 62:1, 5.

OCT.
12

In Christ God was reconciling the world to himself, not counting their trespasses against them.

In him all the fullness of God was pleased to dwell, and through him to reconcile to himself all things, whether on earth or in heaven, making peace by the blood of his cross. ❖ Steadfast love and faithfulness meet; righteousness and peace kiss each other.

"I know the plans I have for you, declares the LORD, plans for wholeness and not for evil." ❖ "Come now, let us reason together, says the LORD: though your sins are like scarlet, they shall be as white as snow; though they are red like crimson, they shall become like wool."

Who is a God like you, pardoning iniquity? ❖ "Agree with God, and be at peace." ❖ Work out your own salvation with fear and trembling, for it is God who works in you, both to will and to work for his good pleasure. ❖ O LORD, you will ordain peace for us; you have done for us all our works.

2 Cor. 5:19. | Col. 1:19, 20. | Ps. 85:10. | Jer. 29:11. | Isa. 1:18. Mic. 7:18. | Job 22:21. | Phil. 2:12, 13. | Isa. 26:12.

OCT. 13

"From the first day that you set your heart to understand and humbled yourself before your God, your words have been heard."

Thus says the One who is high and lifted up, who inhabits eternity, whose name is Holy: "I dwell in the high and holy place, and also with him who is of a contrite and lowly spirit, to revive the spirit of the lowly, and to revive the heart of the contrite." ❖ The sacrifices of God are a broken spirit; a broken and contrite heart, O God, you will not despise. ❖ Though the LORD is high, he regards the lowly, but the haughty he knows from afar. ❖ Humble yourselves, therefore, under the mighty hand of God so that at the proper time he may exalt you. ❖ "God opposes the proud, but gives grace to the humble." Submit yourselves therefore to God.

You, O Lord, are good and forgiving, abounding in steadfast love to all who call upon you. Give ear, O LORD, to my prayer; listen to my plea for grace. In the day of my trouble I call upon you, for you answer me.

Dan. 10:12. | Isa. 57:15. | Ps. 51:17. | Ps. 138:6.
1 Pet. 5:6. | James 4:6, 7. | Ps. 86:5-7.

OCT. 14

Christ died and lived again, that he might be Lord both of the dead and of the living.

It was the will of the Lord to crush him; he has put him to grief; when his soul makes an offering for sin, he shall see his offspring; he shall prolong his days; the will of the Lord shall prosper in his hand. Out of the anguish of his soul he shall see and be satisfied; by his knowledge shall the righteous one, my servant, make many to be accounted righteous, and he shall bear their iniquities. ❖ "Was it not necessary that the Christ should suffer these things and enter into his glory?" ❖ We have concluded this: that one has died for all, therefore all have died; and he died for all, that those who live might no longer live for themselves but for him who for their sake died and was raised. ❖ "Let all the house of Israel therefore know for certain that God has made him both Lord and Christ, this Jesus whom you crucified." ❖ He was foreknown before the foundation of the world but was made manifest in the last times for your sake, who through him are believers in God.

Rom. 14:9. | Isa. 53:10, 11. | Luke 24:26.
2 Cor. 5:14, 15. | Acts 2:36. | 1 Pet. 1:20, 21.

OCT. 15

You, O God, are my fortress.

"The Lord is my rock and my fortress and my deliverer, my God, my rock, in whom I take refuge, my shield, and the horn of my salvation, my stronghold and my refuge, my savior." ❖ The Lord is my strength and my shield; in him my heart trusts, and I am helped; my heart exults, and with my song I give thanks to him.

He will come like a rushing stream, which the wind of the Lord drives. ❖ We can confidently say, "The Lord is my helper; I will not fear; what can man do to me?"

The Lord is my light and my salvation; whom shall I fear? The Lord is the stronghold of my life; of whom shall I be afraid?

As the mountains surround Jerusalem, so the Lord surrounds his people, from this time forth and forevermore. ❖ For you have been my help, and in the shadow of your wings I will sing for joy.

For your name's sake you lead me and guide me.

Ps. 59:9. | 2 Sam. 22:2, 3. | Ps. 28:7. | Isa. 59:19.
Heb. 13:6. | Ps. 27:1. | Ps. 125:2. | Ps. 63:7. | Ps. 31:3.

OCT.
16

Do not be slothful in zeal, be fervent in spirit, serve the Lord.

Whatever your hand finds to do, do it with your might, for there is no work or thought or knowledge or wisdom in Sheol, to which you are going. ❖ Whatever you do, work heartily, as for the Lord and not for men, knowing that from the Lord you will receive the inheritance as your reward. You are serving the Lord Christ. ❖ Whatever good anyone does, this he will receive back from the Lord.

"We must work the works of him who sent me while it is day; night is coming, when no one can work." ❖ "Did you not know that I must be in my Father's house?" ❖ "Zeal for your house will consume me."

Brothers, be all the more diligent to make your calling and election sure, for if you practice these qualities you will never fall. ❖ We desire each one of you to show the same earnestness to have the full assurance of hope until the end, so that you may not be sluggish, but imitators of those who through faith and patience inherit the promises. ❖ So run that you may obtain it.

Rom. 12:11. | Eccl. 9:10. | Col. 3:23, 24. | Eph. 6:8. | John 9:4. Luke 2:49. | John 2:17. | 2 Pet. 1:10. Heb. 6:11, 12. | 1 Cor. 9:24.

OCT.
17

Who exult in your name all the day
and in your righteousness are exalted.

"Only in the LORD, it shall be said of me, are righteousness and strength; to him shall come and be ashamed all who were incensed against him. In the LORD all the offspring of Israel shall be justified and shall glory." ❖ Be glad in the LORD, and rejoice, O righteous, and shout for joy, all you upright in heart!

But now the righteousness of God has been manifested apart from the law, although the Law and the Prophets bear witness to it – the righteousness of God through faith in Jesus Christ for all who believe. ... It was to show his righteousness at the present time, so that he might be just and the justifier of the one who has faith in Jesus.

Rejoice in the Lord always; again I will say, Rejoice. ❖ Though you have not seen him, you love him. Though you do not now see him, you believe in him and rejoice with joy that is inexpressible and filled with glory.

Ps. 89:16. | Isa. 45:24, 25. | Ps. 32:11.
Rom. 3:21, 22, 26. | Phil. 4:4. | 1 Pet. 1:8.

OCT.
18

One of the soldiers pierced his side with a spear, and at once there came out blood and water.

"Behold the blood of the covenant that the LORD has made with you." ❖ "The life of the flesh is in the blood, and I have given it for you on the altar to make atonement for your souls." ❖ It is impossible for the blood of bulls and goats to take away sins. ❖ And he said to them, "This is my blood of the covenant, which is poured out for many." ❖ He entered once for all into the holy places, not by means of the blood of goats and calves but by means of his own blood, thus securing an eternal redemption. ❖ Peace by the blood of his cross. ❖ Knowing that you were ransomed … not with perishable things such as silver or gold, but with the precious blood of Christ, like that of a lamb without blemish or spot. He … was made manifest in the last times for your sake. ❖ I will sprinkle clean water on you, and you shall be clean, … from all your idols I will cleanse you. ❖ Let us draw near with a true heart in full assurance of faith, with our hearts sprinkled clean from an evil conscience.

John 19:34. | Exod. 24:8. | Lev. 17:11. | Heb. 10:4.
Mark 14:24. | Heb. 9:12. | Col. 1:20. | 1 Pet. 1:18-20.
Ezek. 36:25. | Heb. 10:22.

OCT.
19

The Lord will be your confidence and will keep your foot from being caught.

Surely the wrath of man shall praise you; the remnant of wrath you will put on like a belt. ❖ The king's heart is a stream of water in the hand of the Lord; he turns it wherever he will. ❖ When a man's ways please the Lord, he makes even his enemies to be at peace with him.

I wait for the Lord, my soul waits, and in his word I hope; my soul waits for the Lord more than watchmen for the morning, more than watchmen for the morning. ❖ I sought the Lord, and he answered me and delivered me from all my fears.

"The eternal God is your dwelling place, and underneath are the everlasting arms. And he thrust out the enemy before you and said, Destroy." ❖ "Blessed is the man who trusts in the Lord, whose trust is the Lord."

What then shall we say to these things? If God is for us, who can be against us?

Prov. 3:26. | Ps. 76:10. | Prov. 21:1. | Prov. 16:7. | Ps. 130:5, 6. Ps. 34:4. | Deut. 33:27. | Jer. 17:7. | Rom. 8:31.

OCT.
20

I delight in the law of God, in my inner being.

Oh how I love your law! It is my meditation all the day. ❖ Your words were found, and I ate them, and your words became to me a joy and the delight of my heart. ❖ With great delight I sat in his shadow, and his fruit was sweet to my taste. ❖ "I have treasured the words of his mouth more than my portion of food."

"I desire to do your will, O my God; your law is within my heart." ❖ "My food is to do the will of him who sent me and to accomplish his work."

The precepts of the Lord are right, rejoicing the heart; the commandment of the Lord is pure, enlightening the eyes. … More to be desired are they than gold, even much fine gold; sweeter also than honey and drippings of the honeycomb. ❖ Be doers of the word, and not hearers only, deceiving yourselves. For if anyone is a hearer of the word and not a doer, he is like a man who looks intently at his natural face in a mirror.

Rom. 7:22. | Ps. 119:97. | Jer. 15:16.
Song of Songs 2:3. | Job 23:12. | Ps. 40:8.
John 4:34. | Ps.19:8, 10. | James 1:22, 23.

OCT. 21

From his fullness we have all received,
grace upon grace.

"This is my beloved Son, with whom I am well pleased." ❖ See what kind of love the Father has given to us, that we should be called children of God.

His Son, whom he appointed the heir of all things. ❖ If children, then heirs – heirs of God and fellow heirs with Christ, provided we suffer with him in order that we may also be glorified with him.

"I and the Father are one. … The Father is in me and I am in the Father." ❖ "My Father and your Father, … my God and your God." ❖ "I in them and you in me, that they may become perfectly one."

The church, which is his body, the fullness of him who fills all in all.

Since we have these promises, beloved, let us cleanse ourselves from every defilement of body and spirit, bringing holiness to completion in the fear of God.

John 1:16. | Matt. 17:5. | 1 John 3:1. | Heb. 1:2.
Rom. 8:17. | John 10:30, 38. | John 20:17.
John 17:23. | Eph. 1:22, 23. | 2 Cor. 7:1.

OCT.
22

My heart is steadfast, O God!

The LORD is my light and my salvation; whom shall I fear? The LORD is the stronghold of my life; of whom shall I be afraid?

You keep him in perfect peace whose mind is stayed on you, because he trusts in you. ❖ He is not afraid of bad news; his heart is firm, trusting in the LORD. His heart is steady; he will not be afraid, until he looks in triumph on his adversaries.

When I am afraid, I put my trust in you. ❖ He will hide me in his shelter in the day of trouble; he will conceal me under the cover of his tent; he will lift me high upon a rock. And now my head shall be lifted up above my enemies all around me, and I will offer in his tent sacrifices with shouts of joy; I will sing and make melody to the LORD.

After you have suffered a little while, the God of all grace, who has called you to his eternal glory in Christ, will himself restore, confirm, strengthen, and establish you. To him be the dominion forever and ever.

Ps. 108:1. | Ps. 27:1. | Isa. 26:3. | Ps. 112:7, 8.
Ps. 56:3. | Ps. 27:5, 6. | 1 Pet. 5:10, 11.

OCT.
23

"One's life does not consist in the abundance of his possessions."

Better is the little that the righteous has than the abundance of many wicked. ❖ Better is a little with the fear of the Lord than great treasure and trouble with it. ❖ Now there is great gain in godliness with contentment ... But if we have food and clothing, with these we will be content. ❖ Give me neither poverty nor riches; feed me with the food that is needful for me, lest I be full and deny you and say, "Who is the Lord?" or lest I be poor and steal and profane the name of my God. ❖ "Give us this day our daily bread."

"Therefore I tell you, do not be anxious about your life, what you will eat or what you will drink, nor about your body, what you will put on. Is not life more than food, and the body more than clothing?" ❖ "When I sent you out with no moneybag or knapsack or sandals, did you lack anything?" They said, "Nothing." ❖ Keep your life free from love of money, and be content with what you have, for he has said, "I will never leave you nor forsake you."

Luke 12:15. | Ps. 37:16. | Prov. 15:16. | 1 Tim. 6:6, 8.
Prov. 30:8, 9. | Matt. 6:11. | Matt. 6:25.
Luke 22:35. | Heb. 13:5.

OCT.
24

"I am driven away from your sight; yet I shall again look upon your holy temple."

Zion said, "The LORD has forsaken me; my Lord has forgotten me." "Can a woman forget her nursing child, that she should have no compassion on the son of her womb? Even these may forget, yet I will not forget you." ❖ I have forgotten what happiness is; so I say, "My endurance has perished; so has my hope from the LORD." ❖ Awake! Why are you sleeping, O Lord? Rouse yourself! Do not reject us forever! ❖ Why do you say, O Jacob, and speak, O Israel, "My way is hidden from the LORD, and my right is disregarded by my God"? ❖ "In overflowing anger for a moment I hid my face from you, but with everlasting love I will have compassion on you," says the LORD, your Redeemer.

Why are you cast down, O my soul, and why are you in turmoil within me? Hope in God; for I shall again praise him, my salvation and my God. ❖ We are afflicted in every way, but not crushed; perplexed, but not driven to despair; persecuted, but not forsaken; struck down, but not destroyed.

Jonah 2:4. | Isa. 49:14, 15. | Lam. 3:17, 18. | Ps. 44:23.
Isa. 40:27. | Isa. 54:8. | Ps. 43:5. | 2 Cor. 4:8, 9.

OCT. 25

"Behold, I am with you always,
to the end of the age."

"If two of you agree on earth about anything they ask, it will be done for them by my Father in heaven. For where two or three are gathered in my name, there am I among them." ❖ "Whoever has my commandments and keeps them, he it is who loves me. And he who loves me will be loved by my Father, and I will love him and manifest myself to him."

"Lord, how is it that you will manifest yourself to us, and not to the world? ... " "If anyone loves me, he will keep my word, and my Father will love him, and we will come to him and make our home with him."

Now to him who is able to keep you from stumbling and to present you blameless before the presence of his glory with great joy, to the only God, our Savior, through Jesus Christ our Lord, be glory, majesty, dominion, and authority, before all time and now and forever. Amen.

Matt. 28:20. | Matt. 18:19, 20. | John 14:21.
John 14:22, 23. | Jude 24, 25.

OCT.
26

The L*ORD* *reigns.*

"Do you not fear me? declares the LORD; do you not tremble before me? I placed the sand as the boundary for the sea, a perpetual barrier that it cannot pass; though the waves toss, they cannot prevail; though they roar, they cannot pass over it." ❖ Not from the east or from the west and not from the wilderness comes lifting up, but it is God who executes judgment, putting down one and lifting up another.

He changes times and seasons; he removes kings and sets up kings; he gives wisdom to the wise and knowledge to those who have understanding. ❖ "You will hear of wars and rumors of wars. See that you are not alarmed."

If God is for us, who can be against us? ❖ "Are not two sparrows sold for a penny? And not one of them will fall to the ground apart from your Father. But even the hairs of your head are all numbered. Fear not, therefore; you are of more value than many sparrows."

Ps. 99:1. | Jer. 5:22. | Ps. 75:6, 7. | Dan. 2:21.
Matt. 24:6. | Rom. 8:31. | Matt. 10:29-31.

OCT.
27

"He took our illnesses and bore our diseases."

"The priest shall command them to take for him who is to be cleansed two live clean birds and cedar wood and scarlet yarn and hyssop. And the priest shall command them to kill one of the birds in an earthenware vessel over fresh water. He shall take the live bird with the cedar wood and the scarlet yarn and the hyssop, and dip them and the live bird in the blood of the bird that was killed over the fresh water. And he shall sprinkle it seven times on him who is to be cleansed of the leprous disease. Then he shall pronounce him clean and shall let the living bird go into the open field."

There came a man full of leprosy. And when he saw Jesus, he fell on his face and begged him, "Lord, if you will, you can make me clean." ❖ Moved with pity, he stretched out his hand and touched him and said to him, "I will; be clean." And immediately the leprosy left him, and he was made clean.

Matt. 8:17. | Lev. 14:4-7. | Luke 5:12. | Mark 1:41, 42.

OCT.
28

He saw that there was no man, and wondered that there was no one to intercede; then his own arm brought him salvation.

Sacrifice and offering you have not desired, but you have given me an open ear. Burnt offering and sin offering you have not required. Then I said, "Behold, I have come; in the scroll of the book it is written of me: I desire to do your will, O my God; your law is within my heart." ❖ "I lay down my life that I may take it up again. No one takes it from me, but I lay it down of my own accord. I have authority to lay it down, and I have authority to take it up again."

"And there is no other god besides me, a righteous God and a Savior; there is none besides me. Turn to me and be saved, all the ends of the earth! For I am God, and there is no other." ❖ "There is salvation in no one else, for there is no other name under heaven given among men by which we must be saved." ❖ You know the grace of our Lord Jesus Christ, that though he was rich, yet for your sake he became poor, so that you by his poverty might become rich.

Isa. 59:16. | Ps. 40:6-8. | John 10:17, 18.
Isa. 45:21, 22. | Acts 4:12. | 2 Cor. 8:9.

OCT.
29

He is altogether desirable.

May my meditation be pleasing to him. ❖ My beloved is … distinguished among ten thousand. ❖ "A cornerstone chosen and precious, and whoever believes in him will not be put to shame." ❖ You are the most handsome of the sons of men; grace is poured upon your lips. ❖ God has highly exalted him and bestowed on him the name that is above every name. ❖ In him all the fullness of God was pleased to dwell.

Though you have not seen him, you love him. Though you do not now see him, you believe in him and rejoice with joy that is inexpressible and filled with glory.

I count everything as loss because of the surpassing worth of knowing Christ Jesus my Lord. For his sake I have suffered the loss of all things and count them as rubbish, in order that I may gain Christ and be found in him, not having a righteousness of my own that comes from the law, but that which comes through faith in Christ, the righteousness from God that depends on faith.

Song of Songs 5:16. | Ps. 104:34. | Song of Songs 5:10.
1 Pet. 2:6. | Ps. 45:2. | Phil. 2:9. | Col. 1:19.
1 Pet. 1:8. | Phil. 3:8, 9.

OCT.
30

It is good that one should wait quietly
for the salvation of the LORD.

"Has God forgotten to be gracious? Has he in anger shut up his compassion?" ❖ I had said in my alarm, "I am cut off from your sight." But you heard the voice of my pleas for mercy when I cried to you for help.

"Will not God give justice to his elect, who cry to him day and night? Will he delay long over them? I tell you, he will give justice to them speedily." ❖ Wait for the LORD, and he will deliver you. ❖ Be still before the LORD and wait patiently for him; fret not yourself over the one who prospers in his way, over the man who carries out evil devices!

"You will not need to fight in this battle. Stand firm, hold your position, and see the salvation of the LORD."

Let us not grow weary of doing good, for in due season we will reap, if we do not give up. ❖ See how the farmer waits for the precious fruit of the earth, being patient about it, until it receives the early and the late rains.

Lam. 3:26. | Ps. 77:9. | Ps. 32:22. | Luke 18:7, 8. | Prov. 20:22.
Ps. 37:7. | 2 Chron. 20:17. | Gal. 6:9. | James 5:7.

OCT. 31

"Not by might, nor by power, but by my Spirit, says the LORD of hosts."

Who has measured the Spirit of the LORD, or what man shows him his counsel? ❖ God chose what is foolish in the world to shame the wise; God chose what is weak in the world to shame the strong; God chose what is low and despised in the world, even things that are not, to bring to nothing things that are, so that no human being might boast in the presence of God.

"The wind blows where it wishes, and you hear its sound, but you do not know where it comes from or where it goes. So it is with everyone who is born of the Spirit." ❖ Born, not of blood nor of the will of the flesh nor of the will of man, but of God.

"My Spirit remains in your midst. Fear not." ❖ "The battle is not yours but God's." ❖ "The LORD saves not with sword and spear. For the battle is the LORD's."

Zech. 4:6. | Isa. 40:13. | 1 Cor. 1:27-29. | John 3:8. | John 1:13. Hag. 2:5. | 2 Chron. 20:15. | 1 Sam. 17:47.

November

NOV. 1

Blessed is the one who listens to me,
watching daily at my gates, waiting beside my doors.

Behold, as the eyes of servants look to the hand of their master, as the eyes of a maidservant to the hand of her mistress, so our eyes look to the LORD our God, till he has mercy upon us.

"It shall be a regular burnt offering throughout your generations at the entrance of the tent of meeting before the LORD, where I will meet with you, to speak to you there." ❖ "In every place where I cause my name to be remembered I will come to you and bless you."

"Where two or three are gathered in my name, there am I among them."

"The hour is coming, and is now here, when the true worshipers will worship the Father in spirit and truth, for the Father is seeking such people to worship him. God is spirit, and those who worship him must worship in spirit and truth."

Praying at all times in the Spirit, with all prayer and supplication. ❖ Pray without ceasing.

Prov. 8:34. | Ps. 123:2. | Exod. 29:42. | Exod. 20:24.
Matt. 18:20. | John 4:23, 24. | Eph. 6:18. | 1 Thess. 5:17.

NOV.
2

Always seek to do good.

To this you have been called, because Christ also suffered for you, leaving you an example, so that you might follow in his steps. He committed no sin, neither was deceit found in his mouth. When he was reviled, he did not revile in return ... but continued entrusting himself to him who judges justly. ❖ Consider him who endured from sinners such hostility against himself, so that you may not grow weary or fainthearted.

Let us also lay aside every weight, and sin which clings so closely, and let us run with endurance the race that is set before us, looking to Jesus, the founder and perfecter of our faith, who for the joy that was set before him endured the cross, despising the shame, and is seated at the right hand of the throne of God.

Finally, brothers, whatever is true, whatever is honorable, whatever is just, whatever is pure, whatever is lovely, whatever is commendable, if there is any excellence, if there is anything worthy of praise, think about these things.

1 Thess. 5:15. | 1 Pet. 2:21-23. | Heb. 12:3.
Heb. 12:1, 2. | Phil. 4:8.

NOV.
3

The ways of the Lord are right, and the upright walk in them, but transgressors stumble in them.

So the honor is for you who believe, but for those who do not believe, … "A stone of stumbling, and a rock of offense." ❖ The way of the Lord is a stronghold to the blameless, but destruction to evildoers.

"He who has ears to hear, let him hear." ❖ Whoever is wise, let him attend to these things; let them consider the steadfast love of the Lord. ❖ "The eye is the lamp of the body. So, if your eye is healthy, your whole body will be full of light." ❖ "If anyone's will is to do God's will, he will know whether the teaching is from God." ❖ "To the one who has, more will be given, and he will have an abundance." ❖ "Whoever is of God hears the words of God. The reason why you do not hear them is that you are not of God." ❖ "You refuse to come to me that you may have life." ❖ "My sheep hear my voice, and I know them, and they follow me."

Hosea 14:9. | 1 Pet. 2:7, 8. | Prov. 10:29. | Matt. 11:15. Ps. 107:43. | Matt. 6:22. | John 7:17. | Matt. 13:12. John 8:47. | John 5:40. | John 10:27.

Now for a little while, if necessary,
you have been grieved by various trials.

Beloved, do not be surprised at the fiery trial when it comes upon you to test you, as though something strange were happening to you. But rejoice insofar as you share Christ's sufferings, that you may also rejoice and be glad when his glory is revealed. ❖ The exhortation that addresses you as sons … "My son, do not regard lightly the discipline of the Lord, nor be weary when reproved by him." ❖ For the moment all discipline seems painful rather than pleasant, but later it yields the peaceful fruit of righteousness to those who have been trained by it.

We do not have a high priest who is unable to sympathize with our weaknesses, but one who in every respect has been tempted as we are, yet without sin. ❖ For because he himself has suffered when tempted, he is able to help those who are being tempted. ❖ God is faithful, and he will not let you be tempted beyond your ability.

1 Pet. 1:6. | 1 Pet. 4:12, 13. | Heb. 12:5. | Heb. 12:11.
Heb. 4:15. | Heb. 2:18. | 1 Cor. 10:13.

NOV.
5

"Take the finest spices. ... And you shall make of these a sacred anointing oil."

"It shall not be poured on the body of an ordinary person, and you shall make no other like it in composition. It is holy, and it shall be holy to you." ❖ One Spirit. ❖ Now there are varieties of gifts, but the same Spirit.

Your God ... has anointed you with the oil of gladness beyond your companions. ❖ God anointed Jesus of Nazareth with the Holy Spirit and with power. ❖ God ... gives the Spirit without measure.

From his fullness we have all received. ❖ But as his anointing teaches you about everything – and is true and is no lie, just as it has taught you – abide in him. ❖ It is God who ... has anointed us, and who has also put his seal on us and given us his Spirit in our hearts as a guarantee.

The fruit of the Spirit is love, joy, peace, patience, kindness, goodness, faithfulness, gentleness, self-control; against such things there is no law.

Exod. 20:23, 25. | Exod. 30:32. | Eph. 4:4. | 1 Cor. 12:4.
Ps. 45:7. | Acts 10:38. | John 3:34. | John 1:16.
1 John 2:27. | 2 Cor. 1:21, 22. | Gal. 5:22, 23.

When Christ who is your life appears,
then you also will appear with him in glory.

"I am the resurrection and the life. Whoever believes in me, though he die, yet shall he live." ❖ God gave us eternal life, and this life is in his Son. Whoever has the Son has life; whoever does not have the Son of God does not have life.

The Lord himself will descend from heaven with a cry of command, with the voice of an archangel, and with the sound of the trumpet of God. And the dead in Christ will rise first. Then we who are alive, who are left, will be caught up together with them in the clouds to meet the Lord in the air, and so we will always be with the Lord. Therefore encourage one another with these words. ❖ When he appears we shall be like him, because we shall see him as he is. ❖ It is sown in dishonor; it is raised in glory. It is sown in weakness; it is raised in power.

"If I go and prepare a place for you, I will come again and will take you to myself, that where I am you may be also."

Col. 3:4. | John 11:25. | 1 John 5:11, 12. | 1 Thess. 4:16-18.
1 John 3:2. | 1 Cor. 15:43. | John 14:3.

NOV. 7

Let them thank the LORD for his steadfast love,
for his wondrous works to the children of men!

Oh, taste and see that the LORD is good! Blessed is the man who takes refuge in him! ❖ Oh, how abundant is your goodness, which you have stored up for those who fear you.

"The people whom I formed for myself that they might declare my praise." ❖ He predestined us for adoption through Jesus Christ, according to the purpose of his will, to the praise of his glorious grace, with which he has blessed us in the Beloved … so that we who were the first to hope in Christ might be to the praise of his glory.

How great is his goodness, and how great his beauty! ❖ The LORD is good to all, and his mercy is over all that he has made. All your works shall give thanks to you, O LORD, and all your saints shall bless you! They shall speak of the glory of your kingdom and tell of your power, to make known to the children of man your mighty deeds, and the glorious splendor of your kingdom.

Ps. 107:8. | Ps. 34:8. | Ps. 31:19. | Isa. 43:21.
Eph. 1:5, 6, 12. | Zech. 9:17. | Ps. 145:9-12.

NOV.
8

But since we belong to the day, let us be sober, having put on the breastplate of faith and love, and for a helmet the hope of salvation.

Therefore, preparing your minds for action, and being sober-minded, set your hope fully on the grace that will be brought to you at the revelation of Jesus Christ. ❖ Stand therefore, having fastened on the belt of truth, and having put on the breastplate of righteousness. … In all circumstances take up the shield of faith, with which you can extinguish all the flaming darts of the evil one; and take the helmet of salvation, and the sword of the Spirit, which is the word of God.

He will swallow up death forever; and the Lord GOD will wipe away tears from all faces, and the reproach of his people he will take away from all the earth, for the LORD has spoken. It will be said on that day, "Behold, this is our God; we have waited for him, that he might save us. This is the LORD; … let us be glad and rejoice in his salvation."

Now faith is the assurance of things hoped for, the conviction of things not seen.

1 Thess. 5:8. | 1 Pet. 1:13.
Eph. 6:14, 16, 17. | Isa. 25:8, 9. | Heb. 11:1.

NOV. 9

"I have granted help to one who is mighty; I have exalted one chosen from the people."

"I, I am the LORD, and besides me there is no savior." ❖ There is one God, and there is one mediator between God and men, the man Christ Jesus. ❖ "There is no other name under heaven given among men by which we must be saved."

Mighty God. ❖ [He] made himself nothing, taking the form of a servant, being born in the likeness of men. And being found in human form, he humbled himself by becoming obedient to the point of death, even death on a cross. Therefore God has highly exalted him and bestowed on him the name that is above every name. ❖ We see him who for a little while was made lower than the angels, namely Jesus, crowned with glory and honor because of the suffering of death, so that by the grace of God he might taste death for everyone. ❖ Since therefore the children share in flesh and blood, he himself likewise partook of the same things.

Ps. 89:19. | Isa. 43:11. | 1 Tim. 2:5. | Acts 4:12.
Isa. 9:6. | Phil. 2:7-9. | Heb. 2:9. | Heb. 2:14.

NOV.
10

Bearing fruit in every good work and increasing in the knowledge of God.

I appeal to you therefore, brothers, by the mercies of God, to present your bodies as a living sacrifice, holy and acceptable to God, which is your spiritual worship. Do not be conformed to this world, but be transformed by the renewal of your mind, that by testing you may discern what is the will of God, what is good and acceptable and perfect. ❖ Just as you once presented your members as slaves to impurity and to lawlessness leading to more lawlessness, so now present your members as slaves to righteousness leading to sanctification. ❖ Neither circumcision counts for anything, nor uncircumcision, but a new creation. And as for all who walk by this rule, peace and mercy be upon them.

"By this my Father is glorified, that you bear much fruit and so prove to be my disciples." ❖ "I chose you and appointed you that you should go and bear fruit and that your fruit should abide, so that whatever you ask the Father in my name, he may give it to you."

Col. 1:10. | Rom. 12:1, 2. | Rom. 6:19.
Gal. 6:15, 16. | John 15:8 | John 15:16.

NOV. 11

He led them in safety.

I walk in the way of righteousness, in the paths of justice.

"Behold, I send an angel before you to guard you on the way and to bring you to the place that I have prepared." ❖ In all their affliction he was afflicted, and the angel of his presence saved them; in his love and in his pity he redeemed them; he lifted them up and carried them all the days of old.

Not by their own sword did they win the land, nor did their own arm save them, but your right hand and your arm, and the light of your face, for you delighted in them. ❖ So you led your people, to make for yourself a glorious name.

Lead me, O Lord, in your righteousness because of my enemies; make your way straight before me. ❖ Send out your light and your truth; let them lead me; let them bring me to your holy hill and to your dwelling! Then I will go to the altar of God, to God my exceeding joy, and I will praise you with the lyre, O God, my God.

Ps. 78:53. | Prov. 8:20. | Exod. 23:20. | Isa. 63:9.
Ps. 44:3. | Isa. 63:14. | Ps. 5:8. | Ps. 43:3, 4.

NOV.
12

*Godly grief produces a repentance
that leads to salvation without regret.*

Peter remembered the saying of Jesus, "Before the rooster crows, you will deny me three times." And he went out and wept bitterly. ❖ If we confess our sins, he is faithful and just to forgive us our sins and to cleanse us from all unrighteousness. ❖ The blood of Jesus his Son cleanses us from all sin.

My iniquities have overtaken me, and I cannot see; they are more than the hairs of my head; my heart fails me. Be pleased, O LORD, to deliver me! O LORD, make haste to help me!

"So you, by the help of your God, return, hold fast to love and justice, and wait continually for your God."

The sacrifices of God are a broken spirit; a broken and contrite heart, O God, you will not despise. ❖ He heals the brokenhearted and binds up their wounds. ❖ He has told you, O man, what is good; and what does the LORD require of you but to do justice, and to love kindness, and to walk humbly with your God?

2 Cor. 7:10. | Matt. 26:75. | 1 John 1:9.
1 John 1:7. | Ps. 40:12, 13. | Hosea 12:6.
Ps. 51:17. | Ps. 147:3. | Mic. 6:8.

NOV.
13

Christ loved the church and gave himself up for her, that he might sanctify her, having cleansed her by the washing of water with the word.

Walk in love, as Christ loved us and gave himself up for us, a fragrant offering and sacrifice to God.

You have been born again, not of perishable seed but of imperishable, through the living and abiding word of God. ❖ "Sanctify them in the truth; your word is truth." ❖ "Unless one is born of water and the Spirit, he cannot enter the kingdom of God." ❖ He saved us, not because of works done by us in righteousness, but according to his own mercy, by the washing of regeneration and renewal of the Holy Spirit. ❖ Your promise gives me life.

The law of the LORD is perfect, reviving the soul; the testimony of the LORD is sure, making wise the simple; the precepts of the LORD are right, rejoicing the heart; the commandment of the LORD is pure, enlightening the eyes.

Eph. 5:25, 26. | Eph. 5:2. | 1 Pet. 1:23. | John 17:17. John 3:5. | Titus 3:5. | Ps. 119:50. | Ps. 19:7, 8.

NOV.
14

You are my help and my deliverer;
do not delay, O my God!

The steps of a man are established by the Lord, when he delights in his way; though he fall, he shall not be cast headlong, for the Lord upholds his hand. ❖ In the fear of the Lord one has strong confidence, and his children will have a refuge. ❖ "Who are you that you are afraid of man who dies, of the son of man who is made like grass, and have forgotten the Lord, your Maker?"

"I am with you to deliver you." ❖ "Be strong and courageous. Do not fear or be in dread of them, for it is the Lord your God who goes with you. He will not leave you or forsake you."

But I will sing of your strength; I will sing aloud of your steadfast love in the morning. For you have been to me a fortress and a refuge in the day of my distress. ❖ You are a hiding place for me; you preserve me from trouble; you surround me with shouts of deliverance.

Ps. 40:17. | Ps. 37:23, 24. | Prov. 14:26. | Isa. 51:12, 13.
Jer. 1:8. | Deut. 31:6. | Ps. 59:16. | Ps. 32:7.

NOV.
15

God is faithful, by whom you were called into the fellowship of his Son, Jesus Christ our Lord.

Let us hold fast the confession of our hope without wavering, for he who promised is faithful. ❖ God said, "I will make my dwelling among them and walk among them, and I will be their God, and they shall be my people." ❖ Indeed our fellowship is with the Father and with his Son Jesus Christ. ❖ Rejoice insofar as you share Christ's sufferings, that you may also rejoice and be glad when his glory is revealed.

That you, being rooted and grounded in love, may have strength to comprehend with all the saints what is the breadth and length and height and depth, and to know the love of Christ that surpasses knowledge, that you may be filled with all the fullness of God.

Whoever confesses that Jesus is the Son of God, God abides in him, and he in God. ❖ Whoever keeps his commandments abides in him, and he in them.

1 Cor. 1:9. | Heb. 10:23. | 2 Cor. 6:16. | 1 John 1:3.
1 Pet. 4:13. | Eph. 3:17-19. | 1 John 4:15. | 1 John 3:24.

NOV.
16

"Sanctify them in the truth; your word is truth."

"Already you are clean because of the word that I have spoken to you." ❖ Let the word of Christ dwell in you richly, ... in all wisdom.

How can a young man keep his way pure? By guarding it according to your word. With my whole heart I seek you; let me not wander from your commandments!

Wisdom will come into your heart, and knowledge will be pleasant to your soul; discretion will watch over you, understanding will guard you.

"My foot has held fast to his steps; I have kept his way and have not turned aside. I have not departed from the commandment of his lips; I have treasured the words of his mouth more than my portion of food." ❖ I have more understanding than all my teachers, for your testimonies are my meditation. ❖ "If you abide in my word, you are truly my disciples, and you will know the truth, and the truth will set you free."

John 17:17. | John 15:3. | Col. 3:16.
Ps. 119:9, 10. | Prov. 2:10, 11. | Job 23:11, 12.
Ps. 119:99. | John 8:31, 32.

NOV.
17

Your thoughts are very deep!

We have not ceased to pray for you, asking that you may be filled with the knowledge of his will in all spiritual wisdom and understanding. ❖ That you, being rooted and grounded in love, may have strength to comprehend with all the saints what is the breadth and length and height and depth, and to know the love of Christ that surpasses knowledge, that you may be filled with all the fullness of God.

Oh, the depth of the riches and wisdom and knowledge of God! How unsearchable are his judgments and how inscrutable his ways! ❖ For my thoughts are not your thoughts, neither are your ways my ways, declares the LORD. For as the heavens are higher than the earth, so are my ways higher than your ways and my thoughts than your thoughts. ❖ You have multiplied, O LORD my God, your wondrous deeds and your thoughts toward us; none can compare with you! I will proclaim and tell of them, yet they are more than can be told.

Ps. 92:5. | Col. 1:9. | Eph. 3:17-19.
Rom. 11:33. | Isa. 55:8, 9. | Ps. 40:5.

NOV. 18

He removed them with his fierce breath in the day of the east wind.

"Let us fall into the hand of the LORD, for his mercy is great." ❖ "I am with you to save you, declares the LORD. … I will discipline you in just measure, and I will by no means leave you unpunished." ❖ He will not always chide, nor will he keep his anger forever. He does not deal with us according to our sins, nor repay us according to our iniquities. … For he knows our frame; he remembers that we are dust. ❖ "I will spare them as a man spares his son who serves him."

God is faithful, and he will not let you be tempted beyond your ability, but with the temptation he will also provide the way of escape, that you may be able to endure it. ❖ "Satan demanded to have you, that he might sift you like wheat, but I have prayed for you that your faith may not fail." ❖ You have been a stronghold to the poor, a stronghold to the needy in his distress, a shelter from the storm and a shade from the heat; for the breath of the ruthless is like a storm against a wall.

Isa. 27:8. | 2 Sam. 24:14. | Jer. 30:11. | Ps. 103:9, 10, 14. Mal. 3:17. | 1 Cor. 10:13. | Luke 22:31, 32. | Isa. 25:4.

NOV.
19

"You will recognize them by their fruits."

Little children, let no one deceive you. Whoever practices righteousness is righteous, as he is righteous. ❖ Does a spring pour forth from the same opening both fresh and salt water? Can a fig tree, my brothers, bear olives, or a grapevine produce figs? Neither can a salt pond yield fresh water. Who is wise and understanding among you? By his good conduct let him show his works in the meekness of wisdom. ❖ Keep your conduct among the Gentiles honorable, so that when they speak against you as evildoers, they may see your good deeds and glorify God on the day of visitation.

"Either make the tree good and its fruit good, or make the tree bad and its fruit bad, for the tree is known by its fruit." ❖ "The good person out of his good treasure brings forth good, and the evil person out of his evil treasure brings forth evil." ❖ What more was there to do for my vineyard, that I have not done in it?

Matt. 7:20. | 1 John 3:7. | James 3:11-13.
1 Pet. 2:12. | Matt. 12:33. | Matt. 12:35. | Isa. 5:4.

NOV.
20

When I sit in darkness,
the Lord will be a light to me.

"When you pass through the waters, I will be with you; and through the rivers, they shall not overwhelm you; when you walk through fire you shall not be burned, and the flame shall not consume you. For I am the Lord your God, the Holy One of Israel, your Savior." ❖ I will lead the blind in a way that they do not know, in paths that they have not known I will guide them. I will turn the darkness before them into light, the rough places into level ground. These are the things I do, and I do not forsake them.

Even though I walk through the valley of the shadow of death, I will fear no evil, for you are with me; your rod and your staff, they comfort me. ❖ When I am afraid, I put my trust in you. In God, whose word I praise, in God I trust; I shall not be afraid. What can flesh do to me? ❖ The Lord is my light and my salvation; whom shall I fear? The Lord is the stronghold of my life; of whom shall I be afraid?

Mic. 7:8. | Isa. 43:2, 3. | Isa. 42:16.
Ps. 23:4. | Ps. 56:3, 4. | Ps. 27:1.

NOV.
21

"Whoever comes to me I will never cast out."

"If he cries to me, I will hear, for I am compassionate." ❖ "I will not spurn them, neither will I abhor them so as to destroy them utterly and break my covenant with them, for I am the LORD their God." ❖ "I will remember my covenant with you in the days of your youth, and I will establish for you an everlasting covenant."

"Come now, let us reason together, says the LORD: though your sins are like scarlet, they shall be as white as snow; though they are red like crimson, they shall become like wool." ❖ "Let the wicked forsake his way, and the unrighteous man his thoughts; let him return to the LORD, that he may have compassion on him, and to our God, for he will abundantly pardon." ❖ "Jesus, remember me when you come into your kingdom." And he said to him, "Truly, I say to you, today you will be with me in Paradise."

A bruised reed he will not break, and a faintly burning wick he will not quench.

John 6:37. | Exod. 22:27. | Lev. 26:44. | Ezek. 16:60. Isa. 1:18. | Isa. 55:7. | Luke 23:42, 43. | Isa. 42:3.

NOV. 22

Pray in the Holy Spirit.

"God is spirit, and those who worship him must worship in spirit and truth." ❖ We … have access in one Spirit to the Father.

"My Father, if it be possible, let this cup pass from me; nevertheless, not as I will, but as you will."

The Spirit helps us in our weakness. For we do not know what to pray for as we ought, but the Spirit himself intercedes for us with groanings too deep for words. And he who searches hearts knows what is the mind of the Spirit, because the Spirit intercedes for the saints according to the will of God. ❖ This is the confidence that we have toward him, that if we ask anything according to his will he hears us. ❖ "When the Spirit of truth comes, he will guide you into all the truth."

Praying at all times in the Spirit, with all prayer and supplication. To that end keep alert with all perseverance, making supplication.

Jude 20. | John 4:24. | Eph. 2:18.
Matt. 26:39. | Rom. 8:26, 27.
1 John 5:14. | John 16:13. | Eph. 6:18.

NOV. 23

"Whoever listens to me will dwell secure and will be at ease, without dread of disaster."

Lord, you have been our dwelling place in all generations. ❖ He who dwells in the shelter of the Most High will abide in the shadow of the Almighty. ❖ His faithfulness is a shield and buckler.

Your life is hidden with Christ in God. ❖ He who touches you touches the apple of his eye. ❖ "Fear not, stand firm, and see the salvation of the LORD. … The LORD will fight for you, and you have only to be silent." ❖ God is our refuge and strength, a very present help in trouble. Therefore we will not fear.

Jesus spoke to them, saying, "Take heart; it is I. Do not be afraid." ❖ "Why are you troubled, and why do doubts arise in your hearts? See my hands and my feet, that it is I myself. Touch me, and see. For a spirit does not have flesh and bones as you see that I have." ❖ I know whom I have believed, and I am convinced that he is able to guard until that Day what has been entrusted to me.

Prov. 1:33. | Ps. 90:1. | Ps. 91:1. | Ps. 91:4. | Col. 3:3.
Zech. 2:8. | Exod. 14:13, 14. | Ps. 46:1, 2.
Matt. 14:27. | Luke 24:38, 39. | 2 Tim. 1:12.

NOV.
24

"My mother and my brothers are those who hear the word of God and do it."

He who sanctifies and those who are sanctified all have one origin. That is why he is not ashamed to call them brothers, saying, "I will tell of your name to my brothers; in the midst of the congregation I will sing your praise." ❖ In Christ Jesus neither circumcision nor uncircumcision counts for anything, but only faith working through love. ❖ "You are my friends if you do what I command you." ❖ "Blessed rather are those who hear the word of God and keep it!"

"Not everyone who says to me, 'Lord, Lord,' will enter the kingdom of heaven, but the one who does the will of my Father who is in heaven." ❖ "My food is to do the will of him who sent me."

If we say we have fellowship with him while we walk in darkness, we lie and do not practice the truth. ❖ Whoever keeps his word, in him truly the love of God is perfected. By this we may be sure that we are in him.

Luke 8:21. | Heb. 2:11, 12. | Gal. 5:6.
John 15:14. | Luke 11:28. | Matt. 7:21.
John 4:34. | 1 John 1:6. | 1 John 2:5.

NOV.
25

Having been set free from sin,
[you] have become slaves of righteousness.

"You cannot serve God and money." ❖ When you were slaves of sin, you were free in regard to righteousness. But what fruit were you getting at that time from the things of which you are now ashamed? The end of those things is death. But now that you have been set free from sin and have become slaves of God, the fruit you get leads to sanctification and its end, eternal life. ❖ Christ is the end of the law for righteousness to everyone who believes.

"If anyone serves me, he must follow me; and where I am, there will my servant be also. If anyone serves me, the Father will honor him." ❖ "Take my yoke upon you, and learn from me, for I am gentle and lowly in heart, and you will find rest for your souls. For my yoke is easy, and my burden is light."

"O LORD our God, other lords besides you have ruled over us, but your name alone we bring to remembrance." ❖ I will run in the way of your commandments when you enlarge my heart!

Rom. 6:18. | Matt. 6:24. | Rom. 6:20-22. | Rom. 10:4.
John 12:26. | Matt. 11:29, 30. | Isa. 26:13. | Ps. 119:32.

NOV.
26

The Lord delights in you.

"Fear not, for I have redeemed you; I have called you by name, you are mine." ❖ "Can a woman forget her nursing child, that she should have no compassion on the son of her womb? Even these may forget, yet I will not forget you. Behold, I have engraved you on the palms of my hands; your walls are continually before me."

The steps of a man are established by the Lord, when he delights in his way. ❖ Delighting in the children of man. ❖ The Lord takes pleasure in those who fear him, in those who hope in his steadfast love. ❖ "They shall be mine, says the Lord of hosts, in the day when I make up my treasured possession, and I will spare them as a man spares his son who serves him."

You, who once were alienated and hostile in mind, doing evil deeds, he has now reconciled in his body of flesh by his death, in order to present you holy and blameless and above reproach before him.

Isa. 62:4. | Isa. 43:1. | Isa. 49:15, 16. | Ps. 37:23. | Prov. 8:31.
Ps. 147:11. | Mal. 3:17. | Col. 1:21, 22.

NOV.
27

"The glory that you have given me
I have given to them."

I saw the Lord sitting upon a throne, high and lifted up; and the train of his robe filled the temple. Above him stood the seraphim. ... And one called to another and said: "Holy, holy, holy is the LORD of hosts; the whole earth is full of his glory!" ❖ Isaiah said these things because he saw his glory and spoke of him. ❖ Seated above the likeness of a throne was a likeness with a human appearance. ... Like the appearance of the bow that is in the cloud on the day of rain, so was the appearance of the brightness all around. Such was the appearance of the likeness of the glory of the LORD.

"Please show me your glory." ... "But," he said, "you cannot see my face, for man shall not see me and live." ❖ No one has ever seen God; the only God, who is at the Father's side, he has made him known. ❖ God, who said, "Let light shine out of darkness," has shone in our hearts to give the light of the knowledge of the glory of God in the face of Jesus Christ.

John 17:22. | Isa. 6:1-3. | John 12:41. | Ezek. 1:26, 28.
Exod. 33:18, 20. | John 1:18. | 2 Cor. 4:6.

NOV.
28

As the body apart from the spirit is dead,
so also faith apart from works is dead.

"Not everyone who says to me, 'Lord, Lord,' will enter the kingdom of heaven, but the one who does the will of my Father who is in heaven." ❖ Holiness without which no one will see the Lord. ❖ Make every effort to supplement your faith with virtue, and virtue with knowledge, and knowledge with self-control, and self-control with steadfastness, and steadfastness with godliness, and godliness with brotherly affection, and brotherly affection with love. For if these qualities are yours and are increasing, they keep you from being ineffective or unfruitful in the knowledge of our Lord Jesus Christ. For whoever lacks these qualities is so nearsighted that he is blind, having forgotten that he was cleansed from his former sins. Therefore, brothers, be all the more diligent to make your calling and election sure, for if you practice these qualities you will never fall. ❖ By grace you have been saved through faith. And this is not your own doing; it is the gift of God, not a result of works, so that no one may boast.

James 2:26. | Matt. 7:21. | Heb. 12:14.
2 Pet. 1:5-10. | Eph. 2:8, 9.

NOV.
29

We shall be satisfied with the goodness of your house.

One thing have I asked of the LORD, that will I seek after: that I may dwell in the house of the LORD all the days of my life, to gaze upon the beauty of the LORD and to inquire in his temple.

"Blessed are those who hunger and thirst for righteousness, for they shall be satisfied." ❖ "He has filled the hungry with good things, and the rich he has sent empty away."

He satisfies the longing soul, and the hungry soul he fills with good things. ❖ "I am the bread of life; whoever comes to me shall not hunger, and whoever believes in me shall never thirst."

How precious is your steadfast love, O God! The children of mankind take refuge in the shadow of your wings. They feast on the abundance of your house, and you give them drink from the river of your delights. For with you is the fountain of life; in your light do we see light.

Ps. 65:4. | Ps. 27:4. | Matt. 5:6. | Luke 1:53.
Ps. 107:9. | John 6:35. | Ps. 36:7-9.

NOV. 30

Now may the Lord of peace himself give you peace at all times in every way. The Lord be with you all.

Peace from him who is and who was and who is to come. ❖ The peace of God, which surpasses all understanding, will guard your hearts and your minds in Christ Jesus.

Jesus himself stood among them, and said to them, "Peace to you!" ❖ "Peace I leave with you; my peace I give to you. ... Let not your hearts be troubled, neither let them be afraid."

"The Helper ... the Spirit of truth." ❖ The fruit of the Spirit is love, joy, peace. ❖ The Spirit himself bears witness with our spirit that we are children of God.

"My presence will go with you, and I will give you rest." And he said to him, "If your presence will not go with me, do not bring us up from here. For how shall it be known that I have found favor in your sight, I and your people? Is it not in your going with us?"

2 Thess. 3:16. | Rev. 1:4. | Phil. 4:7. | Luke 24:36. | John 14:27.
John 15:26. | Gal. 5:22. | Rom. 8:16. | Exod. 33:14-16.

December

DEC.
1

Each will be like a hiding place from the wind, a shelter from the storm.

Since therefore the children share in flesh and blood, he himself likewise partook of the same things. ❖ "The man who stands next to me," declares the LORD of hosts. ❖ "I and the Father are one."

He who dwells in the shelter of the Most High will abide in the shadow of the Almighty. ❖ There will be a booth for shade by day from the heat, and for a refuge and a shelter from the storm and rain. ❖ The LORD is your shade on your right hand. The sun shall not strike you by day, nor the moon by night.

From the end of the earth I call to you when my heart is faint. Lead me to the rock that is higher than I. ❖ You are a hiding place for me; you preserve me from trouble. ❖ You have been a stronghold to the poor, a stronghold to the needy in his distress, a shelter from the storm and a shade from the heat; for the breath of the ruthless is like a storm against a wall.

Isa. 32:3. | Heb. 2:14. | Zech. 13:7. | John 10:30. | Ps. 91:1. Isa. 4:6. | Ps. 121:5, 6. | Ps. 61:2. | Ps. 32:7. | Isa. 25:4.

DEC.
2

But you have been anointed by the Holy One, and you all have knowledge.

God anointed Jesus of Nazareth with the Holy Spirit and with power. ❖ For in him all the fullness of God was pleased to dwell. ❖ And from his fullness we have all received, grace upon grace.

You anoint my head with oil. ❖ But the anointing that you received from him abides in you, and you have no need that anyone should teach you. But as his anointing teaches you about everything – and is true and is no lie, just as it has taught you – abide in him.

"But the Helper, the Holy Spirit, whom the Father will send in my name, he will teach you all things and bring to your remembrance all that I have said to you."

Likewise the Spirit helps us in our weakness. For we do not know what to pray for as we ought, but the Spirit himself intercedes for us with groanings too deep for words.

1 John 2:20. | Acts 10:38. | Col. 1:19. | John 1:16.
Ps. 23:5. | 1 John 2:27. | John 14:26. | Rom. 8:26.

DEC.
3

"I would seek God, and to God would I commit my cause."

"Is anything too hard for the Lord?" ❖ Commit your way to the Lord; trust in him, and he will act. ❖ Do not be anxious about anything, but in everything by prayer and supplication with thanksgiving let your requests be made known to God. ❖ Casting all your anxieties on him, because he cares for you.

Hezekiah received the letter from the hand of the messengers, and read it; and Hezekiah went up to the house of the Lord, and spread it before the Lord. And Hezekiah prayed to the Lord.

"Before they call I will answer; while they are yet speaking I will hear." ❖ The prayer of a righteous person has great power as it is working.

I love the Lord, because he has heard my voice and my pleas for mercy. Because he inclined his ear to me, therefore I will call on him as long as I live.

Job 5:8. | Gen. 18:14. | Ps. 37:5. | Phil. 4:6. | 1 Pet. 5:7.
Isa. 37:14, 15. | Isa. 65:24. | James 5:16. | Ps. 116:1, 2.

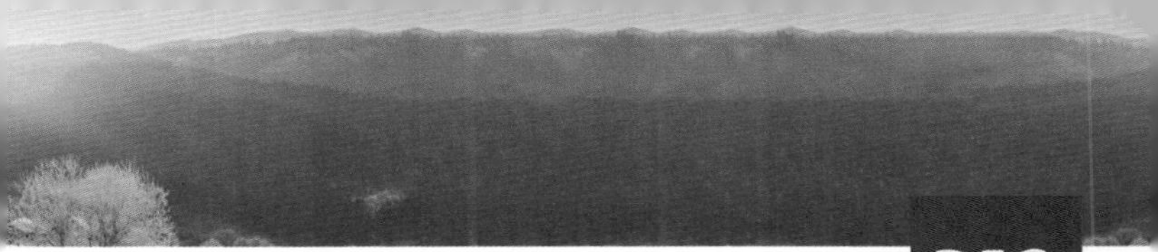

DEC.
4

"Where shall wisdom be found?"

If any of you lacks wisdom, let him ask God, who gives generously to all without reproach, and it will be given him. But let him ask in faith, with no doubting. ❖ Trust in the LORD with all your heart, and do not lean on your own understanding. In all your ways acknowledge him, and he will make straight your paths. ❖ The only [KJV: wise] God. ❖ Be not wise in your own eyes.

"Ah, Lord GOD! Behold, I do not know how to speak, for I am only a youth." But the LORD said to me, "Do not say, 'I am only a youth'; for to all to whom I send you, you shall go, and whatever I command you, you shall speak. Do not be afraid of them, for I am with you to deliver you, declares the LORD."

"Whatever you ask of the Father in my name, he will give it to you. Until now you have asked nothing in my name. Ask, and you will receive, that your joy may be full." ❖ "And whatever you ask in prayer, you will receive, if you have faith."

Job 28:12. | James 1:5, 6. | Prov. 3:5, 6. | 1 Tim. 1:17.
Prov. 3:7. | Jer. 1:6-8. | John 16:23, 24. | Matt. 21:22.

DEC.
5

It is good for me that I was afflicted,
that I might learn your statutes.

Although he was a son, he learned obedience through what he suffered. ❖ We suffer with him in order that we may also be glorified with him. For I consider that the sufferings of this present time are not worth comparing with the glory that is to be revealed to us.

"But he knows the way that I take; when he has tried me, I shall come out as gold. My foot has held fast to his steps; I have kept his way and have not turned aside."

"And you shall remember the whole way that the Lord your God has led you these forty years in the wilderness, that he might humble you, testing you to know what was in your heart, whether you would keep his commandments or not. … Know then in your heart that, as a man disciplines his son, the Lord your God disciplines you. So you shall keep the commandments of the Lord your God by walking in his ways and by fearing him.

Ps. 119:71. | Heb. 5:8. | Rom. 8:17, 18.
Job 23:10, 11. | Deut. 8:2, 5, 6.

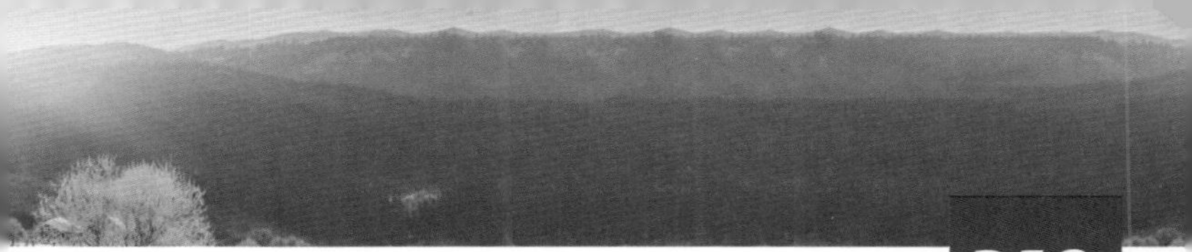

DEC.
6

It is God who works in you.

Not that we are sufficient in ourselves to claim anything as coming from us, but our sufficiency is from God. ❖ "A person cannot receive even one thing unless it is given him from heaven." ❖ "No one can come to me unless the Father who sent me draws him. And I will raise him up on the last day." ❖ "I will give them one heart and one way, that they may fear me forever."

Do not be deceived, my beloved brothers. Every good gift and every perfect gift is from above, coming down from the Father of lights with whom there is no variation or shadow due to change. Of his own will he brought us forth by the word of truth, that we should be a kind of firstfruits of his creatures.

For we are his workmanship, created in Christ Jesus for good works, which God prepared beforehand, that we should walk in them.

O Lord, you will ordain peace for us; you have done for us all our works.

Phil. 2:13. | 2 Cor. 3:5. | John 3:27. | John 6:44.
Jer. 32:39. | James 1:16-18. | Eph. 2:10. | Isa. 26:12.

DEC.
7

For our sake he made him to be sin who knew no sin, so that in him we might become the righteousness of God.

The LORD has laid on him the iniquity of us all. ❖ He himself bore our sins in his body on the tree, that we might die to sin and live to righteousness. By his wounds you have been healed. ❖ As by the one man's disobedience the many were made sinners, so by the one man's obedience the many will be made righteous.

But when the goodness and loving kindness of God our Savior appeared, he saved us, not because of works done by us in righteousness, but according to his own mercy, by the washing of regeneration and renewal of the Holy Spirit, whom he poured out on us richly through Jesus Christ our Savior, so that being justified by his grace we might become heirs according to the hope of eternal life. ❖ There is therefore now no condemnation for those who are in Christ Jesus.

"The LORD is our righteousness."

2 Cor. 5:21. | Isa. 53:6. | 1 Pet. 2:24. | Rom. 5:19.
Titus 3:4-7. | Rom. 8:1. | Jer. 23:6.

DEC. 8

Through love serve one another.

Brothers, if anyone is caught in any transgression, you who are spiritual should restore him in a spirit of gentleness. Keep watch on yourself, lest you too be tempted. Bear one another's burdens, and so fulfill the law of Christ. ❖ My brothers, if anyone among you wanders from the truth and someone brings him back, let him know that whoever brings back a sinner from his wandering will save his soul from death and will cover a multitude of sins. ❖ Having purified your souls by your obedience to the truth for a sincere brotherly love, love one another earnestly from a pure heart. ❖ Owe no one anything, except to love each other, for the one who loves another has fulfilled the law. ❖ Love one another with brotherly affection. Outdo one another in showing honor. ❖ Likewise, you who are younger, be subject to the elders. Clothe yourselves, all of you, with humility toward one another, for "God opposes the proud but gives grace to the humble."

We who are strong have an obligation to bear with the failings of the weak, and not to please ourselves.

Gal. 5:13. | Gal. 6:1, 2. | James 5:19, 20. | 1 Pet. 1:22.
Rom. 13:8. | Rom. 12:10. | 1 Pet. 5:5. | Rom. 15:1.

DEC.
9

To do righteousness and justice is
more acceptable to the LORD than sacrifice.

He has told you, O man, what is good; and what does the LORD require of you but to do justice, and to love kindness, and to walk humbly with your God? ❖ "Has the LORD as great delight in burnt offerings and sacrifices, as in obeying the voice of the LORD? Behold, to obey is better than sacrifice, and to listen than the fat of rams." ❖ "And to love him with all the heart and with all the understanding and with all the strength, and to love one's neighbor as oneself, is much more than all whole burnt offerings and sacrifices."

"So you, by the help of your God, return, hold fast to love and justice, and wait continually for your God." ❖ Mary … sat at the Lord's feet and listened to his teaching. … "One thing is necessary. Mary has chosen the good portion, which will not be taken away from her." ❖ It is God who works in you, both to will and to work for his good pleasure.

Prov. 21:3. | Mic. 6:8. | 1 Sam. 15:22. | Mark 12:33.
Hosea 12:6. | Luke 10:39, 42. | Phil. 2:13.

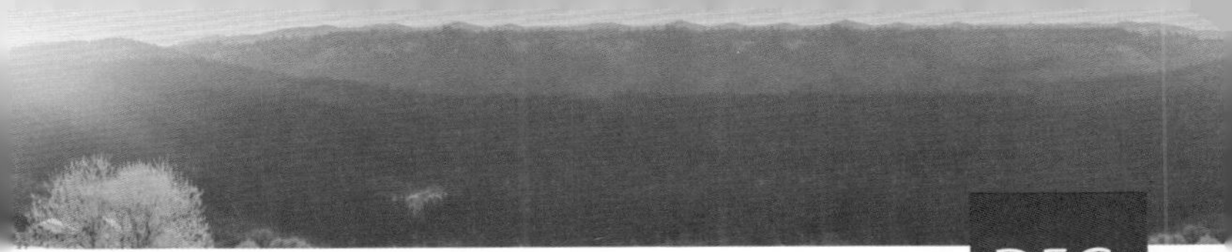

DEC.
10

"No one is able to snatch them
out of the Father's hand."

I know whom I have believed, and I am convinced that he is able to guard until that Day what has been entrusted to me. ❖ The Lord will rescue me from every evil deed and bring me safely into his heavenly kingdom. ❖ We are more than conquerors through him who loved us. For I am sure that neither death nor life, nor angels nor rulers, nor things present nor things to come, nor powers, nor height nor depth, nor anything else in all creation, will be able to separate us from the love of God in Christ Jesus our Lord. ❖ Your life is hidden with Christ in God.

Has not God chosen those who are poor in the world to be rich in faith and heirs of the kingdom, which he has promised to those who love him?

Now may our Lord Jesus Christ himself, and God our Father, who loved us and gave us eternal comfort and good hope through grace, comfort your hearts and establish them in every good work and word.

John 10:29. | 2 Tim. 1:12. | 2 Tim. 4:18. | Rom. 8:37-39.
Col. 3:3. | James 2:5. | 2 Thess. 2:16, 17.

DEC.
11

So do not let what you regard
as good be spoken of as evil.

Abstain from every form of evil. ❖ We aim at what is honorable not only in the Lord's sight but also in the sight of man. ❖ For this is the will of God, that by doing good you should put to silence the ignorance of foolish people.

But let none of you suffer as a murderer or a thief or an evildoer or as a meddler. Yet if anyone suffers as a Christian, let him not be ashamed, but let him glorify God in that name.

For you were called to freedom, brothers. Only do not use your freedom as an opportunity for the flesh, but through love serve one another. ❖ But take care that this right of yours does not somehow become a stumbling block to the weak. ❖ "But whoever causes one of these little ones who believe in me to sin, it would be better for him to have a great millstone fastened around his neck and to be drowned in the depth of the sea." ❖ "As you did it to one of the least of these my brothers, you did it to me."

Rom. 14:16. | 1 Thess. 5:22. | 2 Cor. 8:21.
1 Pet. 2:15. | 1 Pet. 4:15, 16. | Gal. 5:13.
1 Cor. 8:9. | Matt. 18:6. | Matt. 25:40.

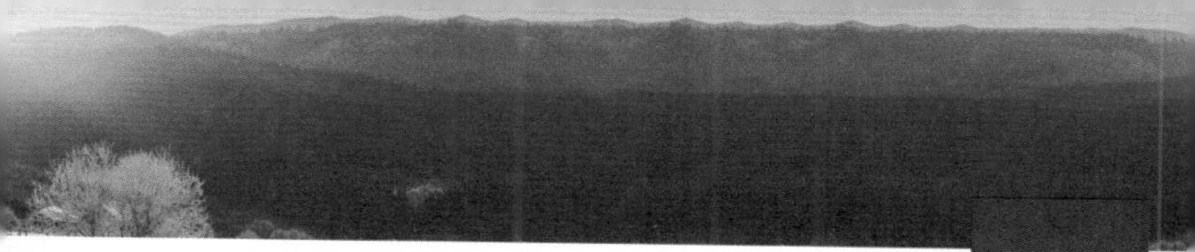

DEC.
12

The Lord, *is in your midst.*

Fear not, for I am with you; be not dismayed, for I am your God; I will strengthen you, I will help you, I will uphold you with my righteous right hand. ❖ Strengthen the weak hands, and make firm the feeble knees. Say to those who have an anxious heart, "Be strong; fear not! Behold, your God will come with vengeance, with the recompense of God. He will come and save you." ❖ The Lord your God is in your midst, a mighty one who will save; he will rejoice over you with gladness; he will quiet you by his love; he will exult over you with loud singing. ❖ Wait for the Lord; be strong, and let your heart take courage.

And I heard a loud voice from the throne saying, "Behold, the dwelling place of God is with man. He will dwell with them, and they will be his people, and God himself will be with them as their God. He will wipe away every tear from their eyes, and death shall be no more, neither shall there be mourning nor crying nor pain anymore."

Zeph. 3:15. | Isa. 41:10. | Isa. 35:3, 4.
Zeph. 3:17. | Ps. 27:14. | Rev. 21:3, 4.

DEC. 13

Be strengthened by the grace that is in Christ Jesus.

May you be strengthened with all power, according to his glorious might. ❖ Therefore, as you received Christ Jesus the Lord, so walk in him, rooted and built up in him and established in the faith, just as you were taught, abounding in thanksgiving. ❖ Oaks of righteousness, the planting of the LORD, that he may be glorified. ❖ Built on the foundation of the apostles and prophets, Christ Jesus himself being the cornerstone, in whom the whole structure, being joined together, grows into a holy temple in the Lord. In him you also are being built together into a dwelling place for God by the Spirit.

"And now I commend you to God and to the word of his grace, which is able to build you up and to give you the inheritance among all those who are sanctified." ❖ Filled with the fruit of righteousness that comes through Jesus Christ, to the glory and praise of God.

Fight the good fight of the faith. ❖ And not frightened in anything by your opponents.

2 Tim. 2:1. | Col. 1:11. | Col. 2:6, 7. | Isa. 61:3. | Eph. 2:20-22. Acts 20:32. | Phil. 1:11. | 1 Tim. 6:12. | Phil. 1:28.

DEC.
14

Give to him glorious praise!

"The people whom I formed for myself that they might declare my praise." ❖ "I will cleanse them from all the guilt of their sin against me, and I will forgive all the guilt of their sin and rebellion against me. And this city shall be to me a name of joy, a praise and a glory before all the nations of the earth." Through him then let us continually offer up a sacrifice of praise to God, that is, the fruit of lips that acknowledge his name. ❖ I give thanks to you, O Lord my God, with my whole heart, and I will glorify your name forever. For great is your steadfast love toward me; you have delivered my soul from the depths of Sheol. ❖ "Who is like you, O Lord, … majestic in holiness, awesome in glorious deeds, doing wonders?" ❖ I will praise the name of God with a song; I will magnify him with thanksgiving. ❖ And they sing the song of Moses, the servant of God, and the song of the Lamb, saying, "Great and amazing are your deeds, O Lord God the Almighty!"

Ps. 66:2. | Isa. 43:21. | Jer. 33:8, 9. | Heb. 13:15.
Ps. 86:12, 13. | Exod. 15:11. | Ps. 69:30. | Rev. 15:3.

DEC.
15

Bear one another's burdens,
and so fulfill the law of Christ.

Let each of you look not only to his own interests, but also to the interests of others. Have this mind among yourselves, which is yours in Christ Jesus, who, though he was in the form of God, did not count equality with God a thing to be grasped, but made himself nothing, taking the form of a servant. ❖ "For even the Son of Man came not to be served but to serve, and to give his life as a ransom for many." ❖ And he died for all, that those who live might no longer live for themselves but for him who for their sake died and was raised.

When Jesus saw her weeping, and the Jews who had come with her also weeping, he was deeply moved in his spirit and greatly troubled. … Jesus wept. ❖ Rejoice with those who rejoice, weep with those who weep.

Have unity of mind, sympathy, brotherly love, a tender heart, and a humble mind. Do not repay evil for evil or reviling for reviling, but on the contrary, bless, for to this you were called, that you may obtain a blessing.

Gal. 6:2. | Phil. 2:4-7. | Mark 10:45. | 2 Cor. 5:15.
John 11:33, 35. | Rom. 12:15. | 1 Pet. 3:8, 9.

DEC.
16

Having loved his own who were
in the world, he loved them to the end.

"I am praying for them. I am not praying for the world but for those whom you have given me, for they are yours. All mine are yours, and yours are mine, and I am glorified in them. ... I do not ask that you take them out of the world, but that you keep them from the evil one. They are not of the world, just as I am not of the world."

"As the Father has loved me, so have I loved you. Abide in my love." ❖ "Greater love has no one than this, that someone lays down his life for his friends. You are my friends if you do what I command you." ❖ "A new commandment I give to you, that you love one another: just as I have loved you, you also are to love one another."

He who began a good work in you will bring it to completion at the day of Jesus Christ. ❖ Christ loved the church and gave himself up for her, that he might sanctify her, having cleansed her by the washing of water with the word.

John 13:1. | John 17:9, 10, 15, 16. | John 15:9.
John 15:13, 14. | John 13:34. | Phil. 1:6. | Eph. 5:25, 26.

DEC.
17

Give us life, and we will call upon your name!

"It is the Spirit who gives life." ❖ Likewise the Spirit helps us in our weakness. For we do not know what to pray for as we ought, but the Spirit himself intercedes for us with groanings too deep for words. And he who searches hearts knows what is the mind of the Spirit, because the Spirit intercedes for the saints according to the will of God. ❖ Praying at all times in the Spirit, with all prayer and supplication. To that end keep alert with all perseverance.

I will never forget your precepts, for by them you have given me life. ❖ "The words that I have spoken to you are spirit and life." ❖ For the letter kills, but the Spirit gives life. ❖ "If you abide in me, and my words abide in you, ask whatever you wish, and it will be done for you." ❖ And this is the confidence that we have toward him, that if we ask anything according to his will he hears us.

No one can say "Jesus is Lord" except in the Holy Spirit.

Ps. 80:18. | John 6:63. | Rom. 8:26, 27.
Eph. 6:18. | Ps. 119:93. | John 6:63. | 2 Cor. 3:6.
John 15:7. | 1 John 5:14. | 1 Cor. 12:3.

DEC.
18

Let us then with confidence draw near
to the throne of grace, that we may receive mercy
and find grace to help in time of need.

Do not be anxious about anything, but in everything by prayer and supplication with thanksgiving let your requests be made known to God. And the peace of God, which surpasses all understanding, will guard your hearts and your minds in Christ Jesus. ❖ For you did not receive the spirit of slavery to fall back into fear, but you have received the Spirit of adoption as sons, by whom we cry, "Abba! Father!"

"I did not say to the offspring of Jacob, 'Seek me in vain.'" ❖ Therefore, ... since we have confidence to enter the holy places by the blood of Jesus, by the new and living way that he opened for us through the curtain, that is, through his flesh, and since we have a great priest over the house of God, let us draw near with a true heart in full assurance of faith, with our hearts sprinkled clean from an evil conscience and our bodies washed with pure water. ❖ So we can confidently say, "The Lord is my helper; I will not fear; what can man do to me?"

Heb. 4:16. | Phil. 4:6, 7. | Rom. 8:15. | Isa. 45:19.
Heb. 10:19-22. | Heb. 13:6.

DEC. 19

Light dawns in the darkness for the upright.

Who among you fears the LORD and obeys the voice of his servant? Let him who walks in darkness and has no light trust in the name of the LORD and rely on his God. ❖ Though he fall, he shall not be cast headlong, for the LORD upholds his hand. ❖ For the commandment is a lamp and the teaching a light.

Rejoice not over me, O my enemy; when I fall, I shall rise; when I sit in darkness, the LORD will be a light to me. I will bear the indignation of the LORD because I have sinned against him, until he pleads my cause and executes judgment for me. He will bring me out to the light; I shall look upon his vindication.

"The eye is the lamp of the body. So, if your eye is healthy, your whole body will be full of light, but if your eye is bad, your whole body will be full of darkness. If then the light in you is darkness, how great is the darkness!"

Ps. 112:4. | Isa. 50:10. | Ps. 37:24. | Prov. 6:23.
Mic. 7:8, 9. | Matt. 6:22, 23.

DEC. 20

He chose us in him before
the foundation of the world.

That we should be holy and blameless before him.

God chose you as the firstfruits to be saved, through sanctification by the Spirit and belief in the truth. To this he called you, … so that you may obtain the glory of our Lord Jesus Christ. ❖ For those whom he foreknew he also predestined to be conformed to the image of his Son, in order that he might be the firstborn among many brothers. And those whom he predestined he also called, and those whom he called he also justified, and those whom he justified he also glorified. ❖ Elect, … according to the foreknowledge of God the Father, in the sanctification of the Spirit, for obedience to Jesus Christ and for sprinkling with his blood. ❖ "And I will give you a new heart, and a new spirit I will put within you. And I will remove the heart of stone from your flesh and give you a heart of flesh." ❖ For God has not called us for impurity, but in holiness.

Eph. 1:4. | Eph. 1:4. | 2 Thess. 2:13, 14. | Rom. 8:29, 30.
1 Pet. 1:1, 2. | Ezek. 36:26. | 1 Thess. 4:7.

DEC.
21

And your days of mourning shall be ended.

"In the world you will have tribulation." ❖ The whole creation has been groaning together in the pains of childbirth until now. And not only the creation, but we ourselves, who have the firstfruits of the Spirit, groan inwardly as we wait eagerly for adoption as sons, the redemption of our bodies. ❖ For while we are still in this tent, we groan, being burdened – not that we would be unclothed, but that we would be further clothed, so that what is mortal may be swallowed up by life.

"These are the ones coming out of the great tribulation. They have washed their robes and made them white in the blood of the Lamb. Therefore they are before the throne of God, and serve him day and night in his temple; and he who sits on the throne will shelter them with his presence. They shall hunger no more, neither thirst anymore; the sun shall not strike them, nor any scorching heat. For the Lamb in the midst of the throne will be their shepherd, and he will guide them to springs of living water, and God will wipe away every tear from their eyes."

Isa. 60:20. | John 16:33. | Rom. 8:22, 23.
2 Cor. 5:4. | Rev. 7:14-17.

DEC.
22

Your work of faith.

"This is the work of God, that you believe in him whom he has sent."

So also faith by itself, if it does not have works, is dead. ❖ Faith working through love. ❖ For the one who sows to his own flesh will from the flesh reap corruption, but the one who sows to the Spirit will from the Spirit reap eternal life. ❖ For we are his workmanship, created in Christ Jesus for good works, which God prepared beforehand, that we should walk in them. ❖ Who gave himself for us to redeem us from all lawlessness and to purify for himself a people for his own possession who are zealous for good works.

We ought always to give thanks to God for you, brothers, as is right, because your faith is growing abundantly, and the love of every one of you for one another is increasing. … To this end we always pray for you, that our God may make you worthy of his calling and may fulfill every resolve for good and every work of faith by his power. ❖ For it is God who works in you, both to will and to work for his good pleasure.

1 Thess. 1:3. | John 6:29. | James 2:17. | Gal. 5:6. | Gal. 6:8.
Eph. 2:10. | Titus 2:14. | 2 Thess. 1:3, 11. | Phil. 2:13.

DEC.
23

"Or let them lay hold of my protection,
let them make peace with me."

"For I know the plans I have for you, declares the LORD, plans for wholeness and not for evil." ❖ "There is no peace," says the LORD, "for the wicked."

But now in Christ Jesus you who once were far off have been brought near by the blood of Christ. For he himself is our peace.

For in him all the fullness of God was pleased to dwell, and through him to reconcile to himself all things, whether on earth or in heaven, making peace by the blood of his cross. ❖ Christ Jesus, whom God put forward as a propitiation by his blood, to be received by faith. This was to show God's righteousness, because in his divine forbearance he had passed over former sins ... so that he might be just and the justifier of the one who has faith in Jesus. ❖ If we confess our sins, he is faithful and just to forgive us our sins and to cleanse us from all unrighteousness.

Trust in the LORD forever, for the LORD GOD is an everlasting rock.

Isa. 27:5. | Jer. 29:11. | Isa. 48:22. | Eph. 2:13, 14.
Col. 1:19, 20. | Rom. 3:24-26. | 1 John 1:9. | Isa. 26:4.

DEC.
24

For if you live according to the flesh you will die, but if by the Spirit you put to death the deed of the body, you will live.

Now the works of the flesh are evident: sexual immorality, impurity, … and things like these. I warn you, as I warned you before, that those who do such things will not inherit the kingdom of God. But the fruit of the Spirit is love, joy, peace, patience, kindness, goodness, faithfulness, gentleness, self-control; against such things there is no law. And those who belong to Christ Jesus have crucified the flesh with its passions and desires. If we live by the Spirit, let us also walk by the Spirit.

For the grace of God has appeared, bringing salvation for all people, training us to renounce ungodliness and worldly passions, and to live self-controlled, upright, and godly lives in the present age, waiting for our blessed hope, the appearing of the glory of our great God and Savior Jesus Christ, who gave himself for us to redeem us from all lawlessness.

Rom. 8:13. | Gal. 5:19, 21-25. | Titus 2:11-14.

DEC.
25

The goodness and loving kindness of God our Savior appeared.

"I have loved you with an everlasting love."

In this the love of God was made manifest among us, that God sent his only Son into the world, so that we might live through him. In this is love, not that we have loved God but that he loved us and sent his Son to be the propitiation for our sins.

But when the fullness of time had come, God sent forth his Son, born of woman, born under the law, to redeem those who were under the law, so that we might receive adoption as sons. ❖ And the Word became flesh and dwelt among us, and we have seen his glory, glory as of the only Son from the Father, full of grace and truth. ❖ Great indeed, we confess, is the mystery of godliness: He was manifested in the flesh.

Since therefore the children share in flesh and blood, he himself likewise partook of the same things, that through death he might destroy the one who has the power of death, that is, the devil.

Titus 3:4. | Jer. 31:3. | 1 John 4:9, 10. | Gal. 4:4, 5.
John 1:14. | 1 Tim. 3:16. | Heb. 2:14.

DEC.
26

Be steadfast, immovable, always abounding in the work of the Lord.

Knowing that in the Lord your labor is not in vain. ❖ As you received Christ Jesus the Lord, so walk in him, rooted and built up in him and established in the faith, just as you were taught, abounding in thanksgiving. ❖ "But the one who endures to the end will be saved." ❖ "As for that in the good soil, they are those who, hearing the word, hold it fast in an honest and good heart, and bear fruit with patience."

For you stand firm in your faith.

"We must work the works of him who sent me while it is day; night is coming, when no one can work."

For the one who sows to his own flesh will from the flesh reap corruption, but the one who sows to the Spirit will from the Spirit reap eternal life. And let us not grow weary of doing good, for in due season we will reap, if we do not give up. So then, as we have opportunity, let us do good to everyone, and especially to those who are of the household of faith.

1 Cor. 15:58. | 1 Cor. 15:58. | Col. 2:6, 7. | Matt. 24:13.
Luke 8:15. | 2 Cor. 1:24. | John 9:4. | Gal. 6:8-10.

DEC.
27

We look not to the things that are seen but to the things that are unseen. For the things that are seen are transient, but the things that are unseen are eternal.

For here we have no lasting city. ❖ You knew that you yourselves had a better possession and an abiding one.

"Fear not, little flock, for it is your Father's good pleasure to give you the Kingdom." ❖ Now for a little while, if necessary, you have been grieved by various trials. ❖ "There the wicked cease from troubling, and there the weary are at rest."

For while we are still in this tent, we groan, being burdened. ❖ "He will wipe away every tear from their eyes, and death shall be no more, neither shall there be mourning nor crying nor pain anymore, for the former things have passed away."

The sufferings of this present time are not worth comparing with the glory that is to be revealed to us. ❖ For this slight momentary affliction is preparing for us an eternal weight of glory beyond all comparison.

2 Cor. 4:18. | Heb. 13:14. | Heb. 10:34.
Luke 12:32. | 1 Pet. 1:6. | Job 3:17. | 2 Cor. 5:4.
Rev. 21:4. | Rom. 8:18. | 2 Cor. 4:17.

DEC.
28

"Your sins are forgiven."

"For I will forgive their iniquity, and I will remember their sin no more." ❖ "Who can forgive sins but God alone?"

"I, I am he who blots out your transgressions for my own sake, and I will not remember your sins." ❖ Blessed is the one whose transgression is forgiven, whose sin is covered. Blessed is the man against whom the LORD counts no iniquity, and in whose spirit there is no deceit. ❖ Who is a God like you, pardoning iniquity?

God in Christ forgave you. ❖ The blood of Jesus his Son cleanses us from all sin. If we say we have no sin, we deceive ourselves, and the truth is not in us. If we confess our sins, he is faithful and just to forgive us our sins and to cleanse us from all unrighteousness.

As far as the east is from the west, so far does he remove our transgressions from us. ❖ For sin will have no dominion over you, since you are not under law but under grace. ... And, [you] having been set free from sin, have become slaves of righteousness.

Mark 2:5. | Jer. 31:34. | Mark 2:7. | Isa. 43:25.
Ps. 32:1, 2. | Mic. 7:18. | Eph. 4:32.
1 John 1:7-9. | Ps. 103:12. | Rom. 6:14, 18.

DEC.
29

Understand what the will of the Lord is.

For this is the will of God, your sanctification. ❖ "Agree with God, and be at peace; thereby good will come to you." ❖ "And this is eternal life, that they know you the only true God, and Jesus Christ whom you have sent." ❖ And we know that the Son of God has come and has given us understanding, so that we may know him who is true; and we are in him who is true, in his Son Jesus Christ. He is the true God and eternal life.

We have not ceased to pray for you, asking that you may be filled with the knowledge of his will in all spiritual wisdom and understanding. ❖ The God of our Lord Jesus Christ, the Father of glory, … give you a spirit of wisdom and of revelation in the knowledge of him, having the eyes of your hearts enlightened, that you may know what is the hope to which he has called you, what are the riches of his glorious inheritance in the saints, and what is the immeasurable greatness of his power toward us who believe, according to the working of his great might.

Eph. 5:17. | 1 Thess. 4:3. | Job 22:21. | John 17:3.
1 John 5:20. | Col. 1:9. | Eph. 1:17-19.

DEC. 30

Guiltless in the day of our Lord Jesus Christ.

And you, who once were alienated and hostile in mind, doing evil deeds, he has now reconciled in his body of flesh by his death, in order to present you holy and blameless and above reproach before him, if indeed you continue in the faith, stable and steadfast, not shifting from the hope of the gospel. ❖ That you may be blameless and innocent, children of God without blemish in the midst of a crooked and twisted generation, among whom you shine as lights in the world.

Therefore, beloved, since you are waiting for these, be diligent to be found by him without spot or blemish, and at peace. ❖ Pure and blameless for the day of Christ.

Now to him who is able to keep you from stumbling and to present you blameless before the presence of his glory with great joy, to the only God, our Savior, through Jesus Christ our Lord, be glory, majesty, dominion, and authority, before all time and now and forever.

1 Cor. 1:8. | Col. 1:21-23. | Phil. 2:15.
2 Pet. 3:14. | Phil. 1:10. | Jude 24, 25.

DEC. 31

"The LORD your God carried you, as a man carries his son, all the way that you went until you came to this place."

"I bore you on eagles' wings and brought you to myself." ❖ In his love and in his pity he redeemed them; he lifted them up and carried them all the days of old. ❖ Like an eagle that stirs up its nest, that flutters over its young, spreading out its wings, catching them, bearing them on its pinions, the LORD alone guided him.

"Even to your old age I am he, and to gray hairs I will carry you. I have made, and I will bear; I will carry and will save." ❖ This is God, our God forever and ever. He will guide us forever.

Cast your burden on the LORD, and he will sustain you. ❖ "Do not be anxious about your life, what you will eat or what you will drink, nor about your body, what you will put on. … For … your heavenly Father knows that you need them all.

"Till now the LORD has helped us."

Deut. 1:31. | Exod. 19:4. | Isa. 63:9.
Deut. 32:11, 12. | Isa. 46:4. | Ps. 48:14.
Ps. 55:22. | Matt. 6:25, 32. | 1 Sam. 7:12.

List of the Daily Texts Arranged in Bible Order

Proverbs

Song of Songs

Isaiah

Jeremiah